Creation's Beauty as Revelation

Creation's Beauty as Revelation

Toward a Creational Theology of Natural Beauty

L. CLIFTON EDWARDS

Foreword by David Brown

PICKWICK *Publications* · Eugene, Oregon

CREATION'S BEAUTY AS REVELATION
Toward a Creational Theology of Natural Beauty

The introduction and first section of chapter 1 appear in modified form in L. Clifton Edwards, "Artful Creation and Aesthetic Rationality," *Theology Today* 69 (2012) 56–72. Used by permission. Information from the first two sections of chapter 5 appears in modified form in L. Clifton Edwards, "Re-envisaging Ruskin's Types: Beautiful Order as Divine Revelation," *Irish Theological Quarterly* 77 (2012) 165–81. Used by permission. A version of the final section and conclusion of chapter 5 appears in L. Clifton Edwards, "'The Beauty of Frontier: A Revelation of the Human Destination in God," *American Theological Inquiry* 3/2 (2010) 15–19. Used by permission.

Pickwick Publications
An Imprint of Wipf and Stock Publishers
199 W. 8th Ave., Suite 3
Eugene, OR 97401

www.wipfandstock.com

ISBN 13: 978-1-62032-368-7

Cataloguing-in-Publication data:

Edwards, L. Clifton.

Creation's beauty as revelation : toward a creational theology of natural beauty / L. Clifton Edwards ; foreword by David Brown.

xviii + 194 pp. ; 23 cm. Includes bibliographical references.

ISBN 13: 978-1-62032-368-7

1. Aesthetics—Religious Aspects—Christianity. 2. Creation. 3. Revelation. I. Brown, David 1948 July 1–. II. Title.

BR115.A8 E29 2014

Contents

Foreword

At a recent meeting of the American Academy of Religion, some scholars expressed surprise at the two apparently unrelated aspects of my academic career, a first half devoted to exploring relations between theology and philosophy and a second half concerned with theology and the arts. However, as I hope to demonstrate in due course, there is far more of a link than may initially appear. With many, if not most, now convinced of the inadequacy of traditional arguments for God's existence, there is need to explore other ways of grounding belief in God, and it is here that the arts become relevant and not least among them, God's own artistry in creation. It was a strategy that was already being explored by Britain's greatest art critic of the nineteenth century, John Ruskin. He not only detected divine craft in nature both great and small (the majesty of the Alps as well as the intricacy of the human hand, for example) but also argued that human art was only good in so far as it reflected that artistry; hence one of his principal arguments for advocating the revival of Gothic architecture in the Britain of his day.

It is into this framework that Clifton Edwards's pioneering work may be set, as he explores suitable theological and philosophical foundations for understanding the natural world as divine art. When the creation narrative in Genesis opens with a word rather more was intended than an indicator of mere divine fiat. It was (and is) a matter of God's speech overflowing in the generosity of a divine creativity painting a good world that can then be read and understood by us. It is this aspect that is taken up in Edwards's re-envisaging of nature as artistic "text" and "image." In a similar way the incarnation itself can also be understood as both image and text, a picture that can be read of God's plans for humanity, the divine being's desire to redeem every aspect of our existence, body no less than soul. Given such a holistic perspective, it comes, therefore, as something of a shock to note how far theology has retreated from areas of human activity that would once have been thought also to be major areas for its concern, the natural world and its aesthetic impact not least among them. It is part of Edwards's aim to reverse that retreat, for in this retreat has come the rise of various forms of spirituality that allow only a rather vague deity to operate in the world (if at all) whose precise relationship to the Christian God remains unclear.

In what follows Edwards attempts to redress the balance by encouraging Christians to pay attention to relationships between Christ and the natural, everyday beauty of the world, thus integrating Christianity with what for most has become a largely secular or even non-Christian sphere of experience. He does this not by simply representing old arguments but by urging readers to think of the world and the experience they derive from it in new ways. The book is thus as much correction as contribution, a correction that is greatly facilitated by Edwards's interdisciplinary approach and background in the natural sciences. Nor are the more negative aspects of that experience ignored, since due attention is given to nature when it appears "red in tooth and claw." So, all in all readers are likely to find this a profound and challenging work that will help them engage with the true character of the natural world that still lies behind the secular lens of the age—a world beautifully crafted by God and able to be read as such by us, if only we allow Edwards to open our eyes once more to that divine handiwork.

David Brown
University of St Andrews, Scotland

Introduction

IN THE *CONFESSIONS*, AUGUSTINE relates how he "questioned" the world implicitly through the attention he gave it. The "response" that he says he received from the world was its beauty. Like Augustine, we all pose our questions to the world in the form of our attention. We pose our "How?" questions through our practical, causal, or scientific investigations and our "Why?" questions *de profundis* of unexpected joy or suffering. What if Augustine's implication is correct that the ultimate answers to our questions are somehow bound up in the response of beauty? Beauty[1] could be a sort of guiding principle or *vade mecum* to God.

Augustine came to believe that his own questioning of the world implicated the God who transcends the world.[2] And Augustine's influence persisted through the Middle Ages, such that theologians assumed the invisible God as seen and known through the visible world, especially through its beauty. Due to this assumption, aesthetics did not exist as a discipline until the eighteenth century, because it was merely an aspect of theology—a visible way of knowing the invisible God. Since modernity, however, we may still concede the Invisible, though often as an unknown.[3] As a consequence, the intimate medieval connection between beauty and ultimate reality is no longer readily accessible, even though people are still powerfully drawn to both natural and artistic beauty.[4] In North America there are only dim echoes of this medieval linking of beauty to God, in some church

1. I use *beauty* and *the beautiful* to refer to beautiful forms—that is, beauty manifested in a context—not to an abstract Platonic form of beauty. A detailed description of what I mean by beauty is forthcoming in chapter 2.

2. Augustine, *Confessions* 10.6.

3. Milbank describes the contours of this decline in the Christian aesthetic from the Middle Ages to the present. "Beauty and the Soul," 2–3. This decrease in knowledge claims about the invisible God is despite science's increasing knowledge of other invisible things: fields, waves, particles, etc.

4. Farley suggests this lost recognition of connection in *Faith and Beauty*, 15.

architecture for instance, while throughout the developed world, in the name of progress and efficiency, modern economics and technology have in some ways removed aesthetic concerns from everyday life.[5] Beauty is also excluded philosophically by those who limit knowledge to the deliverances of the empirical sciences and linguistic analysis: for if we reject metaphysics, and if "God is dead" or made relative to an individual's beliefs, so goes beauty.[6] On top of these cultural impediments is the conviction that beauty is an objectionable mask for a world that on the whole is evil or indifferent toward us.[7] Beauty can even be seen as embodying the more invidious side of our human nature—the side produced by a natural selection rejecting the weak and the unlovely. In light of the world's evil and suffering, we must take such objections to beauty seriously.

In this cultural and ideological context, the marginalization of beauty could speak of our culture's lost orientation toward God.[8] The loss of beauty as a symbol, which once spoke of God to Augustine, characterizes a society that now seeks alternative symbolisms, various quests for meaning, to infuse its daily life with significance. For instance, the range of economic and social "status symbols" seems to function in this way.[9] And as beauty becomes intertwined with status, fashion, and other pursuits, we can observe that beauty's symbolism has not ceased to function, but has instead relocated: culture has suppressed beauty in its former theological context only to have it emerge in other contexts. Commercialism has appropriated and manipulated both natural and artistic beauty, recognizing its inherently communicative function,[10] and thus advertisers seem to be telling us constantly that paradise is attainable if only we buy the product of choice. As Gesa Thiessen notes, "the aestheticization of everyday life in postmodern society through the powerful impact of images in mass media, the arts and culture, the constant presence of music, mostly of the popular variety, and the cult of the body and youth, are now ever-present features in our lives. The hunger for instant gratification, be it through exotic food, travel, films, music, body-cult, as well as the desire for religious or quasi-religious

5. Fuller notes this effect of technology in *Aesthetics After Modernism*, 19.

6. Cf. Farley on beauty's connection to God and metaphysics in *Faith and Beauty*, 64.

7. Muth suggests this influence of evil upon our understanding of beauty in "Beastly Metaphysics," 244.

8. Chittister suggests this lost orientation in "Monastic Wisdom," 173–81.

9. McIntyre notes society's need for revitalized symbolisms in *Theology and Imagination*, 170.

10. Green emphasizes commercialism's appropriation of beauty in *Imagining God*, 150.

experiences, ranging from crystal-gazing to traditional forms of Christian worship, are all based in aesthetics, i.e. sensuous, experience."[11] But even as much as contemporary society exploits beauty, it may also be that beauty appropriates culture and speaks through it in spite of its apparent shallowness. Thiessen also notes how aesthetics can invite even a cynical, post-Christian public to envisage the invisible God, through venues such as the well-attended "Seeing Salvation" exhibition at the National Gallery, London.[12] But such interest is not surprising if beauty is of God's design and fundamental to human existence, for surely then beauty cannot be easily suppressed, even if its message can be easily misunderstood. As Jean-Louis Chrétien says, beauty is "in its very manifestation, a call, a vocation, and a provocation."[13] If beauty is always communicating something, then theology should offer its own interpretations rather than abandoning beauty's message to secularism.

Inevitably, beauty's message invites divergent interpretations and understandings, especially as postmodernity's subjective emphasis frustrates agreement on what beauty is or does. This lack of agreement makes describing what we mean by *beauty* a complex task, and consequently, our theological understanding and systemization of the beautiful is impeded. Theological understanding is also complicated because aesthetics maps onto such a broad range of experiences. And while much has been written on the theology of art (that is, art produced by human beings), art often has aims other than beauty, and can become a roundabout path to a theology of beauty, leaving unclear beauty's relationship to God, creation, and redemption.[14] For this reason, to avoid confusion with artistic excellence and other kinds of aesthetic experience, I develop a more limited concept of "perceptual" beauty, which nonetheless finds application in both art and nature.

Beauty also deserves more theological attention as a perceived, experiential phenomenon, as opposed to a highly theologized concept, such as von Balthasar's or David Bentley Hart's in *The Beauty of the Infinite*.[15] *Natural* beauty, in particular, is also an underdeveloped theological topic, especially in a culture that values nature so highly. Thus I focus on natural beauty partly in an effort to promote dialogue with contemporary culture. In addition, Edward Farley makes the important observation that "whatever our culture, and

11. Thiessen, introduction to *Theological Aesthetics*, 1.

12. Ibid., 5. Finaldi, *Catalogue of Exhibition.*

13. "What is beautiful is what gives itself to be seen by giving itself from the start to be heard, by already speaking" (Chrétien, *Call and Response*, 3, 9).

14. Farley suggests this relationship between art and the theology of beauty in *Faith and Beauty*, 67

15. Hart, *Beauty of the Infinite.*

however little we pay attention to or value nature, we never wholly suppress or escape earth, sky, land, forests and seasons. . . . When we try to imagine a nature-less existence, we soon realize how much the quality of life is bound up with an endless succession of everyday beauty that we take for granted."[16] Certainly if "the heavens declare the glory of God," and the skies "pour fourth speech" and "display knowledge," we must consider the revelation of natural beauty in particular (Ps 19:1–2, NIV). Of course, the natural sublime is also a relevant aesthetic (and perhaps pre-Enlightenment religious) category, which I discuss in relation to natural beauty. But I focus on beauty-experience in particular because of its widespread and ordinary character. Experience of the sublime, in contrast, is somewhat less commonplace.

Beyond methodological difficulties with beauty, there are also theological objections. Christian iconoclasm, asceticism, and the tendency to push aesthetic concerns into the "next world," can subtly marginalize beauty as a devotional and theological focus. Protestant approaches to beauty also tend to set up unnecessary dichotomies between paganism or medieval Christianity and that which is considered to be the true prophetic and transcendent faith. Beauty then survives for theology only after much warning and qualification.[17] Yet such marginalization of the human experience of beauty only succeeds in making our theology poorer and less relevant to our lives in all their aesthetic richness and complexity. In addition, beauty is neglected due to a Protestant (especially Reformed) minimization of natural revelation, along with the marginalization of any theology that focuses on natural revelation rather than the Bible. This de-emphasis is somewhat surprising considering some of Calvin's comments about the natural world and its revelatory function.[18] As a Protestant myself, I wish to address this lack of emphasis, and offer a position that commends itself to Protestant theology.

One Protestant from whom I draw much inspiration regarding natural beauty is John Ruskin. Concerning the evangelical teachers of his day, he lamented that "though they insist much on [God's] giving of bread, and raiment, and health (which He gives to all inferior creatures), they require us not to thank Him for that glory of His works which He has permitted us alone to perceive: they tell us often to meditate in the closet, but they send us not, like Isaac, into the fields at even; they dwell on the duty of self-denial, but they exhibit not the duty of delight." Ruskin thought such teachers "in their struggle with nature fallen" should seek "more aid from nature undestroyed." He believed that such oversight resulted not so much from

---

16. Farley, *Faith and Beauty*, 16.

17. See ibid., 12, 68, on these theological difficulties with beauty.

18. See Calvin, *Institutes* 1.5.1–2.

godliness but from inward anxiety, from selfish introspection rather than grateful contemplation of creation, and from a utilitarianism that ignored whatever did not appear to serve immediate religious ends. In this climate, Ruskin saw the dangers of appeal to fear without appeal to desire, God's wrath unbalanced by his goodness, and a distant God to whom we cannot relate rather than a God revealed in earthly beauty.[19] Ruskin's criticisms are also relevant today.

But if God is revealed in creation's "divine art," to use Augustine's phrase,[20] then the experience of beauty as a universal phenomenon could provide a significant bridge between human experience and Christian theology. And theology might also suggest a more meaningful way to perceive beauty, since as Phillip Blond asserts, "only theology can, in the fullest sense of the word, *see at all*, since only theology can provide an account of what is actually seen that might be adequate to the vision and the reality of the perceptual world that we all share. . . . There is a world whose reality and disclosure constantly exceeds any secular attempt to describe it."[21] Theology can draw out more adequate meaning from our beauty-experience, as weighty and piercing as it sometimes is. And while theology helps find meaning in our experience, which does not interpret itself, our beauty-experience also contributes to this meaning in a way that suggests revelation. For, our beauty-experience often re-presents life to us as a meaningful gift and rare opportunity.[22] So it is not that theology determines beauty's message or beauty determines theology's, but there is a mutually beneficial interchange of meaning.

So how then does beauty deliver such a message? Natural beauty seems to access transcendent meaning by involving us in symbolic epistemic practices. I use *symbol* and *image* interchangeably to describe presentations of beauty; but *symbol* conveys the communicative, (re)presentational nature of an object, while *image* conveys its non-verbal, artistic character.[23] Mircea Eliade notes how a symbolic approach to revelation fosters a worldview that can pierce through our surface level reality without undervaluing its importance: such symbolism cultivates an awareness that we live in an "open" universe that suspends objects in webs of interconnectedness and mutual regard, while infusing them with meaning. Without this symbolic "'opening-out'

---

19. Ruskin, *Modern Painters*, 2:216–17.

20. Augustine, *On the Trinity* 6.12.

21. Blond, "Perception," 232.

22. Cf. Häring on this presentation of beauty in *Truth*, 108.

23. My use of *image* is not restricted to the visual. I understand aural "images" and other combinations of sense impressions as potential sense "images." I do not use *image* or *representation* in the Platonic sense of imperfect copies. Rather, I give beautiful forms a proper artistic status of their own instead of an inferior status as "copy."

into the transcendent," we can become hemmed in and grounded by even the noblest of cultures. But Christianity provides this symbolic and trans-cultural opening-out, and becomes particularly accessible to a culture through universally accessible symbols within its proclamation, such as, in the experience of nature, images of beautiful order, repose, and boundless-ness. By incorporating and refining such images, Christianity's vision of the world becomes not only local, historical, and particular but exemplary and universally applicable.[24] In this way, Christianity can take up and refine natural beauty as a category of images revealing God's nature[25] and inten-tions within creation's artistic "text."[26]

I offer an account of this revelatory natural beauty, taking revelation to mean *anything* that communicates something of God's presence, nature, or actions to us, even if revelation is not the primary purpose of the me-dium that reveals. Chapter 1 outlines a "creational theology" that sources this natural revelation, which I describe in terms of *logos*, or the rationally aesthetic structure of created reality. Beauty as a matter of course is an aspect of natural revelation described in these terms, because beauty fits within the artful character of a creation designed to facilitate (among other things) our aesthetically charged knowing of God and the world. After all, beauty-experience is a common, meaning-laden human experience, akin to experiences of child-birth, romantic love, sublimity, ugliness, and suffering. Creational theology engages such common experiences through a Christian vision, not simply to impose an interpretation, but with the conviction that the resources of the Christian worldview will enable better understanding of these experiences, as well as deepen them.

I refine this understanding of creational theology through interac-tion with Thomas Aquinas's theory of knowledge, drawing from Aquinas the interrelational dynamic of knowing God, the world, and the beauti-ful. I apply this understanding of knowledge by beginning to describe the relationship between beauty and God's nature, and by engagement with the doctrine of the incarnation. These general approaches to revelatory beauty provide an essential framework, which I bring into more detailed focus with each succeeding chapter: a broadly analogical framework be-gins to open up space for creation to function as a revelatory work of art—an artwork that invokes the beautiful as a pointed instance of God's self-expression. An incarnational framework, with the incarnation as the

24. See Eliade, *Images and Symbols*, 168–69, 174, 178.

25. By God's nature I mean simply what God is like, how we can best describe him.

26. I use *text* as a literary metaphor related to the theological concept of creation's "book." By text I mean a significant (but not necessarily verbal) reality in need of interpretation.

paradigmatic instance of relationship between God and creation, points ahead to beauty as a redemptive image.

In chapter 2 I describe the created side of this relationship between God and beauty by characterizing a physical, sensory, "perceptual beauty." I do not seek to diminish the many other senses in which the word *beauty* is used, nor do I want to devalue aesthetic phenomena related to beauty. In Wittgenstein's terms I cannot address all of beauty's "family resemblances," but I focus on one aspect of human experience of the beautiful with the hope of improving our concepts (and perhaps our experience) of beauty. I characterize perceptual beauty by example and distinguish it from related concepts such as the sublime, moral goodness (Richard Viladesau), the excellence of art (Harold Osborne), generic goodness or value (John Navone), and a romantic outlook on the nature of being (David Bentley Hart). I also describe both objective and subjective constituents of beauty, rejecting G. E. Moore's objective-only understanding. I then consider how this perceptual beauty could serve as a created framework through which God reveals something of his nature.

Chapters 3–4 sharpen my focus further by describing human experience of perceptual beauty at higher existential levels. Beyond the heightened perceptual awareness of beauty, human beings often ascribe meaning to beauty-experiences, by interpreting them according to various religious or non-religious frameworks. These meaningful beauty-experiences form patterns of common human experience—patterns that contribute to the development of mythologies and theologies of natural beauty. I describe one such pattern in terms of beauty's "excess"—that is, the tendency for beauty-experience to suggest deeper meanings for the world and human existence. Beauty's excess could consist in a tacit knowledge of transcendence—a knowledge that is given tacitly through perception though not shown explicitly.

Such experience also gives rise to more extensive reflection as human beings apply their mythologies and theologies to make sense of beauty. By seeking out "harmonies" and "resonances" between beauty-experience and a Christian vision of the world, we can make sense of beauty from a Christian perspective, and also deepen and enrich our experience. We make sense of beauty, not simply by inference from our experience, but more realistically, in Michael Polanyi's terms, by personally "indwelling" a communal "epistemic vision" that seeks to know God through nature. Indwelling this vision requires entering into its epistemic practices, beauty-skills, aesthetic desires, and poetic idioms, all of which contribute to our knowing of God through natural beauty. Such an epistemic vision also involves engaging beauty through a symbolic practice, such that beauty begins to "image" God within creation's "book" or artistic "text." This sort of aesthetic communication through images is characteristic of the Bible and ordinary human communication, as well as the incarnation as a paradigmatic image. Thus it is reasonable to suppose that natural beauty functions similarly in our experience, imaging divine transcendence and promise through an artistic interplay between the human psyche and the natural world. This epistemic vision of natural beauty becomes workable insofar as we indwell it, work with it, and find it to illuminate and give order to human experience in relation to both God and nature.

Chapter 5 is a further indwelling of this same epistemic vision, through a re-envisaging of Ruskin's concept of "typical beauty." The chapter builds upon, and seeks to substantiate through use, this symbolic practice engaging beauty-experience—experience that lends itself readily to religious interpretation. Ruskin considers experiences of beautiful order, purity, repose, color, and boundlessness, and offers his personal epistemic vision for understanding these experiences. His vision can be fruitfully indwelt, adapted, and furthered toward a creational theology of natural beauty.

In Ruskin's typology, beautiful forms image specific aspects of God's nature, and one such aspect is divine harmony. This harmony is imaged by a profound and multifaceted *order* in natural beauty. In discussing natural order, I critique both Ruskin's typology and classical understandings of order that would deny beauty to much of nature. But even with this more modern understanding of natural beauty, ordered beauty contrasts with nature's entropy and decay, which contribute to ugliness and highlight creation's more sinister pole. Natural beauty finds its context at both poles, amid both the powerful and the fragile, the destructive and the procreative in creation, integrating itself fully with evil and ugliness in the created order, yet still opposing them through a sort of artistic and redemptive leitmotiv. Natural beauty consorts artistically with fallenness; nevertheless, beauty's commingling with destructiveness, and its indifference to suffering, do not eclipse beauty's revelation, but channel it toward theological verities. Within an unsettled creation, a "reposeful" beauty discloses God's permanence, creation's fallenness, and eschatological resolution: it resolves eschatologically into the divine self-existence that is reflected in a human repose within creation. And such repose images the redemption of both the natural and the human. I thus expand Ruskin's concept of repose by contextualizing it within nature's flux and decay, and by rejecting the Augustinian tendency to include death and decay within the compass of the beautiful.

Building further upon Ruskin, I take up his approach to the sky's unbounded and beautiful distance. This image speaks to God's infinitude, while pointing to a human destiny within an eschatologically unbounded creation. Humankind pushes creation's bounds, vaguely longing to integrate with a natural beauty imaging God. This longing, in turn, images an eschatological integration with God, which, in human experience, takes on the form of a "frontier"—an endlessly expansive interface between nature and humanity. Here beauty and knowledge unfold with the landscape, unveiling the divine mystery that is displayed aptly in the beautiful. I conclude by commending the power of this interrelationship of God, beauty, and humanity: it is a relationship calling for response to beauty as a phenomenality of God for his creatures.[27]

27. Blond describes beauty as a phenomenality of God in "Theology before Philosophy," 57.

1

Creational Theology
Artful Creation and Aesthetic Rationality

DESPITE BIBLICAL TEXTS DISCUSSING the beauty and revelatory function of the natural world, (e.g., Ps 19:1–4, Acts 14:17, and Rom 1:20), and despite a contemporary culture that values the natural world so highly, contemporary Protestant theology has not emphasized a natural revelation through beauty.[1] But a more "creational" theology is surely in order—a theology engaging the natural world as a potential theological "source" akin to Scripture, tradition, reason, and religious experience.[2] Toward this end, I present a preliminary and formative account of how human beings might gain a better understanding of God through an examination of the world's beauty—that is, an account of how God is revealed in, and understood through, creation, especially through natural beauty.

Such an account is appropriate, because our knowledge of God is creationally mediated. That is, creatures know God through the medium of creation—a created transmission of knowledge that has for its pinnacle the

1. For the purposes of this chapter, I use *beauty* in a broad and general sense that could include even an imperceptible, incorporeal *kalokagathia*, or "beautiful goodness." In the following chapter, however, I develop a narrower category of corporeal, "perceptual beauty," in an effort to address specific issues in creational theology.

2. Patrick Sherry suggests that beauty could be a theological "source." *Spirit and Beauty*, 69. John Wesley's methodological emphasis on Scripture, tradition, reason, and religious experience has taken on the name "Wesleyan Quadrilateral," coined by Albert C. Outler in his editorial introduction to the collection, *John Wesley*, iv.

incarnate body of Christ. Creation's mediation of all knowledge becomes apparent when creation is understood in the broadest sense. In this broad sense, creation encompasses not only what we think of as "nature"—that is, the non-human—but also the part of "nature" that is human: the mind-body, with its various capacities. As the conduit for our knowledge, this aesthetically rich creation mediates any understanding we have of God. And we might expect, given the arresting, even "saturated," character of many experiences of beauty, that such experience could point to God in some intelligible way. The beauty of the world is, after all, an aspect of *God's* creation—an ontology that is (at least partly) addressed to God's ends, and in which God is intimately involved. A rich understanding of created beauty,[3] then, might reveal something of God, especially considering how human knowledge functions through aesthetic modalities. By engaging our "aesthetic rationality," the multifaceted phenomenon of beauty might even reveal various aspects of the divine nature, as well as aspects of humankind's place within God's reality.[4] But, more modestly, my initial aim is simply to outline a methodological approach to a "creational theology" engaging a beautiful world.[5]

This development of creational theology and revelatory beauty is a full-blooded Christian picture of knowledge and revelation. But it is not therefore inappropriately metaphysical or theological, since every episte-mology presupposes a metaphysics or a theology; we must at least begin with a metaphysical or theological framework for understanding knowers in a reality that can be known. I describe creational theology from a Christian standpoint, but I also understand it to be partially applicable, in various ways and to varying extents, to non-Christians and even atheists. In fact, I maintain that Christians and non-Christians come to know the world, and God through the world, in remarkably similar ways.

Part one of this chapter outlines my methodological approach to "creational" theology, as opposed to a more traditional "natural" theology. Part two refines this approach through interaction with Thomas Aquinas's theory of knowledge. I draw from Aquinas the interrelational dynamic of knowing God, knowing the world, and knowing the beautiful. I begin to

---

3. By *created beauty*, I mean the beauty of creation as opposed to the category of un-created, divine beauty. The term applies in different ways to both nature and human art.

4. I develop this claim in chapter 5.

5. This is not to suggest that all of creation is beautiful, including its abundance of natural evil, death, decay, and suffering, not to mention moral evil. I am only claim-ing here that *on the whole* the *natural* world is experienced *aesthetically* as beautiful, recognizing at the same time that the natural world is often also experienced as cruel, unsafe, and unfair.

apply this understanding of creational theology in part three by considering beauty in relation to God's nature, and by engagement with the doctrine of the incarnation. This theological framework for understanding revelatory beauty continues to develop with each chapter: the broadly analogical relationship between God and creation provides space for creation to function as a revelatory work of art—an artwork that invokes the beautiful as an image of God's nature and intentions. The incarnation, as the paradigmatic instance of relationship between God and creation, incorporates beauty redemptively, pointing ahead to a beautiful images of creation's redemption.

AESTHETIC CREATIONAL THEOLOGY

Of course some will question the significance and feasibility of knowing God through creation's beauty: beyond what Scripture or tradition might reveal, why should we pursue additional, and perhaps riskier, avenues into that which is ultimately incomprehensible? Are these time-tested theological sources insufficient for rendering knowledge of God? In contrast to more traditional theological sources, some might say of creation with Job, "Behold, these are the fringes of His ways; / And how faint a word we hear of Him!"—God's later response regarding creation notwithstanding (Job 26:14, NASB). But Scripture, as in Job, and tradition do point us beyond themselves toward creation. Furthermore, these more conventional sources of religious knowledge do not offer us by themselves all that we would like to know about God, nor do they always offer knowledge in the most existentially compelling ways. Such knowledge, rather than simply dispelling God's mystery, also deepens it, and bids us enter the depths.[6] As that which both deepens and partially fathoms God's depths, revelation need not be an expressly stated or unmistakable datum. Rather, revelation in the broadest sense can be *anything* that communicates something of God's presence, nature, or actions to us, even if revelation is not the primary purpose of the medium that reveals.

Moreover, our mind-bodies are also a created "medium" through which we must access revelation. And such mediation of revelation deepens God's mystery further, because our minds are uniquely personal vantage points on the world, often mysteriously shaped by our biology, culture, and language.[7] We thus experience God and the world only through this "created subjectivity,"[8] which also mediates even direct religious or mystical

---

6. See Viladesau on revelation inviting us into mystery. *Theological Aesthetics*, 93.

7. Viladesau highlights these subjective factors mediating revelation. Ibid., 93.

8. By subjective I do not mean arbitrary or relativistic; I mean phenomenal and

experience by means of the soul's spiritual capacities. Thus, it is fair to say that creation "circumscribes" our knowledge of God, while at the same time making it possible. Creation also makes possible a subjectively colored but real knowledge of many other objectivities.

Given that all revelation is mediated, if Scripture affirms that we see God's nature through what he has made (Rom 1:20),[9] a reasonable question would be, "How, or in what ways, does creation (and specifically, natural beauty) reveal God?" If the natural world is recognized almost universally to be (at least in large part) beautiful, and many have affirmed that God is beautiful in some sense, what might be the connection?[10] An examination of our epistemology should aid us in establishing a connection.

But if we undertake a theology of created beauty focusing on creation itself rather than on what Scripture or tradition say about creation (though we can certainly draw on both), we will not be able to say much without someone questioning the whole enterprise as a form of "natural theology." Many different types of projects have been placed under this heading, and many have elicited negative responses from Protestant theologians. Some theologians have limited the scope of natural theology to theistic arguments and have accepted or rejected it on the basis of the perceived success of these so-called proofs for God's existence. For many, the pens of Hume and Kant have rendered such arguments obsolete, but this limited understanding of natural theology is probably a holdover from seventeenth- and eighteenth-century England. Natural theology at this time was responding to biblical criticism, the success of the Newtonian worldview, and dissatisfaction with organized religion and its appeals to authority. The strictly empirical, quasi-scientific approach to natural theology at this time led many to deism.[11] Probably with this Enlightenment style of natural theology in mind, some Reformed theologians such as Millard Erickson deny the appropriateness of natural theology, contending that it detracts from Scripture as the proper foundation of theology.[12] Others such as Alvin Plantinga believe that natural

---

shaped by personality. Karl Rahner asserts that all theology must be "subjective," meaning that "it cannot speak about objects which lie outside the realm of the personal, spiritual and free reality of human existence itself." "Theology and the Arts," 17–29.

9. See Wisdom 13:5, NEB: "The greatness and beauty of created things gives us a corresponding idea of their Creator."

10. I will deal with the question of God's beauty more specifically in the following chapter.

11. On the history of natural theology, See McGrath, *Nature*, 242–44.

12. See his discussion of Barth's, Calvin's, and his own position in *Christian Theology*, 177–99.

theology depends upon an overconfident and misguided epistemology, and therefore fails to arrive at knowledge about God.[13]

To avoid confusion with some of the more limited and extreme forms of natural theology, I will refer to my approach as creational theology. We would do well to entertain an approach to nature that includes much besides theistic arguments (I actually do not even discuss them), especially considering the shifts away from Enlightenment epistemology that have occurred since natural theology's heyday. Unlike Enlightenment epistemology, my approach is not strictly rationalistic or empirical, and unlike theistic arguments, it is not apologetic or an attempt to work outside of the Christian worldview. In contrast, creational theology assumes a Creator, even an incarnate Creator, in accord with Scripture's creation and incarnation narratives.

But even with these assumptions, my approach draws not exclusively upon Scripture but also upon our experience[14] of the world as a source for theology—"the world" meaning whatever falls normally outside of traditional theological sources, such as Scripture, tradition, and reason narrowly understood. This approach involves understandings drawn consciously or unconsciously from natural revelation, which I understand to be creation's *logos*, or the rational and aesthetic structure of reality—a structure that, for poet Kathleen Raine, is "word traced in water," "inscribed on stone," and the "Grammar of five-fold rose and six-fold lily."[15] Beauty is an aspect of this structured reality that could reveal something about God, if, as Henry Vaughan says, we "would hear / The world read" to us.[16] And this beauty of the world is a structured reality present not only in the objective world that we see around us, but also within us—within the structure of our subjective experiencing of that world. In other words, we could say that beauty is a combined objective-subjective phenomenon, bridging gaps between the (objective) structure of the world outside of us and the (subjective) realities and meanings that obtain within us. We have a certain structure of experiencing phenomena such as beauty, and we have created structures of thinking and reasoning about such experiences.[17]

---

13. Plantinga, "Reformed Objection," 187–98.

14. I use the word *experience* in a very broad way to mean the way the world is for us, not to suggest a theoretical development of empiricism.

15. Raine, "Word Made Flesh," 45.

16. Henry Vaughan, "The Tempest," 84.

17. I use "reasoning" in a very loose sense having to do with the healthy functioning of the mind. I mean thinking about, processing, and generally seeking to understand our experience. This reasoning involves aesthetic rationality and modes of artistic communication. Such reasoning does not necessarily require argumentation. Neither does it always require "rational" inferences in the narrow sense of the word, which might

These created structures also involve certain rational "disciplines" in any articulate thinking we might undertake, including theology—including those theological topics that are not based directly on special revelation, such as questions of how to recognize or interpret revelation. Whatever theological topic we engage, our experience, our worldview, and the structure of reality are at work in the process of engaging and interpreting revelation in order to formulate our theology.

As we formulate this theology, we abide by certain rational disciplines: for example, we cannot violate the law of non-contradiction; we cannot rest content with informal fallacies in our reasoning (such as the post hoc and false dilemma fallacies); we need some sort of reasons for the things we say, rather than merely wild assertions; we must be circumspect about our biases and our willingness to know the truth; we need to arrive at some level of confidence about what we claim to be true; and we need to do our enquiring within a collaborative community where others can test and sharpen our reasoning. These rational disciplines apply across cultural divides. This is why there is no eastern or western way of doing physics or mathematics; rather, the structured realities of the physical and mathematical worlds demand a certain structure of reasoning and discourse. Spiritual realities show a parallel continuity in our common human experiences: we all experience love and indifference, joy and suffering, good and evil, beauty and ugliness, and the rational disciplines apply to these spiritual matters as well, whether we are reasoning from special revelation or some other bit of knowledge about the world. So there is continuity among our theological reasonings from different sources, even if someone like Erickson, who claims Scripture as the proper source of theology, would minimize such continuity.

Still, our theological reasoning from creation complements but does not overrule theology based upon special revelation, since special revelation enjoys a privileged epistemic position as *theopneustos*, or "God-breathed" (2 Tim 3:16).[18] It is still essential that we conform our reasoning to God's understandings, as far as we understand them, since God is the only one who is not a part of creation and therefore not confined to a perspective from within it. God's understandings, as made available to us, correct our finite, limited, and often defective understandings. This conformity to special revelation is part of the discipline of a distinctively Christian creational theology. But just as special revelation is privileged as God-breathed, the created order also holds an important epistemic status

---

exclude the highly imaginative.

18. I leave the precise locus of special revelation intentionally open, since this locus differs with different theological systems.

as God-created. If the structure of the created world did not correspond intelligibly to the structure of the created mind, knowledge[19] would be impossible. Moreover, modern science could not have arisen without presupposing an ordered creation to be known, and could not continue to progress without continuing to assume an ordered reality. Fortunately and surprisingly for science, so much of the world is describable mathematically and by other means. Based on this describable structure of reality, this *logos*, creational theology is still a matter of speaking about God that is based on God's speaking, even if not based directly on special revelation.[20] This continuity of God's speech makes sense especially if, as Athanasius teaches, the *logos* revealed in creation is continuous with, and preparatory for, the *Logos* revealed in incarnation.[21] And through the incarnation, the rationality of God's "speech" plays out not just verbally but aesthetically through Christ, "the image of the invisible God" (Col 1:15). Accordingly, a creational focus on revelation by no means detracts from the christocentricity of revelation. In fact, it is the very possibility of incarnation—that God could put on flesh and identify with matter to this extent—that vindicates the concept of revelation through that matter. The incarnation changes forever our understanding of the physical world.[22] And with this insight, creational theology also becomes "incarnational" theology and at once that far removed from the category of natural theology. An incarnational-creational theology focuses on the ontological and aesthetic implications of the incarnation more so than the moral work of Christ (that is, on ontological participation more so than our moral imitation or justification, although the latter is not excluded but rather bound up with the former). But this ontological focus is more than appropriate, if, as David Bentley Hart notes, the primal fact of existence is the divine

19. Some of what I discuss under the broad heading of "knowledge" takes more the form of tacit awareness or understanding rather than conscious, propositional belief. After all, we do not normally think or experience the world in terms of "propositional belief" except at an artificial level of abstraction. The attempt to define knowledge only in terms of propositional belief is too simplistic and confining, and does not account for different types or domains of knowledge.

20. See Bauerschmidt's notion of God's speech. "Aesthetics," 201.

21. "He sojourns here as man, taking to Himself a body like the others, and from things of the earth . . . so that they who would not know Him from His Providence and rule over all things, may even from the works done by His actual body know the Word of God which is in the body, and through Him the Father." Athanasius, *On the Incarnation 14.8*. It is Christ who sums up creation, and as creation's Word, becomes accessible to us through creation. Compare Irenaeus's emphasis on "the summing up of all things in Christ" through *logos*, incarnation, and redemption (Eph 1:10, NASB). Irenaeus, *Against Heresies* 4.4.2–7; 4.20.1–8 (*ANF* 1:468–69; 487–90).

22. See Wynn, *Faith and Place*, 249.

aesthetic pleroma, upon which the moral category is merely an intrusion brought about by sin.[23]

An incarnational-creational theology also speaks to traditional debates between Protestants and Catholics on such topics as natural revelation and the *imago Dei* by refusing to enter into the "either-or" dilemmas that are often posed. Yes, nature and humanity are fallen, and our knowing is affected adversely; but this is not the end of the matter or the answer to a question: it is only the beginning of the matter and the question itself. For within creation, grace is also at work (whether common, special, prevenient, or irresistible is less important). And it is certainly not an essential tenet for Protestants (though perhaps for the more Barthian than Barth) that nothing can ever be known about God through creation. As to the extent of creation's fallenness and the epistemological effects, we must continue to discuss these questions. And in so doing, Protestants can and should consider Catholic answers, which are often not as "either-or" as one might suppose. In fruitful dialogue, we must continue the discussion on a case-by-case basis, remaining in touch with our embodied experience of the world, and resisting theological generalizations or abstractions that would impose Procrustean molds upon our actual experience of reality.

What is clear is that a creational-incarnational understanding of nature's ontology demands a theological engagement with the natural world around us.[24] We would certainly be remiss to allow non-Christians a monopoly in interpreting this natural revelation. Furthermore, the beauty of creation deserves particular attention, since both Christians and non-Christians engage this common reality of zebra stripes, meteor showers, and dandelion seeds. And both Christians and non-Christians find that merely studying the natural world puts us in touch with a reality that can cause us to start contemplating ultimate reality.[25] Scientific study of nature can even awaken quasi-religious emotion and reverence. Take for instance the BBC documentary "Lost Land of the Tiger" aired in 2010, in which scientists and photographers grew emotional and tearful upon seeing photographs of tigers, either recently killed by poachers or recently photographed alive in the wild.

Our experience of creation's beauty and divine spokenness certainly does seem to pose religious questions to us, and we wonder how much special revelation would interest us if it did not provide at least some answers to these questions already posed by our experience.[26] In fact, we recognize the

---

23. Hart, *Beauty*, 253.

24. McGrath makes a similar point in *Nature*, 24.

25. Lewis notes the religious implications of scientific study in *Screwtape Letters*, 4.

26. See Brown, *Continental*, 13–14.

value and uniqueness of special revelation by comparing it with our knowledge of the larger creation. Our experience of this creation poses questions about beauty—there is an aesthetic dimension to this reality in which we find ourselves—and so we discover that special revelation also meets us on an aesthetic level, through poetry, through symbols, in a way that engages the aesthetic dimension of our being in the process of delivering a meaning. In a similar way, natural beauty fits within the artistic character of a creation designed to facilitate (among other things) our knowledge of God and the world. It may even be that as aesthetic creatures, we see revelation, at least in part, through the lens of our questions about, and our desire for, beauty. This is because human beings are lovers as much as, or more than, we are knowers, and what we know is bound up in what we desire. This desire involves our aesthetic sense and rationality, and quite appropriately so, if, as Ruskin asserts, both art and philosophy, beauty and knowledge, are aspects of "the Heavenly Wisdom" manifest in creation. Heavenly wisdom so construed is not only concerned with beauty, but by virtue of that concern also "rejoices in the Truth."[27] Indeed, the ways in which beauty functions in our experience suggest that beauty could be a sort of divine "operation" within creation[28]—an operation pointing us toward theological truth that we can practice believing with our intelligent bodies. Beauty is a human *telos*, part of the goal of human flourishing, and as such, instead of merely pushing our knowledge forward by certain beliefs, beauty draws our embodied knowledge along by desire, toward the world's meaning, which is God.[29] In this way the beauty of creation evokes the idea of epistemic, and even eschatological, journeying toward God—a theme that I take up in the final chapter.

In view of these epistemic possibilities in a beautiful creation, we should reconcile what we think of as creational theology with what we think of as theology of special revelation, with the recognition that the two are not entirely separable. Scripture and creation illuminate one another, and each confirms the other's testimony.[30] Our understanding of creation contributes to our understanding of Scripture, as Jesus confirmed in his use of earthy parables, and the psalmists assumed in their descriptions of nature. And, of course, our understanding of Scripture also influences our outlook on creation. These two sources interpenetrate one another, sharing the same

27. Ruskin, Preface to *Amiens*, 24.

28. Graham Ward suggests the idea of beauty as a divine "operation" within creation in "Beauty," 57–59.

29. Wynn holds that places draw our embodied knowledge teleologically toward the world's meaning, namely God. *Faith and Place*, 79–80.

30. Carol Harrison suggests this relationship between Scripture and creation in *Beauty and Revelation*, 114.

divine light that illumines everyone (John 1:9). This relationship of sharing and interpenetration requires further refinement and formulation.[31] But one rather immediate implication is that revelation and reasoning are both based on created structures, whereas any duality between reason and revelation arises from an unduly secular epistemology that does not begin with creation's *logos*. Neither the church fathers[32] nor the early scholastics (as we shall see in Aquinas) would have posed such a duality, but saw both our reasoning and our response to revelation as a participation in God's own rationality: to "reason correctly"[33] is already to be enlightened by God. Revelation is but a higher, more concentrated enlightenment. It is an enlightenment tied intrinsically to a created, symbolic event that discloses transcendent reality—the same reality to which other aspects of creation point, to some lesser degree.[34] Such an understanding of revelation also invites beauty to function symbolically as revelation.

But, again, our engagement with this revelation requires certain disciplines. We must approach reality in a critical way rather than a naïve or skeptical way. We cannot expect to know all or even most of reality with absolute certainty or without the colorings of our subjective vantage points. And these colorings can be both positive and negative, sometimes leading us toward knowledge, sometimes away from it. Our knowledge is also limited by our finitude, which limits possibilities, and by our fallenness, which limits actualities—that is, fallenness limits what we actually do come to know out of what is possible for us to know. But, on the other hand, we cannot say responsibly that we know only very little of the reality that confronts us, or that we only "know" it in terms of its "cash value"—that is, what "works" by serving our own very limited ends. On the contrary, we apprehend reality subjectively but truly, with varying degrees of accuracy, but not with total relativity.

31. For example, special revelation can communicate very specific information that creation cannot. Special revelation also aids in distinguishing "is" from "ought" in the natural world in ways that might be unavailable in an examination of the natural world alone. See also the above remarks about special revelation's epistemological preeminence.

32. In addition to Athanasius (previously cited), see for example, Justin Martyr, *First Apology* 5, 46 (*ANF* 1:164, 178); *Second Apology* 13 (*ANF* 1:193); and Irenaeus's *Against Heresies* 4.4.2–7; 4.19.1; 4.20.1–8 (*ANF* 1:468–69, 487–90). See also the forthcoming citations of Augustine.

33. That is, to come to know the world in concert with grace and the divinely ordained structures within the mind and within the world, not in willful defiance against them.

34. John Milbank draws this contrast between secular epistemology and the functions of reason and revelation in the church fathers and early scholastics. "Knowledge," 24.

We also come to know the world in very diverse and subtle ways. We cannot reduce all knowledge to propositions or beliefs about information, or even to exact verbal descriptions; for how could we so reduce our knowledge of riding a bicycle, or of the yen in someone's eyes? Our knowledge of individual people is not a matter of analytically reading their words and gestures—knowing a person is something much higher and stranger that is hardly comparable. We come to know people and things produced by people, not so much through arguments, verbal information, or inferences from premises, but through a broad range of images or symbols displayed artistically—through a person's dress, vocal tones, facial expressions, body-language, and through our own interactive employment of the same. These "images" can communicate personality and social standing to such a degree that we often form judgments about someone's character based solely upon her hairstyle, or upon whether his belt matches his shoes. Such details of personal appearance may at first glance seem small and insignificant, yet they open up onto vast worlds of social skill, psychological health, identity formation, and meaning apprehension.

Communicative images of this sort are by no means statically "Platonic" but are "active," in ways that might be compared functionally to Christ's active living and interrelating in the world, or the *imago Dei* actively playing out through physicality and interpersonality.[35] We engage these images and socially mediated symbols in ways similar to our experiential engagement with art, in ways that surpass conscious, discursive reasoning. Hence, I use *reasoning* in a broad sense that includes an aesthetic rationality. And in line with this aesthetic rationality, Mark Wynn, in his religious epistemology of place, points to "various habitual modes of seeing-feeling-and-acting" oriented to the artful and the beautiful.[36] Such holistic perception of images allows for what is often a more direct and powerful communication. And it is the directness of this aesthetic communication that enables media and advertising to pique our desires and draw our tacit knowledge, despite ourselves, along certain tracks toward certain commercial, but also mythological, goals.[37] Advertising piques our desires for beauty, for human flourishing, even for paradise and godlikeness. Advertisers, perhaps better than anyone, understand how human beings come to know through desire, and advertisers are able to convey information effectively apart from didacticism. In a similar way, we would expect our knowledge of "soft winds, and

35. Viladesau suggests the idea of the *imago Dei* manifesting itself through physicality and interpersonality in *Theological Aesthetics*, 90–93.

36. Wynn, *Faith and Place*, 128.

37. I understand *myth* as "any symbolic story that underlies and shapes the collective life of a group" (Dulles, *Models of Revelation*, 134).

ringing streamlets, and shady coverts . . . the violet couch and plane-tree shade,"[38] and knowledge of God through such beauties, to be personal and aesthetically rational rather than discursive and propositional. Such knowledge would function not simply through propositions and inferences but through "beauty-skills" that require training and development. And by functioning in this way, the beauty of Christian art and liturgy reflects the wisdom and skill of the Christian tradition.

So our knowledge is indeed deeper, richer, and more existentially grounded than any formalism will allow. But we do obtain knowledge, because, as I will draw out from Aquinas's epistemology, the mind-body's created structures, in all their aesthetic richness, correspond intelligibly to the world's created structures in all their artful complexity. We find certain explanations, interpretations, and understandings—certain "pictures," "fittings," and "shapings"—to apply immediately to our experience of the world. These interpretations or pictures are *underdetermined* by experience; however, they are not underdetermined *equally*. That is, by testing, reasoning, observation, and education we are able to choose among interpretations and understandings, because we ask which ones best explain, or fit along with, our skills, knowledge, and experience of the world.[39] Without this ability to choose among understandings and interpretations, we would be in a very awkward and unlivable quandary as to what to believe about anything. But we do continue to modify these interpretations as necessary to fit our continuing experience. In this way *imagination* also becomes an important rational discipline—even, for Wordsworth, "reason, in her most exalted mood"[40]—because our knowing requires us to explore and consider new possibilities continually. Imagination both receives *and* interprets reality and this is distinct, on one hand, from merely analyzing and cataloguing the world, and, on the other, from departing from it into groundless faith.[41] Through imaginative exploration, every moment of life becomes a sort of study, and all study becomes a sort of imaginative yet disciplined play. Even science demands this creative knowing in its theorizing and postulating of

38. Ruskin, *Modern Painters*, 2:50.

39. See David Clark, *Know and Love*, 140, 161–63, on underdetermined interpretations. Epistemological approaches that do not emphasize this sort of reasoning become counterintuitive and incongruous to the way human beings think. In this regard creational theology is compelling, in that it accounts for theological knowledge similarly to the way that it accounts for other knowledge, such that knowing God is not drastically different from knowing people or other things about the world. See Meek, *Longing to Know*, 41.

40. Wordsworth, Fourteen Book *Prelude* 14.192.

41. Thomas O'Meara, "Aesthetic Dimension," 213, describes this function of imagination.

explanations for the world. We find knowledge, then, not naively in surface impressions of the world, nor esoterically in the depths of our own interpretations, but in the interlocution or resonance between these two (objective and subjective) spheres of reality.[42] We find knowledge in a beautiful world but also in and through ourselves as percipients made in God's image to perceive beauty as part of the created order. We find revelation in beauty not only in the way that its structure may reflect God, but also in the way that structure affects us. In this way, beautiful pearls, sea spray, or mossy glades, as Wordsworth says, "do speak, at Heaven's command, to eye and ear, / And speak to social Reason's inner sense, / With inarticulate language," bringing "authentic tidings of invisible things."[43]

If our knowledge operates through skilled interpretations of experiences such as beauty, then we are not inferring or deducing our knowledge "from the ground up" based on unquestionable "foundational" beliefs. By contrast with this view of foundations as starting points for our reasoning, we find ourselves reasoning already, and if we begin anywhere, it is with potentially modifiable (defeasible) and often tacit working presuppositions resulting from our experience and acting in the world. For most of our reasoning (outside the spheres of mathematics and formal logic), these presuppositions, these starting points, are not sacrosanct and immoveable; they need not be certain or yield certainty as "foundations." We modify them as we learn and experience more. Our theological starting points are thus not necessarily "properly basic beliefs" delivered by a presumed "proper functioning" of the mind within conducive environments.[44] Rather, our knowledge of God through creation is richer aesthetically and more nuanced epistemologically than such models (like Reformed epistemology) might suggest. The "proper functioning" of our reasoning from creation requires the development of aesthetic, epistemic, and religious skills with which to engage the world.

Here we may use Calvin to supplement what is called "Reformed" epistemology. Calvin, borrowing from Augustine,[45] emphasizes the aesthetic dimension of our reasoning about God—our survey of creation's

---

42. See Bauerschmidt, "Aesthetics," 207, for a similar description of interlocution between interpretation and objectivity.

43. Wordsworth, *Excursion* 4.1199–1201, 1138. Against the charge that Wordsworth was a pantheist, Stephen Prickett, *Romanticism and Religion*, 85–86, argues that Wordsworth's ambiguous mixture of naturalistic and Platonic statements was a poetic formulation that was neither pantheism nor Platonism, but an effort to hold God's transcendence and immanence in tension.

44. Plantinga, *Warranted*, 175.

45. See Augustine, *Free Will* 2.16.43, and *On the Trinity* 6.12.

"divine art" and "workmanship"—the "visible splendor" and engraved "insignia whereby he shows his glory to us, whenever and wherever we cast our gaze." Such an account suggests that sin has neither annihilated creation's revelation of God nor expunged human ability to receive such revelation. On the contrary, the aesthetic appreciation of divine art, for Calvin, leads to "admiration of the Artificer."[46] And much as this may call into question certain theological models, the same goes for epistemological models: the appreciation and interpretation of divine art is not quite on the order of basic or foundational belief any more than our appreciation and interpretation of human art is. On the contrary, such understanding of creation's art must be learned and developed through the use of aesthetic, religious, and epistemic skills that connect with our past experience and total human context. For example, we might see red, orange, and yellow leaves without really appreciating the beauty of autumn foliage, and we might appreciate a summer breeze without having the skill to compose Shelley's "Ode, to the Breath of Summer." In a similar way, human beings have always known God through creation by engaging or creating symbols as part of storied, aesthetic understandings of the world. We modify these storied and aesthetic understandings, these pictures of the world, to fit our experience with aesthetic and epistemic skill, such that metaphysics is always a properly poetic discourse. And as we continue to engage the beautiful in this way, we find that new interpretations emerge, including theological ones, especially if we allow for the "re-mythologizing" of a symbolic natural beauty (an approach to be developed in chapters 4 and 5). We must allow such beauty-experience to produce religious beliefs in its own way rather than merely confirm beliefs supposedly delivered more directly by, say, "faith-knowledge," input-output proper functioning, or some other model approaching an epistemological *deus ex machina*.

After all, our aesthetic perception certainly requires skill development, as exemplified by some Africans who are accustomed to seeing only in three dimensions, and so do not automatically recognize a photograph to be a two-dimensional representation of three-dimensional objects.[47] As a result of their environment and prior range of experience, they must "learn how to see" a photograph. Most life-situations seem to require learning of this sort, and our culture influences our aesthetic and epistemic skill sets. Similarly, we come to adopt religious beliefs through a long process of learning that begins in early childhood. Parents and culture impart religious ideas to us, and we grow to reflect upon this "training" and to evaluate it based on our

---

46. Calvin, *Institutes*, 1.5.1–2.

47. The source of this information is an African colleague named Michael Partridge.

own learning and experiences. Such upbringing comes with its own sort of "reasoning" processes (such as accepting authority and parental testimony) however limited in scope they may be. This experience of how religious beliefs are actually formed speaks to the need for skilled reasoning and revising of religious beliefs. Such a process parallels our ordinary revising of aesthetic beliefs and practices as we grow and develop and acquire more aesthetic attunement to the world.

Beyond our own individual skill in perception and belief formation, we also need others to confirm our beliefs and interpretations once they see how we arrived at them. If we are all alone in our unique interpretation, we should be cautious. This is not to say that we must convince everyone or even be able to demonstrate how we know something. We might simply have a feeling about what beauty is and about how it speaks of God without making arguments and without being able to articulate our feeling precisely. Our fuzziness does not make our experience any less veridical, but such fuzziness is always in need of questioning and refinement. We do need help, training, and interaction with others in order to refine our feelings, hunches, and intuitions. This is another rational discipline—a communal one. So if I am to be justified in my understanding of revelatory beauty, I do need to deal with any counterevidence honestly, and invite others to criticize or modify my understanding. That is, I need to be intellectually honest and circumspect.

Of course there are those who are intellectually dishonest about their experience of the world, and who "suppress the truth" in unrighteousness (Rom 1:18). But such defective reasoning cannot account for all incorrect conclusions about God, because people also apply different culturally inherited interpretations to their experience. Thus, some non-monotheists might experience "splendour in the grass . . . glory in the flower"[48] in much the same way as monotheists, and function cognitively quite well in that respect, while still explaining their experience in terms of the Tao or some other non-monotheistic concept. But these differing explanations should not be seen simply as the result of truth suppression or "epistemic malfunction," as Plantinga, rather patronizingly, maintains of non-monotheists.[49] On the contrary, non-monotheists could be functioning well epistemically given the cultural resources available to them. But by learning different explanations and interpretations, different ways of looking at creation, non-monotheists could begin to understand their experience of a beautiful world in monotheistic ways. Some people will suppress the

48. Wordsworth, "Ode," 181.
49. Plantinga, *Warranted*, 184.

truth, but the noetic effects of sin are certainly not a sufficient or appropriate explanation for monistic belief. Neither do such effects of sin minimize the importance of an aesthetic sort of reasoning in religious belief formation—an aesthetic rationality through which non-monotheists are already appropriately engaged with the world. This engagement can also certainly inform Christian theology. Still, the Protestant emphasis on sin does suggest that virtue, including epistemic virtue, is an important factor in how we reason about God and the world.

So, while creational theology reasons about beauty from within the Christian worldview, fully deploying its intellectual riches and epistemic resources, we should seek more than a rational but incommensurable "faith-knowledge" of beauty's revelation. That is, we should seek to describe a knowledge through beauty that is at least partly accessible (even if not acceptable) to those outside the Christian worldview as well.[50] As a created end and "image" of divine things, beauty speaks transculturally according to the logos of creation and human experience. And in this way, the experience of beauty, as a universal phenomenon, could provide a significant bridge between human experience and Christian theology.

In response to a beautiful world, we should not expect passivity to guide us into all truth, but instead, we should train our mind-bodies—our intellectual virtue and aesthetic skills—and take part in the improving of our own epistemic function through practice and education. So, as creation confronts us with its beauty, we should apply ourselves and our aesthetic rationality to the world in intellectually virtuous ways. In so doing, we should entertain the possibility, with Wordsworth, of a "conformity to," or an aesthetic and epistemic harmony with, "the end and written spirit of God's works,/Whether held forth in Nature or in Man,/Through pregnant vision."[51] Or in Augustine's terms, we should pose our questions to the world, and investigate beauty's response. And in interpreting beauty's response, we should paint the most complete and vibrant picture—that is, the most compelling interpretation—that we can. In this way, theology, like art, apprehends truth by eschewing the oversimplified and the cliché.[52] But all of this is merely a starting point for an aesthetic creational theology to be developed in everything that follows—a theology engaging an artful and beautiful world, fully expecting to encounter the divine artist.

50. But the fuller accessibility that God intends comes through an interpretation of beauty informed by all the theological resources of the Christian worldview. Cf. McGrath on the relationship between the Christian worldview and natural theology. *Open Secret*, 248.

51. Wordsworth, Fourteen Book *Prelude* 4.350–53.

52. On art and cliché, see Richard Harries, *Art*, 11.

THOMISTIC CREATIONAL THEOLOGY

Having outlined a creational theology of beauty, I now refine this understanding through interaction with Aquinas's distinctively creational epistemology. In the *Summa Theologica*, Aquinas, following Augustine, emphasizes a "divine light" present in the human mind-body that is integral to knowledge. This divine light is a noetic reference to the transcendent, an innate capacity that leads to knowledge of God when trained and used properly. Aquinas also describes a natural revelation in the ordered structures of reality—a reality that encompasses the transcendent.[53] This divine light in the mind-body and divine order in creation together reveal God, in that they reflect God's nature and make knowledge of God possible. For Aquinas, knowledge is the aesthetic harmony between these two aspects of revelation in accordance with the *logos* principle outlined above. This aesthetic harmony of knowing is a "proper functioning" that applies to Christian and non-Christian, the sinful and the saintly, and it furthers the vision of an aesthetic creational theology. This Thomistic model of knowing also begins to relate God's nature to created beauty. So my approach is first to describe knowledge of God through creation in general, and then to show how beauty lends itself appropriately to a revelatory function.

Protestant theologians and epistemologists do not typically discuss knowledge under the heading of natural revelation, since perhaps it is not obvious to post-Cartesian epistemology and post-Barthian theology that divine revelation could be woven into the fabric of created being. Nevertheless, a theological recasting of the "problem" of knowledge is in order, even if Aquinas's "solution" proves fairly commonsensical: his solution is to relate aspects of creation to God's nature as part of his doctrine of creation.

Like Aquinas, when biblical writers make claims about God's nature, they rely upon an understanding of creation, especially the profundities of the human and natural worlds. They presuppose that we understand created goods such as beauty before they apply these qualities to God in some way. Similarly, in Aquinas's argument from gradation, as well as in Anselm's *Monologion*, the apprehension of some quality of creation, such as beauty, anticipates an absolute source of that quality: "something which is to all beings the cause of their being, goodness, and every other perfection" (1.2.3).[54] Of course, the mere anticipation of an absolute perfection

---

53. See especially Aquinas, *Summa Theologica* part 1, questions 13, 76, 84. Future references will be parenthetical and in the following form corresponding to part, question, and article: (1.2.3). Although this edition has been superseded, I use the older translation because it is a more literal, and therefore more accurate, translation.

54. See Anselm, *Monologion*, 11–12.

in no way requires that such an Absolute exist. Yet assuming metaphysical materialism, it would be a curious state of affairs in which human beings, who had evolved from particulars and are themselves nothing more than complex configurations of particulars, however deluded they might be, made such a categorical leap by even for a moment entertaining a belief in absolute beauty, goodness, or absolute anything. After all, according to the naturalistic evolutionist, we highly evolved primates are concerned only with survival and genetic immortality, gathering our knowledge empirically by perceiving the world from which we arose. But we have never once seen an absolute. We have never heard, touched, or tasted an absolute anything—goodness and beauty relative to our own appraisals, yes, but no absolute goods or beauties. Why then have philosophers spilt so much ink cogitating on the absolute? Why expend so much effort trying to escape mentally from an impenetrable universe of particulars and relative qualities? Such effort would seem a strange and illogical outworking of the blind materialistic forces that brought human beings into existence. As an explanation, Freud's wish-fulfillment hypothesis takes for granted the category of absolutes, and does not explain how human beings could invent the category without having the capacity to think in such terms already.

But all of this is simply to raise the question of how human beings can know absolute, transcendent qualities—an absolutely perfect God for instance. Human beings are creation-bound, or epistemically "embedded" and "embodied" as knowers.[55] Whatever human beings know, we know through the medium of our created being with its cognitive and spiritual faculties. But the absolute divine perfection transcends creation, and the created mind of itself would seem to have no resources for reaching beyond creation to grasp this transcendent reality. For if knowledge were the product of created particulars only, and mediated through particulars only, then human beings would only comprehend relative qualities; there would be no genuine knowledge of absolute qualities—unless God in some way endowed the mind-body with this transcendent category.

By presupposing this divine endowment, Aquinas begins his epistemology. He admits frankly that "for the knowledge of any truth whatsoever man needs Divine help" (1–2.109.1). Without it, the logical consequence seems to be skepticism, especially with regard to the transcendent realm. For there would be no assurance that the mind grasps reality faithfully. There would be no assurance that the mind could even grasp a specially revealed word from God, mediated as it is through our subjective vantage points on the world shaped by our culture, language, and biology.[56]

55. Westphal, "Hermeneutics," 420, emphasizes our epistemic embeddedness.

56. Viladesau, *Theological Aesthetics*, 93, emphasizes these factors shaping our

How then does the mind-body know the transcendent, and what does Aquinas mean by "divine help"? God does not seem to infuse ideas directly into the mind as is the case in occasionalism.[57] Aquinas, following Aristotle, holds that knowledge begins with experience of the world, through the senses. So any understanding of divine beauty, for example, would rely on our prior grasp of created beauty. This prior grasp is what Aquinas has in mind when he says that "grace presupposes nature" (1.2.2); or, in other words, our knowledge of divine things presupposes our knowledge of natural things, and the grace of special revelation presupposes the grace of creation in its naturally-revealed order. In this sense, "nature never fails in necessary things" for human knowledge (1.76.5). Aquinas elaborates on this principle in regard to knowledge of the incorporeal: "Incorporeal things, of which there are no phantasms [i.e., sensible images], are known by us through comparison with sensible bodies, of which there are phantasms. . . . And, therefore, when we understand something about these things, we need to turn to phantasms of bodies, although there are no phantasms of the things themselves" (1.84.7). For Aquinas, knowledge of God requires some kind of comparison with the sensible images of creation: "since our intellect knows God from creatures, it knows him as far as creatures represent Him," that is, "as He is represented in the perfections of creatures"—their goodness, beauty, etc. (1.13.4). Thus, if only such "perfections" can "represent" the Godhead, we would do well to pay close attention to these qualities and consider *how* they might (re)present God.

But Aquinas seems to recognize a potential problem with this empirical account of knowledge. He knows that we make mistakes, and his realism is not entirely naïve. He states that "material things, as to the being which they have outside the soul, may be actually sensible, but not actually intelligible."[58] But in so claiming, Aquinas seems to anticipate a problem similar to Kant's *Ding an sich*: how can we know the "thing in itself"—exactly what the thing is—and not just our limited perceptions of the thing? How can we know the thing exhaustively? And how do we know that we are actually understanding the thing that we perceive? Certainly we have no non-circular justification for the reliability of our senses (should we come to look for such justification). Indeed, any evidence we can muster for sensory reliability is itself obtained through the very senses whose reliability is in question. The only escape from this proposed conundrum seems to

subjectivity.

57. See Jonathan Edwards, "The Mind," 36.

58. Aquinas thereby denies that immaterial Forms exist independently outside the soul: these Forms are not known directly, as Plato thought, but indirectly through their manifestation in matter (1.84.4).

be the presupposition of an epistemic "reliabilism," whereby we trust that our senses do *normally* function reliably in connecting us with the "extramental" world (should we come to invent this category)—that is, the world as it is "in itself," apart from our understandings of it.[59]

Divine Light: Revelation through the Mind-Body

Given this epistemic boat in which the philosophers might intend to place us, Aquinas's presupposition of a created framework for knowledge does not seem quite so unreasonable. His presupposition resembles a sort of epistemic reliabilism. He argues that in order for humans to attain knowledge via particulars, God must have "endowed" the intellectual soul with "the power of understanding," operating through intrinsic abilities of the mind-body (1.76.5). This is in contrast to any remedy for skepticism that posits special revelation alone and not the mind-body as that which informs us of reality, and so requires God to establish some extraordinary, supernatural link between our minds and reality. Even Descartes, beginning only with *ego cogito* (I think), falls back on the reliability of perception to connect with the world.[60] But we all fall back on the reliability of our perception, because our *ego cogito* presupposes prior knowledge based upon our acting in the world and perceiving it.

Yet if one believes that perception cannot really connect us to the world, then one might (with Barth) enlist special revelation to perform this function. Such a view of revelation's radical immediacy traces perhaps to Luther, as reflected in his choice of "*Offenbarung*" to translate *revelatio* and *apokalupsis*. John Montag believes that Luther was as concerned with the absolute certainty of religious knowledge as Descartes was with that of all knowledge. This concern for absolute certainty led eventually to an arbitrary faith confirming the validity of an esoteric revelation, as opposed to the Thomistic paradigm of a reasonable revelation making possible, and giving rise to, faith in what has been revealed. For Aquinas, revelation is not alien to nature's economy.[61] But in Luther's emphasis on *personal* faith, revelation, as an exclusively personal phenomenon, can become alien to nature. This is

---

59. "*Normally*" allows of course for errors, misperceptions, misjudgments, lack of training, etc. See William Alston, *Perceiving God*, 143, on reliabilism.

60. Cf. Karl Barth on revelation as the supernatural link between mind and world. Barth goes on to fault Descartes for his lack of skepticism and his reliance on perception. *CD* 3/1:346, 349, 363. See Fergus Kerr, *After Aquinas*, 24–26, on this point.

61. See John Montag, "Revelation," 50–51, 55–56, on this contrast between Luther and Aquinas.

especially true when the Renaissance's purely human backdrop for theology eclipses the medieval backdrop of a cosmos imbued with *logos*.[62] Yet it is our perception of this cosmos, rather than an egocentrically personal faith, that should inform our understanding of revelation.

In keeping with this sensitivity to perception, Aquinas could agree with Barth in requiring revelation for all knowledge, while giving that revelation a different locus within creation. Aquinas's view of God and creation precludes any fear of Descartes's evil demon, who would deceive the mind with an illusory world. For Aquinas, the mind-body is dependable, because it is not only created by God, it is also a "participated likeness of Him who is the first intellect. Hence also the intellectual power of the creature is called an intelligible light, as it were, derived from the first light" (1.12.2). This intellectual participation in God is "the spirit in man, the breath of the Almighty, that makes him understand" (Job 32:8, ESV), and it is necessary because Aquinas says that "we must not expect the entire truth from the senses. For the light of the active intellect is needed, through which we achieve the unchangeable truth of changeable things and discern things themselves from their likeness" (1.84.6). This innate capacity for understanding is "a participated likeness of the uncreated light, in which are contained the eternal types. . . . By the seal of the Divine light in us, all things are made known to us." Through this divine light we do not behold God himself in his perfect goodness or glory, because this knowledge is reserved for the state of the blessed (1.84.5). Nevertheless, "the intellectual soul as comprehending universals, has a power extending to the infinite." This is in contrast to animals, whose souls "are endowed with knowledge and power in regard to fixed particular things" only (1.76.5).

Karl Rahner draws out further implications from Aquinas's "divine light" of understanding. Aquinas says that the intellect in the process of reasoning "necessarily compares one thing with another by composition or division" (1.85.5). Through this comparing, Rahner argues that the intellect recognizes a particular as "finite, and as failing, by reason of its limitations. . . . It is shown to be *a* being as compared with being itself." By recognizing the particular in this way, that which transcends the particular is implicitly recognized as well.[63] This cognitive feat would seem impossible in a universe without transcendence or without a noetic reference to transcendence. For without an innate reference, we, like animals, would recognize particulars

62. Cf. Bauerschmidt, "Aesthetics," 206.

63. Rahner, "Thomas Aquinas," 24–25. Here I use Rahner's interpretation of Aquinas, because I find it plausible. I realize fully that it is heavily indebted to the transcendental Thomism of Maréchal, but discussing details of interpretation is not relevant to my present development of creational theology.

only. But the mind-body's transcendent reference enables abstraction from the particular to the transcendent absolute, and thus enables judgment—that is, our understanding of "something as a 'something.'" In other words, our connection to an infinite God gives us an elevated perspective from which to view objects in the world critically and recognize their finitude. In contrast to the Infinite, all that we experience is provisional and potentially in need of improvement.[64] We must understand these finite parts in light of the whole, and only God's impinging upon us can provide us with a true whole.

It is this transcendent whole that also shapes and makes possible human imagination as it contributes to knowledge. Our noetic reference to the transcendent whole allows us to arrange the particulars of our experience creatively rather than have particulars arrange us determinatively. Particular facts and experiences do not imaginatively interpret themselves, yet our imagination, with its aesthetic capacities and divine enlightenment, is a substantive way of integrating and interpreting particulars, and thus a way of arriving at meaning. In this way Aquinas's epistemology allows insight to arise from perceptual images.[65] To obtain such insight and to explain the world, we require an element transcending our perception to give various and imaginative meanings (i.e., theories, stories, and myths) to what we perceive. Thus the transcendent reference makes us creative knowers within a creative reality. And this creative aspect to knowing becomes especially important as we look for meaning in a beautiful world—for each sunny day and starlit night invites imaginative interpretations.

The transcendent reference is then an a priori, an innate function, like first principles that one cannot deny without invoking.[66] This innateness is reflected in Aquinas's statement that "the natural light bestowed upon the soul is God's enlightenment" yet is distinct from the additional "light of faith or prophecy" (1–2.109.1; 1.12.2). Through this innate capacity, "the intelligent being is naturally adapted to have also the form of some other thing; for the idea of the thing known is in the knower" (1.14.1; cf. 1–2.109.1). The intellectual soul "is such that it agrees with every being" by its constitution.[67]

In this account of knowing, Aquinas is both a rationalist and an empiricist. He is a rationalist in that knowledge is shaped by a priori categories, so the mind is not purely a *tabula rasa*. Though Aquinas uses this term, quoting Aristotle, he uses it only of the "passive" intellect, which merely

64. Cf. Rahner, "Faith," 68.

65. Viladesau connects meaning and insight to a non-determinative imagination. *Theological Aesthetics*, 82–83, 243.

66. See Rahner, "Thomas Aquinas," 24, 26.

67. Aquinas, *De Veritate*, 1.1.

receives perceptual data, and not of the "active" intellect, which abstracts form and meaning from particulars (1.79.2). Aquinas is also an empiricist in that knowledge begins with sense experience. His biblical anthropology shapes both his rationalism and empiricism, because he sees human beings as rational, embodied souls. Thus Aquinas could agree with Kant that "all our knowledge begins with experience," but "it by no means follows that all arises out of experience."[68] But in sharp contrast to Kant's a priori categories, Aquinas's a priori not only facilitates abstractions and imaginative interpretations of the perceptual world, it also partakes of the transcendent, grasping Being in relation to beings and making metaphysics possible.[69]

In bringing together rationalism and empiricism, epistemology unites with ontology—a union that was firm in the Middle Ages but severed into separate intellectual pursuits by the Enlightenment.[70] Descartes pursued rationalism apart from empiricism, while Hume pursued empiricism apart from rationalism. Alarmed by Cartesian dogmatism and Humean skepticism, Kant attempted a synthesis of these two approaches.[71] But as the medievals would insist, human knowledge finds true explication only within a divinely created and ordered reality. Indeed, knowledge has an ontological and creational foundation.

In a similar way, Martin Heidegger also sees an inseparable connection between knowing and being. He understands knowing as "a mode of Dasein founded upon Being-in-the-world."[72] In the Thomistic understanding as well, knowing is an aspect of our created being. Similarly, the world's status as "being known" is a function of its design.[73] But to disregard these implications of the doctrine of creation is to disregard our epistemic "embodiment" and "embeddedness" with its inherent precognitive categories. This oversight can become ultimately a futile Luciferian attempt to escape from finitude.[74] This creational perspective on epistemology is threatened not only by Cartesianism but also in the same way by the neoplatonic, nonsensory knowledge that Aquinas attacked so vigorously. Aquinas may have seen in this version of Neoplatonism a demand to know immediately as God knows—the same demand made by a disembodied Cartesian skepticism.

---

68. Kant, *Reason*, 41.

69. See Rahner, "Thomas Aquinas," 25.

70. See Ward, "Beauty," 64, on unified epistemology and ontology.

71. See Brown, *Philosophy*, 93.

72. Heidegger, *Being and Time*, 90.

73. Kerr, *After Aquinas*, 30.

74. See Westphal on embeddedness and the Luciferian attempt to escape from finitude. "Hermeneutics," 419–20.

And he may also have sensed that chronic dissatisfaction with the human epistemic situation leads directly to this sort of skepticism.[75] But for Aquinas, knowledge of the world and of God is not a meritorious achievement of Descartes's *res cogitans*; it is simply part of the graced existence of humanity, which entails the divinely arranged correspondence between mind-body and reality (cf. ST 1–2.109.1). It is grace that makes God approachable both salvifically and epistemically, even if virtue is an important factor in whether we actually do attain to salvific knowledge of God. Thus revelation through the mind-body and world is a matter of graced rationality.[76]

Knowledge, then, requires a noetic reference to, or category for, God, but in most cases is also mediated unavoidably through perception. And along with physical perception, the soul's spiritual faculties are also an element of creatureliness that mediates even direct mystical experience. As far as such experience might render knowledge, it requires the processing and conceptual categories of the created mind. God could infuse new categories into the mind, for we might assume that glorification entails this infusion: Aquinas recognizes that "our intellect . . . can be raised up above its own nature to a higher level by grace" (1.12.5). But even this type of experience is not purely transcendent, due to these newly created categories for receiving transcendence. In fact, the mind and even the senses might never become irrelevant, might always be indispensable, to our apprehension of a transcendent God. In this vein, C. S. Lewis declares that "there is . . . no vision of Deity Himself so close and so far beyond all images and emotions, that to it also there cannot be an appropriate correspondence on the sensory level."[77] This sensory mediation suggests a role for revelatory "images," even for sense-perceived beauty—one of the "perfections" by which Aquinas says that creatures represent God. But it is this mediation that is so easily ignored by an exclusive emphasis on special revelation or "faith-knowledge." Without such mediation, however, we would be left with the sort of Platonism in which Aquinas says the soul "would not need the body in order to understand: wherefore to no purpose would it be united to the body" (1.84.4).[78] But the body is integral to God's original ends and design in creating.

<hr>

75. Kerr, *After Aquinas*, 28, links Aquinas, Neoplatonism, and Cartesianism in this way. But of course Aquinas was not opposed to all strands of Neoplatonism, since he draws extensively on Pseudo-Denys.

76. See Rahner, "Rationality," 68–69, on the grace of rationality.

77. Lewis, "Transposition," 115.

78. Even without bodily mediation, in a disembodied state, we would still need the faculties of the immaterial soul to understand God; otherwise the I-Thou distinction would break down. Regarding mediation in mystical experience, Dulles believes that the great Christian mystics "are best interpreted as affirming that God makes himself

Aquinas suggests that the creatureliness that mediates knowledge of God can also be described in terms of the *imago Dei*. He says that "the image of God is found in the soul according as the soul turns to God, or possesses a nature that enables it to turn to God" in both knowledge and love (1.93.8; 3.4.1). This "turning" to God suggests an "active" view of the *imago*. Actively, the *imago Dei* manifests itself within the context of a physical, historical, and interpersonal world, such that our physicality and interpersonality contribute to who we are spiritually and individually. It is this image of God playing out within creation's context that makes God knowable.[79] The image of God also understands and is oriented toward the "(re)presentations" of God in the good and the beautiful, and this understanding and orientation are a significant part of what it means to be human.[80] Being human entails a "trans-traditional rationality" regarding the beautiful—a rationality that is appropriated and developed but not merely invented by human traditions.[81] So it is the Creator of the divine image who makes possible knowledge of himself, the world, and the beautiful—perhaps even knowledge of a relationship between himself and the beautiful.

Divine Order: Aesthetic Revelation in the World

Not only does Aquinas describe a God-implanted reference to the transcendent in the mind-body, he also describes revelation in the world. Though creation exhibits a certain "fallenness," it is not chaos, wherein we must pose the Humean question of whether effects really arise from causes. Rather, nature operates "only on the presupposition of created principles"; "for there is a good belonging to the very substance of nature, which good has its mode, species and order, and is neither destroyed nor diminished by sin" (1.45.8; 1–2.85.4). In creation, "each thing has a relation of *order* to something else" (1–2.85.4). It is for this reason that "nature never fails in necessary things," and "we receive knowledge from natural things" (1.76.5; 1.14.8). Creation is not a deceitful ontology but exhibits a divine order that is a condition and starting point for thinking and knowing.[82]

known by producing signs and effects of his presence in the soul" (Dulles, *Models of Revelation*, 148).

79. See Viladesau, *Theological Aesthetics*, 90–93, on this "active" *imago Dei*.

80. See Ward, "Beauty," 40, on human nature's link to the good and the beautiful.

81. McGrath, *Reality*, 96, holds to a "trans-traditional rationality" regarding beauty.

82. The terms *knowledge* and *revelation* presuppose that God is not a deceiver. As Phillip Blond points out, this is in contrast to William of Ockam's vision of a God who "owed no debt to man." Ockam entertained the possibility that "given reality and perception were illusory, arbitrary and liable to negation at any moment by the Creator"

Aquinas relates this divine order to *logos*, or participation in the Word of God, "the exemplar likeness of all creatures" (3.3.8). He also relates order to a "trace of the Trinity" at work "in every creature . . . according as it has a certain relation of order" (1.45.7). Thus, through their order, creatures can represent God imperfectly, even as names can describe God imperfectly (1.13.2). And through their ordered perfections especially, creatures represent God and are like him, because, in some sense, "all created perfections are included in the perfection of being," which is God: "*whatever good we attribute to creatures, pre-exists in God*, and in a more excellent and higher way" (1.13.2, 4; 1.4.2). These "perfections pre-exist in God unitedly and simply, whereas in creatures they are received, divided and multiplied" (1.13.4).[83]

Aquinas's relating of created perfections to God's perfection speaks directly to the idea of revelatory beauty.[84] The medievals saw beauty as an aspect of God's goodness that he had woven into his creation; so rather than distinguish beauty and goodness, theologians integrated them in the Greek term *kalokagathia*.[85] Human art, then, was seen as tapping into this divine aesthetic order: Boethius, for example, spoke of the "music of the spheres." Art was therefore sacred in its re-presenting of God's goodness.[86] As the human soul recognized the divine aesthetic order in material objects, that order harmonized with the soul's own structure, and this harmony was the essence of aesthetic experience.[87]

In a similar way, given what Aquinas says about the mind-body, we might also say that the soul's transcendent reference recognizes in creation an aesthetic harmony with its own structure. And, further, we could say that this recognition is the essence of knowledge, especially knowledge of God. Aquinas implies as much in *De Veritate*, where he says, "by its form a thing existing outside the soul imitates the art of the divine intellect; and, by the same form, it is such that it can bring about a true apprehension in the human

---

(Blond, "Perception," 234).

83. In addition, Aquinas, *Summa Contra Gentiles* 3.41.1, 3.19.4, draws on Aristotle to conclude that "the likeness of the cause must be found in the effects," such that creation must bear some likeness to its Creator. On the face of it, however, this is a more questionable line of argument.

84. Nonetheless, in the next chapter I question whether "perceptual beauty," as I describe it there, can really "pre-exist in God unitedly and simply" as Aquinas would seem to suggest. It is better to understand beauty here in a broader sense (e.g., *kalokagathia*) than I describe it in chapter 2. Here beauty relates to much broader aspects of knowing than does the symbolic practice of perceptual beauty that I develop later.

85. See Eco, *Aesthetics of Aquinas*, 13. Cf. ST 1–2.27.1.

86. Viladesau, *Theological Aesthetics*, 150–51.

87. See Eco, *Aesthetics of Aquinas*, 11.

intellect."[88] Our intellect does not project an arbitrary order upon the world; rather, the world impresses its created order, "the art of the divine intellect," upon the mind-body.[89] Thus, Aquinas holds together the "order of nature" and the "order of reason" in close relation, because they must harmonize to bring about knowledge (1–2.77.3; 1.84.5). But notably, the "order of reason" does not primarily concern propositions, inferences, and arguments, but our grasp of divine art, our aesthetic rationality. The order of nature and the order of reason also correspond to two "suns": "The material sun sheds its light outside us," illuminating the created order; "but the intelligible Sun, Who is God, shines within us" (1–2.109.1). This combined subjective-objective account of knowledge also prepares the way for a combined subjective-objective account of beauty, forthcoming in the next chapter.

Aquinas's epistemology is, then, also theology—the natural outworking of his doctrines of creation and humanity. Aquinas makes knowledge the proper fulfillment of both the mind-body and the world: that is, God has made everything for a purpose and destined it to certain ends. It is the final cause of the mind-body to know and of the world to be known. Aquinas's doctrine of creation encompasses humanity, such that, as knowers we are at home in the world and the world is at home within us in terms of our apprehension of its meaning.[90] Creation thus, in an artful way, accommodates the ends of a God who reveals himself according to an aesthetic rationality.

There is good reason to follow Aquinas in supposing that human knowledge, especially knowledge of God, depends upon natural revelation. Knowledge of God seems unlikely apart from an image of God in humanity with some implanted reference to the transcendent. Even the mind-body's grasp of transcendent categories may in itself be revelatory (in my deliberately broad sense of the term). Given that human beings are creation-bound, knowledge of things beyond creation would seem impossible unless God penetrates those bounds by means of revelation. If human beings are thoroughly embedded knowers, revelation embeds the transcendent within the embedded knower. This noetic reference to the transcendent harmonizes with an aesthetic order (including the beautiful) embedded in creation: this is the essence of knowing. And by knowing, both the mind-body and the world move toward their divinely appointed ends. Moreover, we are well within our epistemic rights to presuppose, and work with and in, this creational epistemology in a way that tests, grounds, and supports it, since secular epistemology does much the same with epistemic reliabilism

---

88. Aquinas, *De Veritate*, 1.8.

89. See Kerr, *After Aquinas*, 27.

90. See Kerr's summary of Thomistic epistemology, ibid., 30–32.

in order to avert skepticism. Aquinas's epistemology amounts to a more fully orbed reliabilism based upon the doctrines of creation and humanity.

This conception of revelation in the mind-body and in the world constitutes a fused horizon, a limen between the transcendent and immanent. Human knowledge, like the medieval understanding of beauty, becomes an operation of the divine in, with, and through creation. Therefore any dichotomy of "the human, worldly and rational alongside that which is Christian" cannot apply, since Aquinas recognizes no substantive conflict between grace and the nature that is but one aspect of grace.[91] As A. N. Williams says of Aquinas's epistemology, it proves "impossible to keep the realms of the natural and the supernatural distinct. . . . "Beyond us, yet ourselves" is one of the great themes upon which the *Summa* is a set of variations."[92] To explain human knowledge, Aquinas would indeed place us within a "haunted" universe that is "beyond us, yet ourselves." We must therefore accept God's revelation in various forms, through the created context in which knowledge operates in all its physicality, interpersonality, aesthetic depth, and richness.[93] Indeed, we must accept it even in the form of a man, Jesus, living and interacting in the world, with all the aesthetic implications of such physical "imaging" of God.

God's Nature and Created Beauty

We can apply Aquinas's epistemology more specifically to knowledge of a beautiful world, and to knowledge of God through beauty. Parallel to knowledge through beauty, Proverbs locates God's wisdom in creation in human intelligence and even in the ant, locust, and lizard (Prov 6:6; 30:24–28). If creation can thus reflect God's wisdom, then surely creation could similarly reflect other aspects of God's nature, perhaps even an aesthetic aspect of his nature.[94] For if the created order indeed reflects "the art of the divine intellect," and corresponds to God through created perfections such as beauty, we find that knowing the world, knowing God, and finding meaning in the beautiful are not entirely separate pursuits. And if aesthetics contributes significantly to knowledge, we should ponder more specifically what it contributes to knowledge of God. For Wynn, aesthetic knowledge

91. Barth, *CD* 3/1:414. See Montag, "Revelation," 45.

92. Williams, "Argument to Bliss," 505–26.

93. Viladesau, *Theological Aesthetics*, 92–93, focuses on the physical and interpersonal context of revelation.

94. Patrick Sherry, *Spirit and Beauty*, 140, makes this comparison between beauty and wisdom.

of the world's meaning, or *"genius loci,"* "is, at least in part, constitutive of knowledge of God";[95] and the medievals also saw aesthetic experience as especially theophanic, because they presumed an aesthetic link between earth and heaven.[96] For instance, Suger, abbot of St.-Denis, understood his experience of ecclesiastical art and Gothic architecture to "transport" him "by the grace of God . . . from this inferior to that higher world in an anagogical manner."[97] And even today, upon entering a dim Chartres cathedral, with its unearthly stained-glass gems piercing the gloom, or upon ascending its carved towers that brood over the landscape, one can experience something similar. Suger's implication is that this higher world, and even God himself, should also be called beautiful in some sense.

Patrick Sherry argues that God's beauty is indeed present in some way in creation, and his analogical approach to beauty takes us part way toward a creational theology of natural beauty. Sherry maintains that the principle of creation in God's image can be extended beyond humanity to all of creation because of texts like Romans 1:20 and Psalms 19:1–6; 104. This scriptural foundation helps allay fears that his approach amounts to Platonic corruption of Christianity.[98] In contrast to Sherry, however, Nicholas Wolterstorff is much more cautious about any transparency or revelation in created objects.[99] His caution is in keeping with the Reformed tradition's concerns about natural theology. Reformed theologians would certainly consider beauty a gift from God, but could maintain that God creates beautiful things without being beautiful himself.[100] Wolterstorff's caution raises the question of how finite, corporeal creation can image an infinite and incorporeal God.

How indeed can so many different kinds of beauty in physically differentiated creatures all reflect the beauty of an incorporeal God? Sherry opts for an explanation based on "cross-categorical comparison" or analogy. He notes that different categories of objects display different kinds of beauty. For example, the beauty of visual art seems quite different in character from the beauty of music or poetry. In a similar way, an incorporeal God might possess a different kind of beauty than that of corporeal objects, yet one might still rightly ascribe beauty to God. Sherry finds support for this cross-categorical comparison in Aquinas, who understands the created order to

---

95. Wynn, *Faith and Place*, 69.

96. Eco, *Aesthetics of Aquinas*, 14.

97. Suger, *Church of St.-Denis*, 65.

98. Sherry, *Spirit and Beauty*, 128, 132.

99. Wolterstorff, *Art in Action*, 49.

100. Sherry, *Spirit and Beauty*, 54, 131.

reflect God's nature analogously (1.13.2; 1.4.2).[101] That is, the perfections that "pre-exist in God unitedly and simply" are "received, divided, and multiplied" in creatures (1.13.4). Thus Anselm also prays, "You have in Yourself, Lord, in Your own ineffable manner, those [qualities] You have given to the things created by You according to their own sensible manner."[102] In other words, God bestows beauty on each creature according to its own unique nature, just as beauty applies in its own way to God's nature.[103] And out of his wisdom and goodness, God has established precisely these differences that we observe between himself and creation (cf. 3.1.1).

This line of argument looks promising; however, we would infer from it a curious difference between perceptible created beauty on one hand and imperceptible divine beauty on the other. And this notion of imperceptible beauty raises some difficulties that I will address in the following chapter, including our quandary as to what divine beauty would be like. The analogy between created beauty and God's nature seems appropriate but only takes us so far in describing God. Yet beauty may have more to say about God and his intentions than this minimal sort of analogy allows. If beauty is to say more about God, we must abandon analogy in the strictest sense and employ it in a much looser way. Interestingly, Sherry also holds out the possibility that created beauties might symbolize God in some way.[104] This is a promising suggestion that could give revelatory beauty more substantial content than a stricter analogy provides, and I will explore possible symbolisms of natural beauty in the following chapters. But symbolism still seems to function best within a broadly-defined analogical relationship between God and created beauty. In other words, symbols seem to communicate best when they, in some sense, "resemble" their referents. Nonetheless, Wynn suggests that "resemblance" in this sense might be more accurately understood as "necessary aesthetic complement." For example, objects in a painting can complement each other without resembling each other, and the painting as a whole can complement the artist without resembling him. This suggestion accommodates the notion of creation as divine art developed in chapter 4.[105]

Aquinas himself does not mention beauty explicitly as an analogical term, but he does suggest that beauty and goodness are really two different ways of looking at the same thing (1–2.27.1).[106] What makes an object good

---

101. Ibid., 134, 137–39. Cf. Aquinas, *Summa Contra Gentiles* 3.41.1, 3.19.4.

102. Anselm, *Prosologion*, 97.

103. Sherry, *Spirit and Beauty*, 37.

104. Ibid., 138.

105. Wynn, "From World to God," 379–94.

106. See Aquinas, *De Veritate* 21.3; Sherry, *Spirit and Beauty*, 39; Eco, *Aesthetics of*

or beautiful for Aquinas seems to be the degree to which it "imitates the art of the divine intellect" without privation.[107] For example, a coral reef is good and also beautiful insofar as it is what God intended and designed it to be. Jacques Maritain goes further than Aquinas by affirming that beauty is an analogous term that can apply to all being in analogous ways—even to what we would normally call ugly.[108] But to take this route seems to rob the term *beauty* of much of its meaning.[109] This concern also relates to our quandary regarding imperceptible beauty, and I return to it in the following chapter.

Despite these sorts of limitations, some analogy from created properties seems essential to our understanding of God. That is, there must be some meaningful relationships between words and referents as applied to God and words and referents as applied to creatures. Otherwise, it is difficult to see how thoughts about God could even begin to enter finite minds unless our mind-bodies were already inclined to understand certain creatures as, in Austin Farrer's words, "symbols or shadows of God."[110] For, even the statement that "no one is good but God alone" (Mark 10:18, RSV) suggests that we know God, the essential good, only by analogy from the created good, since all knowledge is mediated. And the better we know the created good, the better our analogies to God will be.[111] For this same reason we should seek to gain a better understanding of created beauty. But along with analogical statements, Scripture also emphasizes what God *is not* and thereby prevents analogy from ascribing created properties inappropriately to God.[112] Analogy, when applied to God, expresses similarity while always assuming an even greater dissimilarity. In this way, through an inherent epistemic humility, analogy finds its contribution to knowledge between a fruitlessly empty apophaticism and a sterilely rigid cataphaticism, in the free spaces of possibility and potentiality. Analogy promotes a vision and a mode of discourse; it responds to the Spirit's leading in the direction of all truth.[113] Analogy, broadly understood, seems to be the mode by which knowledge of God through creation operates, and Farrer maintains that

---

Aquinas, 31.

107. Aquinas, *De Veritate* 1.8.

108. Maritain, *Art and Scholasticism*, 30. Cf. Sherry, *Spirit and Beauty*, 37.

109. Cf. Sherry, *Spirit and Beauty*, 40.

110. Farrer, *Glass*, 88–89.

111. Bernard Lonergan, *Topics*, 30–31, discusses this relationship between divine and participating good.

112. Viladesau, *Theological Aesthetics*, 99–100, emphasizes Scripture's constraint upon analogy.

113. Cf. Hart, *Beauty*, 242, 311, 314–15, on the function of analogy.

"'analogies' is only another name for sober and appropriate images."[114] Thus our vision of creation's beauties, if taken as "images" or "symbols," could cultivate a greater symbolic vision that begins to grasp forward into the knowledge that God has for us.

The analogical approach to beauty also has the advantage of being a metaphysically weaker claim than might result from a theoretical development of Platonic forms. Just as it is difficult to encompass all beauties, including the incorporeal, under the same term, it would be even more difficult to describe a Platonic essence of beauty in which all beauties share.[115] Nevertheless, if we emphasize only God's transcendence and difference from all created things, we shall have very little to say about God that is meaningful and convincing given our creaturely outlook.[116] We do need verbal and other sorts of links, relations, correspondences, between God and our created nature. Without them, we also run the risk of seeing the world merely as a collection of data that says nothing about God and therefore tacitly excludes him.[117] But why should we not expect creation to reflect the richness and profundity of God's nature in manifold ways?[118] After all, says Aquinas, "it belongs to the essence of goodness to communicate itself to others," and "it would seem most fitting that by visible things the invisible things of God should be made known; for to this end was the whole world made, as is clear from the word of the Apostle (Rom. i. 20)." Even so, Aquinas avers that this communication of God "is brought about chiefly by *His so joining created nature to Himself*" in the incarnation (3.1.1).

Incarnation and Redemptive Beauty

The doctrine of the incarnation makes even stronger the link between God and his creation presupposed by the *imago Dei* and texts like Romans 1:20. For in the incarnation, God "puts on" his own created matter, becoming a man born of woman while remaining at the same time uncreated God. Anselm expresses this idea poetically in his third "Prayer to St. Mary": "God who made all things made himself of Mary. . . . that all nature in you [Mary] might be in him."[119] If doubts persist about whether God's nature can really be seen

114. Farrer, *Glass*, 71.

115. See Sherry, *Spirit and Beauty*, 38, 140, concerning an analogical versus Platonic understanding of beauty's relationship to God.

116. Sherry raises a similar concern in ibid., 139–40.

117. Ward, "Beauty," 36, notes the problem of an "opaque" creation excluding God.

118. Cf. Sherry, *Spirit and Beauty*, 140.

119. Anselm, "Prayer to St. Mary," 120–21.

through creation, these doubts are alleviated by the incarnation, in which God's nature is revealed through the incarnate body of Christ. The incarnation demonstrates that God is at least partially expressible through created, physical realities. While the totality of Christ's living and acting in the world is not strictly *analogous* to God, Christ as *Logos* and image does relate God to creation properly, rationally, and communicatively. And if "all nature" becomes part of Christ through Mary, then this divine incorporation of nature blurs the lines between the seen and unseen, the physical and the spiritual, the created and the Creator. For Christ encompasses both the created and uncreated realms, and offers them both to us, so to speak, as gifts through him.[120] The incarnation thus has direct implications for natural, aesthetic revelation, because Christ's giving of himself to the world makes possible the revelation of God through the world's forms. Because of the incarnation, as Wynn says, the world's "storied identity" is "changed fundamentally," and the world need not be seen as opaque data that tacitly excludes God.[121]

Aquinas also seems to regard the incarnation as central to aesthetics. Quoting Augustine, he claims that Christ is *"so to speak, the art of the omnipotent God"* (1.39.8).[122] But beyond his "artistic" representation of God's immaterial nature, Christ also establishes a much more tangible created beauty. In the resurrection, Christ has, in Richard Harries' words, "raised earthly beauty to everlasting life."[123] And by ascending to the right hand of God, Christ has actually established the place of physical beauty within the divine fellowship. Therefore, in opposition to the Gnostic devaluing of the physical, we can value Christ's physicality as a suitable expression of God. And since beauty is part of Christ's human physicality,[124] we can also value

120. See Ward, "Beauty," 47–48, on Christ's "giving" of the created and uncreated.

121. Wynn, *Faith and Place*, 249.

122. But, again, a work of art is not strictly analogous to the artist, even though it is still logically connected to the character of the artist.

123. Harries, *Art*, 37.

124. That is, Christ would seem to possess, at the very least, an ordinary, general sort of beauty of the human body in his pre-glorification humanity. And his glorified body, as truly glorified in every respect, would seem to require an ideal physical beauty. In both cases beauty receives value christologically, even without Christ's pre-resurrection body being exceptionally beautiful, although different positions have been taken on this point. While some have emphasized Isaiah 53:2 in relation to Christ, others emphasize Psalm 45:2. Cyril of Alexandria, emphasizing the former text, saw no need for human splendor in Christ's pre-resurrection body. Similarly, Eusebius of Caesarea, student of Origen, stressed the complete transformation of Christ's humanity in the transfiguration. Compatible with this position is the stress on Christ's spiritual rather than physical beauty in Augustine, Bonaventure, Barth, and von Balthasar. Taking the opposite position, Nicephorus the iconophile saw the incarnation as raising human nature to perfect bodily beauty, and Theodore the Studite implies the same by suggesting

the created and physically beautiful in all its physicality, looking beyond this particularity to its source in the divine nature, and looking also for expressions of the divine nature in the beautiful.[125] For, as Simone Weil suggests, all beauty may be "as it were an incarnation of God in the world."[126]

The incarnation thus becomes a guiding principle for our aesthetics and epistemology. The incarnational receiving of all things, created and uncreated, including the beautiful, as gifts through Christ recalls the Thomistic theory of knowledge, in which knowledge is also a gift of grace. The doctrine of the incarnation further reintegrates epistemology and aesthetics with ontology, because both beauty and knowledge find true explication only within a divinely created reality that includes an enfleshed God. The incarnation reaffirms the impossibility of separating the natural and the supernatural, and reasserts the theme of "beyond us, yet ourselves."[127] And this theme also resounds when we apprehend the creation in aesthetic experience, because much as Christ is "beyond us, yet ourselves," created beauty is also "ourselves" and yet grounded meaningfully "beyond us" in the nature of God. Because beauty relates in this way to Christ's redemptive duality—his manhood and Godhood—we might, as one possibility, read beauty christologically[128] as a sign of Christ's redemption of the world. For, as Roger Scruton says, "nobody who is alert to beauty is without the concept of redemption—of a final transcendence of mortal disorder into a 'kingdom of ends.'"[129] We might also begin to receive beauty redemptively in a way parallel to our reception of Christ's redemption—that is, through the world Christ entered and indwelled. For, like the incarnate Christ, beauty as a redemptive sign and divine operation in no way lifts us inappropriately out of the world, but returns us more profoundly to a compelling world from which Christ's redemption is inseparable.

---

that whatever is characteristic of Christ's humanity must be characteristic of God the Word. Gerard Manley Hopkins also claims physical beauty for Christ on the grounds that he was conceived by the Holy Spirit. Aquinas, on the other hand, seems to take a cautious mediating position, suggesting that Christ possessed whatever physical beauty was proper to the dignity of his station and role. See discussions in Sherry, *Spirit and Beauty*, 73–75; Nichols, *Art of God*, 66, 85–86; and Hopkins, *Sermons*, 34–38.

125. Harries, *Art*, 43, emphasizes both valuing and looking beyond particular beauties.

126. Weil, *Gravity and Grace*, 137.

127. Williams, "Argument to Bliss," 522.

128. That is, in the eschatological sense of Christology relating to Christ's glorified, beautiful physicality, not in the sense of Christ's suffering being "beautiful," as some would call it.

129. Scruton, *Beauty*, 188.

Beauty, then, could be not just a static relationship between God and creation, but an active operation—an operation that we receive simply as part of creation, and that we can learn to receive in more profound and revelatory ways.[130] Rahner refers to such operations as "the analogy of being, meaning that all realities have an inner connection, refer to each other, are in some way related, and can in the final analysis be understood only when we transcend them, as individual things, in the direction of the whole of reality." If beauty connects to God in this way, and we can transcend created beauty through our noetic reference to the transcendent, then we can understand beautiful pinions, starfish, or whistling loons as "revelation of a higher, different, more comprehensive reality."[131] And in light of the incarnation's redemptive focus, we can also understand beauty as a revelation and operation by which we strive desirously toward the totality of redemption, toward the comprehensive divine reality that integrates the beautiful with ourselves, just as Christ's body integrates beauty with glorified humanity. In this incarnational and redemptive integration of beauty with humanity, the beautiful (*kalon*) not only calls (*kalein*) to us through desire, but perhaps also calls (*kalein*) or *names* us redemptively.[132] That is, beauty could be an expression of the redemptive "new name" ("beautiful one," "desirable one") given on a white stone by Christ to those who overcome (Rev 2:17; cf. Isa 62:4–5, 12). These suggestive ideas on beauty and redemption lead into further development of natural beauty as a sign and operation of redemption, and I return to these ideas later.

Such meaning in a beautiful creation reaches beyond Aquinas's own epistemology and doctrine of analogy, but it does not seem opposed to his thinking. At the other end of the spectrum, however, the rejection of any meaning-laden connectivity between God and creation has rather serious implications.[133] Such a rejection implies that creaturely nature cannot relate to God's nature except through negation, and therefore cannot readily apprehend revelation. This situation fosters agnosticism toward God by implying that we can only "understand" God by negating creation, including its beauty. It even calls into question whether creation can truly express God's love for us, even in the incarnation. And rather than protect

130. Ward, "Beauty," 57–59, suggests that beauty is a receivable divine operation that returns our attention to the world redemptively.

131. Rahner, "Art Against the Horizon," 164.

132. See Chrétien, *Call and Response*, 7–8, 13–14, on beauty calling and naming. This link between the Greek words is unfortunately implausible etymologically, although it is very suggestive and employed by Pseudo-Denys in his *Divine Names*.

133. See for example Laurence Hemming's criticisms of the analogy of being in, "*Analogia non Entis*," 119–32.

God's transcendence, it seems to oppose God to creation as an absent or contradictory subcategory of being instead of the prolific primal Being in which all else subsists.[134]

God would indeed seem to be an epistemically elusive contradiction to humankind if the only analogy between God and humankind is an inscrutable "faith-knowledge." In contrast, the *analogia entis* grounds and makes possible theological knowledge as but a reply in kind to creation—an aesthetic response to match and describe creation's artistry. This understanding of theology certainly accords with Aquinas's creational epistemology. And further, this analogically-inclined relating of God and creation, with the incarnation as the prime instance, becomes ultimately part of creation's artistry, functioning as the overarching logic of both language and creation.[135] This theme unfolds in chapters 3–5 through the idea of creation as a revelatory work of art requiring our aesthetic and theological response.

CONCLUSION

Creation circumscribes humankind, giving us aesthetic form and function. And God must reveal himself through this artful created medium, through which he has given us a uniquely aesthetic rationality to apprehend his revelation. Since beauty is a prominent quality of creation that can be understood as corresponding to God, there is reason to believe that beauty functions as a form of revelation. The corporeal beauty of creation may very well express the incorporeal nature of God, and could also have a redemptive disclosure and function. Moreover, God's participation in creation through the incarnation makes the transcendent and revelatory character of beauty all the more fitting. But this general framework for revelatory beauty requires a more detailed formulation to follow.

Nonetheless, these conclusions may not be convincing if one stresses the qualitative distinction between God and creation so as to rule out meaningful interrelations. Or even without posing this extreme gulf between God and creatures, one might still reject my overall epistemological approach to creational theology in favor of, on the one hand, a more "Reformed" epistemology or, on the other, a traditional natural theology.[136] But apart from objections along these lines, a creational theology of natural beauty holds

134. Cf. Hart's objections to the rejection of the *analogia entis* in *Beauty*, 242.

135. See Hart, ibid., 306, 311, 315, on the *analogia entis* as a rationality making possible an artistic theology.

136. Traditional natural theology, however, does not make superfluous an additional creational theology.

promise for theological knowledge, and will gain strength and support through further heuristic development and practical use. Through such development and use, the relationship between God and created beauty begins to imply more for our conception of God than has yet been explored.

2

The Phenomenon of Beauty,
A Reflection of the Divine Nature

I HAVE PROPOSED A relationship between created beauty and the divine nature, but to describe that relationship more fully requires a thorough investigation of the concept of beauty. The first part of this chapter pursues an understanding of how we use the word *beauty*, which is, after all, a notoriously slippery word. I map out different ways of using this word and other related words in an effort to describe our actual experience of the beautiful more adequately. From among these diverse understandings, I choose and develop a particular understanding of beauty for the purpose of examining its revelatory potential: an understanding of what I call "perceptual beauty"—a framework that is suitable to the common human experience of natural beauty. This begins a description of beauty that continues in various ways through the remaining chapters, while keeping in focus our creation-bound knowledge and experience. In light of creation's mediation of knowledge, before we attempt to understand what "divine beauty" might mean, we should first elucidate beauty as creatures perceive it. That is, rather than impose an understanding of beauty "from the top down" through metaphysical or theological speculation, we should seek to understand what beauty is at the level of our experience before we then attempt to theologize it. For, we might expect that the beautiful creation, as we experience it, and as it facilitates knowledge of God, reveals God intelligibly.[1] This experiential, perceptual beauty contrasts with historical, theologi-

---

1. Of course, one might first attempt to describe God's beauty and then apply this

cal usage of the word, which connects beauty explicitly with God's essence. But this traditional usage fits neither our normal contemporary use of the word, nor our generally accepted descriptions of beauty-experience. Thus a reconnecting of beauty-phenomena with God is necessary in order for our theology of beauty to make sense based on our aesthetic experience of the world. The second part of the chapter moves toward this reconnecting, exploring especially how and to what extent perceptual beauty might reflect and reveal God's nature. This discussion builds upon the preliminary one in chapter 1 regarding the relationship between God and created beauty.

I proceed along these lines by first arguing for the inadequacy of wholly subjective understandings of beauty. I then propose a combined subjective-objective understanding of perceptual beauty, the "subjective-objective" nature of which follows from my epistemology in the first chapter. I characterize this understanding of beauty by example, and distinguish it from related beauty-concepts. As part of this characterization, I describe objective beauty-properties, and I defend the need for subjective properties in opposition to G. E. Moore's objective-only position. I also suggest that a combined subjective-objective understanding borrows strengths from both classical and Romantic intuitions about beauty. Finally, in the second part of the chapter, I consider how this understanding of perceptual beauty, developed within the context of creation, might also give further insight into the divine nature, even if beauty is not understood to be an essential divine attribute.

But I do not pretend that my understanding of perceptual beauty is a final and definitive description of what beauty is. My category of beauty is a specific, and hence, narrowed one, and I recognize that there are other profitable ways to speak about beauty (or other kinds of beauty) than the one I have chosen. I also acknowledge significant and closely related aesthetic phenomena, such as the sublime, that fall outside my category. But I want to distinguish perceptual beauty from related concepts such as goodness, moral goodness, and sublimity, partly because I believe that theology can deal with these ideas better in other ways than through beauty, and partly because such distinctions sharpen our concept of beauty as we use the term theologically. Simply by recognizing these different modes of discourse on beauty, or different "beauties," we enrich our theological aesthetics.

---

concept of beauty to creation; but this approach does not avoid creaturely mediation, and raises other difficulties regarding what we mean by beauty, which I address in the second part of the chapter.

AN UNDERSTANDING OF PERCEPTUAL BEAUTY

We require an understanding of beauty before proceeding with a theology of beauty, and yet the difficulty of describing the beautiful always confronts us. Multiple, highly-nuanced theories of beauty claim authority—there are least sixteen definitions of beauty categorized by Harold Osborne—and the difficulty of choosing among these accounts is compounded by the different meanings attached to the word in common parlance. People can hold different conceptualizations of beauty even if their actual experience of a glassy alpine lake or a sea lion cavorting is roughly equivalent.[2] Add to this, diverse intuitions, sensitivities, and cultural preferences, and the obstacles to definition lead David Bentley Hart to conclude that beauty cannot be defined either abstractly or from a theological standpoint. He believes that such attempts always end in unproductive verbiage.[3] In a similar spirit, Kant asserts that "to seek for a principle of taste which shall furnish, by means of definite concepts, a universal criterion of the beautiful, is fruitless trouble; because what is sought is impossible and self-contradictory."[4] But notwithstanding Hart and Kant, we require some attempt at empirical descriptions of common human experiences of beauty. For without such commonality, aesthetics cannot move beyond reports of how individuals and cultures have used the word *beauty*.[5] But rather than put forward another definition, I will seek out a better description of the common human experience of perceptual beauty—a range of human experience that is narrower and more pertinent to an enquiry into natural beauty.

Subjective Beauty-Theories Rejected

I propose an understanding of beauty that recognizes objective beauty-properties, as opposed to understandings that do not. I reject these "subjective" theories, primarily because, if there are no objective beauty-properties, it is

---

2. See H. Osborne, *Theory of Beauty*, 33, 78, on conflicting beauty-theories and word usages.

3. Nonetheless, Hart, *Beauty*, 17, attempts "to describe a general "thematics" of the beautiful" using Christian dogmatics as his starting and reference point for beauty. This is in contrast to my own starting point in human experience of creation, which I then relate to other points of doctrine.

4. Kant, *Critique of Judgment*, 17. Patrick Sherry, *Spirit and Beauty*, 44, also notes the tendency of some theorists to dismiss theories of beauty as contrary to the inherent mystery of aesthetic experience.

5. Osborne, *Theory of Beauty*, 12, emphasizes description of experience as the alternative to merely linguistic discussions.

difficult to explain the broad consensus in human beauty-judgments. But, on the other hand, if there are objective beauty-properties, it is not as difficult to explain disagreements of beauty-judgment.[6] Even so, many still assume that beauty-judgments vary widely among epochs and cultures. Yet psychological studies have opposed this assumption. For instance, long before society and upbringing can influence beauty standards, infants prefer the same types of human faces as do adults, as evidenced by their lengthier and more attentive gazing at beautiful faces.[7] In addition, studies have demonstrated a preference for savannah-type landscapes, both in children and across cultures.[8]

Corroborating the experimental evidence are several theoretical considerations. While disagreements about what is beautiful abound, these disagreements only hold force against an objective theory of beauty when several conditions are met. For one, the disagreements must stem from a shared understanding of beauty: disagreements that assume different understandings, while they may at first seem important, may actually be irrelevant. So if Smith believes that beauty consists in order and splendor, and Jones believes that beauty consists in a power to evoke emotion, then their contradictory judgments about the beauty of a certain painting do not necessarily cast doubt upon the painting's objective beauty-properties. Their disagreement means only that Smith and Jones understand beauty differently, or perhaps simply verbalize their experience differently. One or both might have idiosyncratic understandings of beauty, or might be focusing on only one aspect of beauty. Moreover, the painting in question may not be beautiful at all.

Relevant disagreements about what is beautiful must also presuppose the existence of objective beauty-properties.[9] That is, true *disagreement* presupposes some objectivity about which to disagree. Purely subjective beauty, on the other hand (if such could still intelligibly be called beauty), entails no true disagreements, and so disagreements between those who hold subjective theories do not count against an objective theory. If Smith and Jones both hold subjective theories of beauty, and they disagree about

6. Osborne, ibid., 70, gives this reason for rejecting subjective theories.

7. Rubenstein et al., "Infant Preferences," 848–55. It is also interesting to note that newborn infants are most attracted visually to lights, colors, patterns, and human faces. An oft-cited counterexample is the modern preference for slender women compared to earlier preferences for fatter women. But Singh, "Adaptive Significance," 293–307, observes that icons of female beauty, new and old, share a waist-to-hip ratio of about 0.7. One might also argue that the earlier preference reflects an understanding of plumpness as a sign of prosperity and blessing, while thinness signified frailty and poverty.

8. See Porteous, *Environmental Aesthetics*, 26–27.

9. Osborne, *Theory of Beauty*, 78–79, notes that relevant disagreements about beauty depend upon a shared understanding of beauty, and must presuppose an objective theory.

the beauty of a painting, their disagreement speaks only to differences between Smith's and Jones's experiences, but says nothing about the painting's objective beauty-properties.

In addition, differing beauty-experiences, to be relevant, must not be merely the result of associative emotion—that is, emotion aroused during the aesthetic activity by associations with similar objects or experiences. If Smith and Jones disagree only because Smith associates the painting with pleasant childhood memories, again the disagreement traces to differences between Smith and Jones. Emotional reactions can vary widely among people, and differing reactions do not entail differing beauty-judgments.[10]

Once we set aside these irrelevant beauty-judgments, we can attempt to explain other differences in judgment. Some differences could be explained in terms of different natural and cultivated aesthetic abilities. Such abilities are relevant, because due to the complexity of most beautiful objects as "systems of ordered relations," not everyone perceives all the relations at any given time. So while different viewers might see the same painting, they might be experiencing different perceptual configurations of the painting based on their skill in perceiving. Those with more aesthetic training and skill will perceive what others do not.[11] Contrast the observations of a group of teenagers touring an art museum with the keen and seasoned observations of the curator. But even among trained critics, disagreements will arise when someone focuses exclusively on either the prominence or obscurity of one particular beauty-property.[12] Beauty-judgments will also differ due to socially conditioned habits of judgment. For example, someone who is conditioned to judge Renaissance art beautiful may judge a painting beautiful simply because it resembles Renaissance style.[13] In addition, beauty-judgments may differ owing to moral differences in the subjects, corresponding to the way that virtue affects reasoning. A taste for sensuality in dancing, for example, might deaden sensitivity toward the beauty of other forms of dancing. According to David Hume, proper circumstances, education, and character are all essential to proper aesthetic appreciation.[14]

When we appreciate beauty, it is notable that we *assume* an objective aspect to this beauty when we desire other people to join in our

---

10. See Osborne, ibid., 81, 84, on variable emotion as indeterminative of beauty-judgments.

11. Osborne, ibid., 87, 126–28, emphasizes differing abilities leading to differing perceptual images and beauty-judgments.

12. Moore, *Principia Ethica*, 249, gives this reason for differing beauty-judgments.

13. See Osborne, *Theory of Beauty*, 87, on social conditioning as a reason for differing beauty-judgments.

14. Hume, "Standard of Taste," 241.

appreciation. We desire that they have not just any aesthetic experience but the one that we are having right now. If this sort of experience is in fact shareable, the most likely explanation is that human beings share similar aesthetic faculties and skills responding to objective constituents of beauty. On the other hand, if beauty were wholly subjective, why then bother trying to communicate our experience to others?[15] Beauty would then be an individualistic phenomenon, and no one can legitimately judge another's subjective experience. Thus, our efforts to educate taste would also be misguided if all tastes should be ranked equally.[16] Nonetheless, even with an objective theory, some diversity of taste is allowable if only because people are different, or even on the theological grounds that God might speak differently to different people.[17] But if we adopt a wholly subjective approach, we limit ourselves to cataloguing historical tastes and individual aesthetic emotions.[18] Moreover, even with this limited aim, lucid descriptions of tastes and emotions would belie the wholly subjective nature of beauty. This is because the very intelligibility of such language requires some shareability of experience.

Perceptual Beauty Described

But if we seek an understanding of beauty empirically that is not wholly subjective, a dilemma confronts us: to recognize objective beauty-properties we must look at what people appreciate as beautiful. But to recognize genuine appreciation we must link appreciation back to objective properties. The solution to this dilemma involves, first of all, finding beauty-properties that coincide with putatively beautiful objects. Secondly, it involves correlating these properties with experiences that coincide with putatively genuine beauty-appreciation.[19] The challenge then comes in describing this unique beauty-experience and these unique objective properties. But despite the reasonableness of this descriptive approach, Kant assures us that there is "no empirical *ground of proof* which would force a judgment of taste upon any one," and further, he would rather discard all commonly accepted

15. Carritt, *Theory of Beauty*, 108–9, observes that we assume objective beauty-properties in our desire for shared, communicable appreciation of beauty.

16. Osborne, *Theory of Beauty*, 82, 89, notes that purely subjective experience of beauty could not be legitimately judged or educated.

17. Sherry, *Spirit and Beauty*, 49, allows that people might have different tastes because God speaks differently to different people.

18. See Osborne, *Theory of Beauty*, 74.

19. See Osborne, ibid., 201–2, on this dilemma and proposed solution.

beauty-properties than permit his aesthetic judgment to be swayed by such principles.[20] But rather than fret about this lack of positive proof, I will aim for a happy resonance between our beauty-experiences and the objective beauty-properties that I have chosen to describe.

I will also narrow the discussion by focusing on what I call "perceptual" beauty rather than beauty as the excellence of art. By *perceptual* beauty, I designate a focus on the perceived physical, sensory properties of objects rather than more abstract properties, such as pathos and allusiveness, found in artistic composition. Although I will later contend that all beauty is produced by art (human or divine), the excellence of a work of art can depend upon its ability to communicate ideas or evoke emotion, and these considerations fall outside the bounds of perceptual beauty as I describe it initially.[21] Good works of art will often contain elements of plainness and ugliness, as well as beauty, which contribute to the overall composition. Many works of art do not aim at beauty at all, and may even focus on the ugly: for example, Francis Bacon paints particularly grotesque figures, yet these unlovely creations may still function quite well as works of art. Excellent art, then, will possess different objective elements than perceptual beauty even if both produce similar subjective responses. This similarity of response may be why some Christians insist on calling very gruesome portrayals of the crucifixion (e.g., Grünewald's) beautiful: they are thinking of the excellence of the artwork, or the character of the person depicted, or of their own emotional response to the work, but not of their perceptual experience of the image's formal properties. Nonetheless, the category of perceptual beauty still applies to much art, and perceptual beauty appears in similar ways in both art and nature.

I also distinguish perceptual beauty from several other related concepts, namely generic goodness or value, moral goodness, the artistry or "romance of being,"[22] and the sublime. Usage of the word *beauty* to describe all of these categories raises the question of what we are doing with the word, how it is functioning. The word *beauty* can be a broad gesture toward any

---

20. Kant, *Critique of Judgment*, 33.

21. Nonetheless, these considerations are very relevant to creation as a divine work of art that includes revelatory beauty. But before addressing divine art and revelatory beauty further, I first characterize our experience and recognition of perceptual beauty *as* beauty—that is, apart from its revelatory function. This separation of beauty from its revelatory function is somewhat artificial, but I wish to maintain that beauty retains its integrity as beauty, and its shareability in human experience, apart from explicit recognition of its revelatory function.

22. I use the term "romance of being" to describe the aesthetic and religious sense of creation's interconnectedness within itself and toward God, as emphasized by John Navone and David Bentley Hart.

number of related categories, and I distinguish perceptual beauty from these categories not to discount the insights of those who speak of beauty in such terms, but to seek out a clearer understanding of beauty that is faithful to our embodied human experience of creation, especially the natural world. So I am acknowledging several "lexical definitions" of beauty, or ways in which the word beauty is commonly used.[23] Or borrowing Wittgenstein's terminology, I recognize that the word beauty represents a very loosely bounded set or "family" of related and overlapping concepts.[24] But I also want to present a stipulative understanding of one sort of beauty, meaning that I am establishing a meaning for the word for the purposes of my investigation into the revelatory potential of natural beauty. Although in theory a stipulative understanding could cover anything, I am not choosing this approach to beauty arbitrarily. Rather, I am trying to capture common usage of the word, along with the range of things that might be called beautiful. I am also trying to highlight the most significant aspects of beauty. The only way to do this is through extended and less-than-systematic descriptions that may not hold in every case. But I do want to recommend an understanding to those involved in similar enquiries in the hope that it will improve understanding of beauty as it relates to disclosure of God in creation. This methodology, however, is not the only way to improve one's understanding; it is one tool among others. Imagination also illuminates metaphorical connections within reality that fall beyond the reach of analysis, and this illumination is fundamental to our knowledge of God as discussed previously.[25] So my current descriptions and distinctions are preparatory for more imaginative engagements to come.

A number of examples should help convey a sense of what I mean by perceptual beauty. Such examples are not only helpful but essential, since we cannot adequately describe non-verbal experience of beauty in abstract, conceptual terms. The breadth and depth of our experience often outstrips or defies our vocabulary. Perceptual beauty is, then, primarily a matter of "sense" or "know-how," not of theory. Thus we can perhaps describe beauty best by saying that it is "like this," "not like that," and "sometimes like this," such that the less systematic our description, the truer to life and to actual word-use it becomes. By perceptual beauty, I have in mind, for example, the experience of listening to and contemplating birdsong or Bach's cantatas; but I do not have in mind the visceral rush one might get at a rock concert (though beauty might be part of what is involved in rock music). By

23. See Robinson, *Definition*, 19, on lexical definitions.
24. Wittgenstein, *Philosophical Investigations*, 66–71.
25. Robinson, *Definition*, 68, describes analysis and imagination as separate tools.

perceptual beauty I mean Wordsworth's rhythmical lines about quiet valleys and murmuring streams and the mental images conjured by those lines—I do not mean the aesthetic power and pathos of T. S. Eliot's *The Waste Land* (though, again, something of beauty may be there in the poetry).[26] I mean the gilded mosaics of the saints in St Mark's Cathedral in Venice, but not the moral examples of those saints' lives. I also mean the curvilinear shapes and patterns plotted in accordance with a mathematical equation, but not the equation itself or any understanding of the equation apart from sense-perceptual imaging. In my understanding of perceptual beauty, I also separate some elements that perhaps cannot be fully separated in our experience, since we do not perceive beauty in isolation from our experience of the rest of the world. For instance, I refer to the perceived curves, hues, and sounds of a great waterfall, but not to the contemplation of the waterfall's tremendous force or my smallness and helplessness in comparison to it. Perceptual beauty also refers to the perceived lines and shapes of a beautiful human body but not to any associated health, strength, affection, or sexual desire, although all of these associations might occur simultaneously.

But while I distinguish perceptual beauty from these associations for the sake of conceptual clarity, I also recognize that beauty's aesthetic (and revelatory) power lies partly in the richness of its associations. Aesthetic training and experience give us greater facility with these associations, and I give special attention to beauty's existential and theological associations in discussing revelatory beauty more specifically in the following chapter. Beauty does relate appropriately to other aspects of our lives—our emotions, our philosophical reflection, our knowing—in ways that have power over us, even a revelatory power that requires further examination. Accordingly, perceptual beauty can expand beyond merely aesthetic concerns to involve all of life.

Along with more examples and case-descriptions to come, I offer the following as a general description of my understanding of perceptual beauty: perceptual beauty is the phenomenon in which certain objective qualities produce a certain heightened perceptual awareness that is an end in itself—that, in other words, can rest content without needing to pursue any further aim, such as moving or acting in the world.[27] When I say that this perception is an end in itself, I mean that it is not necessarily used for practical purposes. As a strictly aesthetic perception, it is a delight in objects themselves, and not an engagement with objects simply in order to survive or to achieve other goals. In other words, our perception of a hanging valley

26. Relevant to poetry, Ruskin, *Modern Painters*, 2:64, distinguishes beauty from "the power bestowing pleasure which objects receive from association."

27. See the formulations in Osborne, *Theory of Beauty*, 69; Ruskin, *Modern Painters*, 2:46; Aquinas, *ST* 1–2.27.1.

lined with spruce and fir has intrinsic value. This aspect of beauty holds despite my claims about beauty's manifold "associations."

This summary description of perceptual beauty can be categorized as a "combined subjective-objective" understanding of beauty, meaning that beauty requires both a unique perceptual state and a specific structure in objects.[28] *Subjective*, as used previously, means phenomenological; it refers to the experience of an individual person (a subject), and this subjective-objective, experiential emphasis follows from my epistemological approach. This stipulative understanding of perceptual beauty continues to develop by distinction and characterization throughout this and the remaining chapters.

Sensory Perception Distinguished from Other "Perceptions"

In speaking of "perceptual awareness" in my understanding of perceptual beauty, I refer to perception through the agency of bodily senses—most commonly vision and audition. But other senses also factor into any experience, because perception is comprehensive, and the senses work in concert.[29] Thus it is not surprising that perception of beauty requires development and learned coordination of the senses. Under the heading of perception I also include inner perception by the mind's eye, ear, or other senses—that is, the faculty of mental imaging. A poem, for example, might evoke a harmonious meter in the mind's ear along with beautiful images in the mind's eye. In similar ways, dreams and memories could also be perceptually beautiful. But this inner perception still depends upon the physical senses, unlike an inner perception of moral goodness, since moral goodness can subsist in dispositions apart from actions. So perceptual beauty may not always be strictly sense-perceived, but is always perceptually connected.

This heightened perceptual awareness of beauty involves both the senses and the intellect. It involves the intellect insofar as it is, in Roger Scruton's words, "contemplative, feeding upon the presented form of its object, and constantly renewing itself from that source."[30] Our awareness of waves breaking on the shore is contemplative and aesthetically rational, unlike a visceral taste or distaste for brussels sprouts.[31] Some gustatory tastes,

28. Osborne, *Theory of Beauty*, 34, describes combined subjective-objective understandings of beauty.

29. Nicholson, "General Revelation," 8, holds to comprehensive perception while emphasizing vision and audition.

30. Scruton, *Beauty*, 31. Unlike Scruton, however, I think that some gustatory tastes might be contemplative.

31. Kant, *Critique of Judgment*, 7, also makes a useful distinction between beauty-judgments and judgments of delight in particular foods or colors.

however, might be aesthetic and contemplative, such as a taste for the best wine cultivated through training and reflection.

The perceptual awareness of beauty is similar to the heightened physical awareness that an athlete experiences in the midst of a perfect golf swing or pole vault. But it is the athlete's physical motion itself that is (potentially) perceptually beautiful rather than the athlete's own kinaesthetic awareness of the motion, because the athlete does not possess the fully integrative awareness of the motion and its context that the spectator does. The athlete's awareness is sensory, but is used to achieve the appropriate movement. Therefore the athlete's awareness is not a fully integrative, contemplative perception of form that is also its own end.

The perceptual awareness of beauty is also analogous to the keen cognitive awareness that a thinker experiences in the midst of a skilful argument or proof. And interestingly, we value beauty in an analogous way to truth, the knowledge of which results from this cognitive awareness much as beauty results from perceptual awareness. Each of these states of awareness (perceptual, kinaesthetic, and cognitive) often produces pleasure, and each pleasure seems unique because it is tied directly to unique objects of awareness. Our aesthetic pleasure seems bound up in beautiful objects; but it is bound to them by our perception of the objects. So it may be that the pleasures deriving from aesthetic, kinaesthetic, and cognitive activities have more in common with each other as pleasures than do the activities themselves, in that the pleasure in each case is in a heightened sense of life or excellence. We could only, in theory, isolate a truly unique aesthetic pleasure empirically by introspection, but not everyone recognizes a distinct kind of pleasure in their own experience.[32] There may also be cases in which circumstances prevent pleasure in beauty from obtaining: I might perceive a symphony to be beautiful but take no pleasure in it due to an intense migraine. Or, under such circumstances, I might be able to take some minimal pleasure in the perception of beauty but have that pleasure sharply curtailed by my intense pain. But it is the perceptual "uplifting" rather than pleasure alone that is indicative of beauty; for people can find pleasure in many things, including the ugly. Pleasure in the beautiful can also give way at a higher existential level to displeasure, for example, in one's sense of alienation from the beautiful. And along with pleasure, various emotions also accompany beauty-experience. Emotions may accompany any kind of pleasure; but neither particular emotions nor a certain kind of pleasure

---

32. Osborne, *Theory of Beauty*, 67–68, 165, compares the aesthetic and cognitive, noting the similar pleasures in life or excellence among these analogous activities and the difficulty in isolating a unique aesthetic pleasure.

seems unique to our experience of the beautiful.[33] What seems unique is a heightened perceptual awareness that is often also pleasurable and emotive.

In speaking thus, I have incorporated Osborne's concept of heightened perceptual awareness into my account of perceptual beauty; however, Osborne uses the concept to describe beauty as "the characteristic and peculiar excellence of a work of art."[34] He recognizes that excellent art is not always pleasurable to perceive, but he claims that even in our perceiving the displeasing in art, we can experience pleasurably the excellence of art, which is beauty.[35] But this approach seems to break down in the case of "shock art," such as Damien Hirst's *A Thousand Years*: a rotting cow's head with flies and maggots.[36] Even if we do receive pleasure or satisfaction by perceiving the excellence of this type of art, one finds it difficult to call this artistic shock treatment "beautiful." Osborne's approach to beauty seems lacking here, but it might work in the case of tragedy: a story might be beautifully told, might exhibit objective qualities of beauty even if the subject matter of the story is not pleasant or beautiful. But even here the adjectives *skilful, artful, emotive,* or *evocative* might be more accurate to describe the story than *perceptually beautiful*. If we ascribe beauty to the storyteller's art—its pattern, integrity, radiance, and intensity—we might as well ascribe beauty to ideas, feelings, and expressions of those ideas and feelings. We could add virtues, moral lives, and relationships to the compass of beauty. The beautiful might be anything good or pleasant for which we can conceive of some metaphorical objective beauty-properties. But now we have moved far from a *sense*-perceptual awareness of beauty and have shifted toward a more affective, moral, intellectual, or other sort of "perception."

By couching beauty in sense-perceptual terms, I intend to delimit perceptual beauty as a subset of the aesthetically good, and avoid conflating it with other sorts of goodness. This can be a difficult distinction to make when "beautiful" is often used as a general compliment, meaning only that a thing is a good specimen of its kind.[37] But workbenches and clods of soil can be quite good specimens of their kind and good for the purposes for which they exist without being beautiful. Beauty possesses a splendor or radiance above and beyond the merely good or useful.

---

33. Osborne, ibid., 69, 163, holds that heightened perceptual awareness rather than pleasure or emotion is central to beauty.

34. Ibid., 201.

35. Ibid., 165.

36. See Nicholson, "Hirst, Damien," n.p.

37. Osborne, *Theory of Beauty*, 11, notes this use of beauty as a general compliment.

A mathematical equation also might be good in that it pleases the mind with its simplicity, integrity, and efficacy. But it would not be perceptually beautiful if it engages only the cognitive faculty without the sense-perceptual faculty. Yet this could explain why mathematicians sometimes attribute beauty to equations: mathematicians are engaged in a cognitive activity that is analogous to the perceptual activity—a cognitive activity that also produces pleasure through a heightened sense of life or excellence tied to external objects. In a similar way to equations, simple geometric shapes are not quite perceptually splendorous. Although we might experience displeasure at an ill-drawn circle, we do not experience a heightened perceptual awareness at a simple circle or trapezoid correctly drawn, even though these basic shapes could contribute to the beauty of a larger whole that contains them. Mathematics surely contributes to the composition of beautiful forms, but when someone speaks of the beauty of an equation or a circle, notwithstanding Plato, *goodness* or *fittingness* would be a more accurate term: we simply recognize when an object is as it should be.[38] Thus Kant says rightly that goodness in an object has to do with our understanding of "what sort of a thing the object ought to be."[39] Even some mathematicians who talk about beauty would probably be reluctant to attribute perceptual beauty as I am describing it to mathematics, because they are merely giving criteria for what good mathematics ought to be.[40]

Mathematics might fit into John Navone's understanding of beauty as "the splendor of the true and the good irradiating from every ordered state of

38. Plato calls geometric figures "eternally and absolutely beautiful" (*Philebus* 51). But Beardsley notes that Plato also extends the range of *to kalon* in some contexts to encompass the "fair or fitting," and Xenophon's *Memorabilia* (3.8) describes beautiful objects as being "well made to perform their function" (*Aesthetics*, 42).

39. Kant, *Critique of Judgment*, 4.

40. Mullins, "Truth plus Beauty," 18, cites "some generally accepted tests that a [mathematical] work must pass to be deemed beautiful—it must employ a minimal number of assumptions, for example, or give some original and important insight, or throw other work into new perspective." He then admits that "elegance is perhaps a better term" than beauty. He also describes the "romance" rather than the beauty of mathematical descriptions of natural phenomena, such as subatomic particles and the birth of stars. There is also a marked difference between my constituents of perceptual beauty and Howell's "aesthetic criteria" for good mathematics. Howell lists "economy of expression, depth, unexpectedness, inevitability and seriousness" as "qualities that also seem to form good standards of poetry" ("Mathematical Beauty," 493–504). MIT mathematician Gian-Carlo Rota takes issue even with some of these criteria, stating that "even a cursory observation shows that the characteristics of mathematical beauty are at variance with those of artistic beauty." He suggests that mathematical "beauty" should rather be called "enlightenment" ("Phenomenology," 171–82). Rota's observations accord with Dirac's identification of mathematical beauty with the explanatory power of geometry, on which see, Thomsen, "Beauty of Mathematics," 137–38.

being."[41] Mathematics might also be beautiful to classicists who understand beauty to consist in proportion alone, and who therefore ascribe beauty to all being, since nothing exists without some form or proportion (although, of course, we speak of bad proportion).[42] For example, Francis Hutcheson understands mathematical beauty to consist in "a compound Ratio of Uniformity and Variety," allowing him to assert that a square is more beautiful than a triangle, because it unifies more angles.[43] But appealing to human experience, many ordered states of being (like squares) seem "good" and perhaps, in some sense, "true," while lacking the splendor we call beauty. This may be why we find it difficult to apply the term *radiance* to an equation, yet often consider radiance to be an objective constituent of beauty.

Something similar could be said for the "beauty" of theological arguments and theories, as well as scientific or mathematical theories that seek to explain reality. Theologians and scientists alike have argued that the beauty of a theory commends its truthfulness. I agree that ordered and artful theories best describe an ordered and artful creation, and the mind finds pleasure in this fit between theory and reality. There is an artistry or romance to creation that plays out even in the theorizing of science and theology. So why should we narrow the range of the beautiful to exclude this intellectual and even romantic fittingness while expanding aesthetic "goodness" to include it? Should we not also call the intellectual and non-sensory fitting "beautiful?" Another example is the poem that employs literary rather than sensory metaphors, or that is so abstract as to resist any sense-imaging of its subject matter. Indeed, the intellectually fitting seems very close to the perceptually fitting, and if the two are not univocally beautiful, they are at least analogous. And surely the intellectually fitting gives rise to the perceptually fitting if the divine intelligence creates beautiful forms. There may even be a seamless connection between the intellectually fitting and the perceptually beautiful with the apparent seam being merely the result of limited human perception. But even this apparent seam is significant when thinking about a prospect of green fields, rolling hills, and purple clouds, because the set of things that human beings can perceive offers a vastly different level of human experience from the set of things that human beings can only think. Indeed, "light is sweet, and it pleases the eyes to see the sun" (Eccl 11:7, NIV)—there is no purely abstract experience that is equivalent. As Edward Farley remarks, "remove the graceful, embodied movements and complex unities of life from us and our world and we remove the world

---

41. Navone, *Theology of Beauty*, 5.
42. See Farley, *Faith and Beauty*, 17, on classical beauty.
43. Hutcheson, *Beauty and Virtue*, 29.

itself."[44] Thus the category of perceptual beauty excludes ideas that cannot be visualized or otherwise sense-imaged. In attempting to describe these wholly abstract ideas, we may simply be borrowing sensory terminology metaphorically. Harvard mathematician Barry Mazur confirms this possibility: "I don't think there is any mathematics radically divorced from some kind of vivid intuition that illuminates it and ties to the sensual. . . . I believe this is the common understanding of just about everyone who practices mathematics."[45] But if someone wishes to attribute beauty analogously to purely intellectual fittingness, I will not object too strongly, because any understanding of beauty we choose produces a range of possible difficulties and counterexamples. Again, my goal is to clarify and improve concepts for the purposes of my enquiry.

Perceptual Beauty Distinguished from Moral Goodness and the "Romance of Being"

I also distinguish perceptual beauty from two other beauty-concepts: John Navone and Richard Viladesau's understanding of moral goodness, and David Bentley Hart's understanding of the "romance of being." The first of these concepts, that of moral goodness-as-beauty, is, I believe, a figurative[46] or sometimes less-than-accurate use of the term. Navone, consciously reflecting the ideas of Hans Urs von Balthasar, asserts that the "Cross, no form of beauty for worldly eyes, reveals what God's beauty and glory are really about."[47] Viladesau, also referencing von Balthasar, says that "the Christ event, is intrinsically beautiful: it is a manifestation of God's glory. This glory is experienced as beauty because of the correspondence of God's

44. Farley, *Faith and Beauty*, 64.

45. Mazur adds that "this type of intuition is very well developed in people who do complex analysis. . . . Our basic intuitions regarding Euclidean geometry . . . become magically available even in contexts where we would hardly have dared to imagine that visualization would have any relevance. . . . Living mathematics is in no way abstract, at least to the people who live it. Intuitions can tie mathematics to the most concrete pictures, sensual experiences, and things that are immediate to all of us" ("Dialogue," 124–30).

46. By figurative, I mean to designate a contrast with the literal meaning of the word. For example, 1 Pet 3:3–5 implies the concept of beauty by the use of "adornment" (*kósmos*), and compares beauty to moral goodness. In the Old Testament beauty or splendor is used figuratively to describe wisdom (Ezek 28:7), salvation (Ps 149:4), and holiness (1 Chron 16:29; 2 Chron 20:21; Pss 29:2, 96:9, 110:3. But these passages could also refer to holy attire).

47. Navone, *Theology of Beauty*, 20. Karl Barth, *CD* 2/1:655, shares this understanding of divine beauty as including the ugly.

being, as ultimate Goodness, to the deepest human desire for happiness."[48] Viladesau's logic here seems to require whatever is rightly desirable to be beautiful, but surely this cannot be the case if beauty is to retain any distinct meaning. He also does not seem to allow that God's glory might manifest itself as dreadful or wrathful. And paradoxically, he also includes the undesirable in the beautiful: "Spiritual beauty for the Christian is not simply unalloyed sensible pleasure, but includes what is ugly and alienating—insofar as it is transformed or transformable by God's triumphant love."[49] Viladesau supports his contention with a well-founded warning that "the Christian message is not merely . . . that God is beautiful and is to be found in the pursuit of what is attractive and desirable in the world." Certainly God has great concern for the "ugly and deformed and unworthy."[50] But the problem with Viladesau's usage of *beauty* is that no one other than a Christian would easily understand it: his usage amounts to a dogmatic change of meaning. Later, however, Viladesau qualifies his understanding of beauty, placing the word "beautiful" tellingly in quotation marks: "Human suffering and need are not beautiful in themselves . . . but for the Christian, the portrayal of suffering and need can be 'beautiful' insofar as it makes us realize the truth of the human situation in need of salvation, evokes the beautiful vision of hope, and stirs up the beautiful moral response of compassion."[51] Nevertheless, this transcendent and paradoxical beauty-as-moral goodness would not seem to encourage acts of mercy toward a fallen world; for if the ugly and deformed can be seen as beautiful, then why bother to improve their state? But Viladesau qualifies once again by distinguishing beauty from "aesthetic power," which seems a better term for what he is describing.[52] His Balthasarean aesthetic treats the "theological sublime" more so than perceptual beauty.[53]

Navone and Viladesau, like von Balthasar, allow Scripture's gospel themes to dictate the nature of a "beauty" that often conflicts with our perception of beauty.[54] But Scripture does not give us as clear an understanding of many things—including the nature of beauty—as we might desire. Navone and Viladesau tend to equate divine beauty with divine glory, and

48. Viladesau, *Theology and the Arts*, 146.

49. Ibid., 147.

50. Ibid., 52–53.

51. Ibid., 148.

52. Ibid., 151.

53. See Bauerschmidt, "Aesthetics," 208, on von Balthasar's theological sublime.

54. David Brown, *Enchantment*, 7–8, notes this a priori gospel and Scripture emphasis in von Balthasar.

to separate divine and created beauty, but their comments about the beauty of the cross seem to be examples of what Osborne calls "cloaking conceptual obscurity beneath spiritual exaltation."[55] When we say that Jesus' undergoing of the crucifixion was a "beautiful" act, we usually mean that it was a loving, moving, meaningful, and morally good act. We do not mean that viewing the crucifixion or contemplating it in the mind's eye is perceptually beautiful. To call the crucifixion beautiful, then, is at best a figurative use of language and at worst a pious platitude along the lines of calling human suffering "good" because God has willed it. If the cross had not been, in fact, ugly, it would not be effectual as an expiatory event.

The relationship between beauty and God's nature requires further exploration, but from the human standpoint, the primary relationship between beauty and morality seems to be that we are better people for understanding beauty, its origins, and its meaning.[56] Beyond this there may be what Hart calls "an aesthetic moment of wakefulness in the ethical," whereby we recognize through beauty, or through an awareness of what ought to be beautiful, the value of creatures other than ourselves and the weightiness of our actions toward those creatures.[57]

But Hart himself also uses the word *beauty* figuratively and problematically. Alluding to the *analogia entis*, Hart says that "in the yielding of each thing to each other, all becomes incandescently beautiful."[58] This is parallel to Navone's use of the phrase "the beauty of all things."[59] Hart uses the word beauty rhetorically to describe the romantic interconnectedness of creation within itself and toward God. He admits that analogical language "thematizes the infinite as beauty," but he also thematizes creation as beautiful.[60] This language goes beyond the weaker claims that God can present himself as beautiful, and that most of creation is beautiful or has potential for beauty. Hart's "thematizing" becomes capable of mystically enveloping the ugly, ignoring its contrasts, and further "cloaking conceptual obscurity."[61] In chapter 4 I return to Hart's concept of beauty to reframe it in terms of creation's artistry rather than beauty. This reframing allows for a more adequate treatment of natural evil and ugliness.

---

55. Osborne, *Theory of Beauty*, 61.

56. Carritt, *Theory of Beauty*, 73, suggests this relationship between beauty and morality.

57. Hart, *Beauty*, 21.

58. Ibid., 316.

59. Navone, *Theology of Beauty*, 3.

60. Hart, *Beauty*, 317.

61. Osborne's phrase, *Theory of Beauty*, 61.

Objective and Subjective Beauty-Constituents Affirmed

To test my understanding of perceptual beauty further, we must consider the possibility of a heightened perceptual awareness of ugliness. Such an experience would certainly be an illegitimate end, but if it were otherwise possible, the objective side of beauty would also distinguish the case from an experience of, say, hoarfrost or geometric phytoplankton. Yet the objective aspects of beauty are difficult to capture and describe. This difficulty, however, in no way speaks against the existence of objective properties, because we struggle to describe many concepts and experiences, from the essence of love to the taste of coffee. We rarely describe such realities exactly as others do, not least because objective reality can be so tremendously complex and of a nature that defies verbal representation. But even if we struggle to describe in common ways what makes objects beautiful, we can much more readily share common "beauty-skills"—that is, common abilities to experience the beautiful. We do not learn these beauty-skills by learning abstract descriptions of what makes objects beautiful; but, in the interest of better understanding, such verbal descriptions can still be of some use. They can point us in appropriate directions, and help us reflect back on our experience of perceptual beauty in productive ways. To this end I borrow and modify four of Michael Nicholson's objective beauty-constituents: symmetry or balance, wholeness or integrity, radiance, and intensity.[62]

"Symmetry," for Nicholson, refers to the visual and mathematical patterns found in both nature and art and recognized across all cultures. Simple bilateral symmetry, for example (among other kinds of symmetry), often manifests itself not as an exact correspondence between halves but as a rough balance, as Ruskin observes in alternating river bends, opposite sides of a tree or valley, and "opposing lines or masses" in art.[63] These observations suggest a continuum of order between exact symmetry and balance or pattern, both of which contribute to "integrity." Integrity or wholeness denotes the quality of completeness as opposed to brokenness—the compositional unity and harmony of appropriate parts to form a whole.

The quality of "radiance" can designate an effulgence of color or luminosity, as well as purity of sound or texture, while the quality of "intensity" describes how any property stands out from its background as a concentrated, ephemeral, or subtle instance of that property. Radiance and intensity work together, since a quality can only be radiant if it is

62. Cf. Aquinas's three conditions of beauty: integrity or perfection, due proportion or harmony, and brightness or clarity; *ST* 1.39.8.

63. Ruskin, *Modern Painters*, 2:125. Nicholson, "General Revelation," 4, notes that nature's geometry may be more fractal than Euclidean.

sufficiently intense; but radiance emphasizes the qualitative aspect, while intensity emphasizes the quantitative. For example, a sunset can display radiant but faint and short-lived colors. And in a portion of a landscape, several different qualities (such as contrasting color schemes in sky, rock, and foliage) may achieve radiance with varying intensities, contributing to the overall intensity of the scene as it stands out from its periphery. In this way, beautiful objects always display an arresting "realness" or quality of "being there," which is intense, even if at the same time subtle and fleeting.[64] Thus, radiance and intensity also spill over into beauty's subjective side, contributing to a sense of awe before the beautiful.

Of these constituents, symmetry or balance becomes the most dispensable as it dissolves into a more loosely defined "wholeness" or "integrity;" however, beauty always involves some sort of order at some level. Granite and opal lack symmetry, but the balance and contrast between shapes, colors, and textures in the stones contributes to their beauty. And certainly these patterns recognizable as "granite" and "opal" arose from the ordering of chemical properties of elements in the environment, acted upon by precise physical forces of heat and pressure. In a similar way, integrity also can appear to be lacking in amorphous objects like the sky. But even a clear blue sky is not a monochromatic patch of color isolated from any frame or context. It consists of various color shades, an apparent texture of medium, and different shapes or frames that give it context as "sky" and not mere "color." All these elements contribute to the compositional integrity of a blue sky.[65] Similarly, a very dim evening sky does not seem to pose a radiant scene, but the deep blue of the sky behind the sharp lines of crooked branches does achieve something like radiance. And an object as commonplace as a tree can be intensely beautiful when we reflect upon it in an appropriate context, with an appropriate state of mind. If we

64. Cf. Nicholson, "General Revelation," 3–5, on symmetry, integrity, radiance, and intensity.

65. Someone might question my emphasis on perceived order or "form" in the beautiful. One might speak of "a beautiful shade of green," meaning that the color is "luminous" or "rich." This could be an objective beauty claim but does not concern what we usually consider to be ordered form. But in my use of *form*, I include properties such as luminosity, richness of texture, and context, which contribute to the "formal composition" even of a single color. Someone will accuse me of abusing the word *form*, but what I wish to point out is that our perception of even the simplest beauty is a complex matter. We cannot quite put our finger on every element of background or context, or all the interrelations of physical properties that go into our perception of even a simple color. Even if color *itself* in the abstract lacks form, we never perceive color itself apart from a context. There is always a "form" to our *perception* of color that is never wholly abstract. For a similar example of "form" regarding sound, compare a single note played on a pipe organ inside a cathedral.

take balance, integrity, radiance, and intensity in the loosest sense, all four may be necessary conditions for beauty. But we can usefully employ two more general descriptors: order (encompassing symmetry and integrity) and splendor (encompassing radiance and intensity).

The Subjective Side of Beauty

Objective properties are necessary conditions for beauty, but could they be sufficient conditions? Could an object be beautiful whether or not anyone could ever perceive it, and irrespective of anything that beauty accomplishes, thus requiring an objective non-relational understanding of beauty? G. E. Moore proposes such an understanding by saying that beauty arises from, and depends solely upon, an object's intrinsic nature.[66] This is not to say that beauty is an intrinsic *property* of objects; it is rather a *value* that supervenes upon certain intrinsic properties.[67] Yet this value depends only on the intrinsic properties of the object and not at all on the properties of the subject. This allows Moore to assert that it is impossible for a beautiful object to be beautiful at one time, or in one set of circumstances, and not to be beautiful at another time, or in other circumstances. Likewise, he holds that it is impossible for an object to possess beauty to one degree in one set of circumstances and possess it to a different degree in other circumstances.[68] Thus the percipient cannot add or take away beauty from an object. Moore rejects the idea that a beautiful object moved to a new set of circumstances becomes a *different* object by virtue of its new relations.[69]

Moore illustrates his concept of beauty by imagining two worlds, one maximally beautiful and the other maximally ugly, both of which no one ever has perceived, or ever can perceive. He argues that the beautiful world maintains the intrinsic value of beauty despite its not being perceived.[70] Moore does not consider, however, that in a theistic universe God would have knowledge of the beautiful world. And though God would not "perceive" the world himself, he would know how creatures *would* perceive it (provided that God can know future counterfactuals). The value of the world's beauty obtains through God's knowledge of that beauty and not through the bare fact of its existence. The subject, in this case, God, still contributes to what beauty is by knowing and valuing it. Similarly, human

66. Moore, *Principia Ethica*, 297.
67. Ibid., 295–96.
68. Ibid., 286.
69. Ibid., 294.
70. Ibid., 135.

beings are not passive receptors of beauty or knowledge but active knowers and valuers. We may judge the beauty of something incorrectly as compared to God's judgment, but our *selves* still contribute to what beauty is as a phenomenon. Through this encounter with a subject, the intrinsic properties of an object do not change, but the value of the object in that circumstance may change. The dynamism of a subject made in God's image brings an inimitable new relation to the object—a unique subject-object event.[71]

Moore's position holds common sense appeal for the realist, since beauty can seem wholly dependent upon the intrinsic properties of objects. Yet perceptual beauty also seems a rather empty notion apart from perception by a subject, and even Moore concedes that the value of such beauty would be miniscule.[72] Moreover, any "beauty" that is *inherently* imperceptible cannot rightly be called perceptual beauty. Perceptual beauty requires perception by a subject,[73] because, strictly speaking, it is not a property of a material source but of an image that we construct cognitively and personally by selecting and integrating, with individual skill, what we find to be the salient elements of a material source. So while two people may look at the same painting, they may not perceive the same image or the same beauty. The painting still has an objective structure or "objective beauty" analogous to the perceptual image, but this analogous structure is outside our purview and therefore "outside the scope of aesthetics."[74] Like the wavelengths of electromagnetic radiation just outside the visible color spectrum, it is an aspect of a complex creation that is not found on our limited perceptual "map" of reality.

This human mapping or framing, which composes beautiful percepts, is exemplified by the idea of landscape. As the environmental philosopher Holmes Rolston notes, "landscape is land-scope, land taken into human scope." In landscape, our subjective framing gives rise to objective-relational properties such as balance, integrity, and intensity where they would not otherwise exist given a different frame. A horizon-line, for instance, though based on objective structure, is ultimately the product of a human frame of reference.[75] Thus, rather than existing in things themselves, beauty is a

---

71. By appealing to perception at this point, I might give the impression of belying my earlier description of beauty as an end in itself. But such an impression overlooks the *combined* subjective-objective nature of my description: it is beauty as a perceptual *phenomenon* that is an end in itself, not merely the objective structures that contribute to this phenomenon.

72. Ibid., 237–38.

73. Or, at least, it requires God's knowledge of what creaturely perception would entail.

74. Osborne, *Theory of Beauty*, 94–95.

75. Science is another way of taking land into human scope. Rolston, "Aesthetic

function of established relationships in creation among both objective and subjective factors.[76] Beauty becomes, then, not a fixed existent but an ongoing possibility, manifesting itself for a time, for us.[77]

We can also mention the human physiological conditions for beauty, namely the sensory and cognitive apparatuses that make raw physical data intelligible, and thus, the perception of beauty possible.[78] Human physiology is an objective reality, but it contributes directly to subjective, experiential reality. This experiential reality of beauty is often synoptic and intuitional— a perceiving of the whole at once rather than adding parts to form a whole, such that the whole gives meaning to the parts and not vice versa. Our perception organizes objective components into "a convergent system of ordered relations"—an organic and meaningful whole that emerges from objects.[79] Denis Diderot understands beauty in this way as a configuration that "awakens in the mind the idea of *rapports*," by which he means the fittingness among parts, for instance, of a building or symphony.[80] When this organic whole is not sufficiently complex (as in the case of simple geometric shapes), attention lapses, and the object is not perceived as beautiful.[81] But synoptic perception alone is inadequate to account for all types of beauty, because the mind can also break beautiful objects into larger or smaller wholes, and can imagine the completion of fragments, such as a piece of music interrupted after only a few measures and without resolution. As another example, Byron says that the moonlight on the Coliseum

> fill'd up
> As 'twere anew, the gaps of centuries;
> Leaving that beautiful that still was so,
> And making that which was not.[82]

Appreciation," 374–86.

76. Nicholson, "General Revelation," 5, understands beauty to be a function of created relationships.

77. Osborne, *Theory of Beauty*, 95, 100, describes beauty as ongoing possibility. This subjective side of beauty also alleviates somewhat the problem of the diverse nature of perceptually beautiful objects (e.g., visible versus audible beauties). Such experiences of diverse beauties resemble each other *as experiences* more so than do the various physical media and sensory mechanisms through which they arise.

78. Nicholson, "General Revelation," 5, notes the physiological conditions for beauty.

79. See Osborne, *Theory of Beauty*, 124, 126–27, on synoptic beauty-perception.

80. Diderot, *Recherches*, 303. Similarly, Jonathan Edwards, "Beauty," 305, says that "the beauty of the world consists wholly of sweet mutual consents, either within itself or with the supreme being."

81. See Osborne, *Theory of Beauty*, 160, on insufficient complexity and lapsed attention.

82. Byron, *Manfred*, 3.4.34–37. I would distinguish the perceptual beauty of the

This completion of patterns is evidence that we perceive beauty not only synoptically but also by connecting parts to form a whole.[83] Yet we can also sometimes appreciate the elemental beauty of parts by themselves, such as a single chord or a shard of a stained glass window.

In addition to this perceptual side of beauty is the affective side. We experience affections accompanying and shaping our experience of beauty—feelings such as delight, peace, longing, awe, and reverence.[84] But these are results or aspects of beauty enjoyed for its own sake, not its essence or goal. I suggested above that emotional associations, such as pleasant childhood memories, could cause someone to attribute beauty to an object that is not beautiful. But this is not to imply that psychological factors play no part in recognizing beauty. Personal factors of disposition and prior experience may sometimes be the key that unlocks the door to an experience of beauty—a key that gathers together objective qualities into an organic whole that someone else would miss. So, in addition to shared subjectivity, beauty-experience can also involve individual (though not arbitrary) subjectivity. Human beings do not receive beauty passively and dispassionately any more than we do knowledge, but participate in beauty. The whole person can interface with such spectacles as birch bark and seascapes, including facets of personhood that might be called existential rather than psychological—a point that I will develop in the following chapter.[85]

It is the relationships among all these objective and subjective factors that give rise to beauty in incredibly complex ways. Supervening upon these interrelationships, beauty becomes a gestalt, surpassing its constituent substrata and emerging from them in surprising and unpredictable ways. One might compare the emergence of beauty to the way that a running computer program "emerges" from software and hardware components.[86] But although beauty supervenes upon its constituents, it is not ultimately reducible to them, because beauty-properties are not the same as the experience or phenomenon of beauty. And this phenomenon is not merely a conglom-

---

stone and the architecture from the Romantic and even neoclassical vision of ruins in which "their irregularity charmed; memorials to antiquity, they evoked dim memories of indefinite time. They became to their devotees 'a little Sublime.'" Nicolson, *Mountain Gloom*, 338.

83. See Charlton, *Aesthetics*, 53, on perceiving beauty through pattern completion.

84. Nicholson, "General Revelation," 6, suggests these affections.

85. Mark Wynn, "Towards a Broadening," 147–66, argues that emotions can alert us to broader existential meanings in places, since emotions work inseparably from our selective perception as well as our bodily posturing and interacting with the world.

86. See Nicholson, "General Revelation," 7, for the computer analogy and beauty as gestalt.

erate but is, from a Christian perspective, a divinely conceived event—an outworking of God's creativity—phenomenally temporal in creation yet enduring in God's intention.

At this phenomenal level, we can experience beauty without referring explicitly to the constituents that make objects beautiful and without an immediate consciousness of why something is beautiful. Similar to the way we can know something without being able to explain exactly how we know it, we often apprehend beauty-properties without conscious reflection.[87] This dispensability of reflection in the moment of experience helps explain how we can so easily disagree about what makes something beautiful. It also begins to explain disagreements about what we may or may not experience in and through the beautiful. I return to this point in chapters 3 and 4.

Classical and Romantic Conceptions of Beauty and Sublimity

This combined subjective-objective approach to beauty speaks to another perceived difficulty in describing beauty, namely the differing conceptions of beauty throughout history. One might struggle to reconcile Romanticism's understanding of beauty with classical and neoclassical understandings, but perhaps somewhat needlessly so, considering beauty's multifaceted and allusive character. Neoclassical theorists sought beauty in a priori order, irrespective of what effect that order might have on a subject. Such theory resulted in a determination either to make experience fit the prescribed order, or to reinterpret the prescribed order to accommodate any unexplained experience.[88] These theorists also found beauty in ideal generic types rather than in unique individuals. Romantics, by contrast, though they could also appreciate much classical art, found beauty in wild landscapes that evoked awe and wonder for their uniqueness and perceived lack of order—the same landscapes that medievals could not call beautiful partly because of their fear of privation or destruction by the elements (raising the question

---

87. That is, beauty-skills, properly developed, can often be performed with unconscious ease. But this is not to say that beauty-skills require no guidance or epistemic development.

88. See Beardsley: "Most of the theorists were united on the a priori approach. 'Every art has certain rules which by infallible means lead to the ends proposed,' says George de Scudéry (in his Preface to Ibrahim [1641]) . . . . 'I know that there are certain eternal rules, grounded upon good sense, built upon firm and solid reason, that will last,' says Charles de St.-Évremond (essay on tragedy [1672]) . . . . When faced with an apparent conflict between experience and the rules (as in a dull play that followed the rules, or a moving one that did not), the theorists were apt to argue either that a play that 'pleases' must really follow the rules, when they are conveniently reinterpreted, or that no one ought to be pleased by it" (*Aesthetics*, 146).

of what prerequisite conditions or situations are required for the perception of beauty).[89] Thus, the meticulously cultivated garden was the ideal natural beauty for neoclassicists, perhaps reflecting an effort to repair the corruption in creation, while untamed mountains embodied the ideal for Romantics. Mountains and other natural forms, for Romantics, displayed the informal and nonhuman "nature" of beautiful order: "Beauty—a living Presence of the earth, / Surpassing the most fair ideal Forms."[90] While the Enlightenment saw in ideal forms imposed upon nature (such as gardens) a reflection of human and divine rationality, Romanticism raised the question of whether undisturbed nature reflects God—even natural forms that were once not thought to be beautiful.[91]

But our concept of beauty has something to gain from both historical emphases—attention to order *and* to one's experience (of nature particularly). This is because the classical emphasis highlights the objective side of beauty, while the Romantic emphasis highlights the subjective side. These emphases on order and experience, though historically seen as opposed, can be seen as complementary, even if their complementariness was easily missed by societies that heavily stressed one or the other. Of course classical and Romantic ideals of beauty could also be opposed: the Romantic emphasis on experience could be taken to mean emotional self-expression, or delight in chaos, or the pitting of imagination against reason, all of which might well be in conflict with order. But more compatibly, the Romantic emphasis could be taken to mean that beauty arises not from order alone but also from the 'felt quality' of objects, even if those objects do not display a classical or readily discernible order. And bound up in this notion of felt quality is Kant's thesis that the mind contributes something to the making of reality[92]—a thesis that I have argued is presented theologically by Aquinas. Drawing on Kant, and like Aquinas, Wordsworth shares the theological sense that the human

> mind
> Even as an agent of the one great mind,

89. Beardsley discusses the differing Romantic and classical beauty-concepts. Ibid., 150, 182–84.

90. Wordsworth, preface to *Excursion*, 42–43.

91. Porteous draws a similar connection between the medieval Aristotelian recovery of science; 17th century Dutch naturalistic painting; 18th century sublime and 19th century irregular Romantic landscapes; and the modern fascination with wilderness. These stand in contrast to neoclassicism, 17th century idealistic painting, 18th century ordered landscapes and gardens, and modern cities and suburbs. In chapter 5, I develop the idea of beauty in irregular natural forms, such as mountains. *Environmental Aesthetics*, 60.

92. Beardsley, *Aesthetics*, 247, 253, suggests the idea of "felt quality" and notes this contribution of Kant.

Creates, creator and receiver both,
Working but in alliance with the works
Which it beholds.—Such verily is the first
Poetic spirit of our human life.[93]

Even in Plato, objective order may not solely constitute beauty. In Monroe Beardsley's view, Plato leaves room for "some abandonment to the creative *eros*, some inspired access to ideal beauty" on the subject's part.[94] And if beauty truly has a subjective, even existential, component, then along with our appreciation of objective order, we can also appreciate the German Romantic emphasis on the subject's "alienation" from the objective order and beauty of nature—an alienation that Boethius too recognizes in himself as he seeks to reconnect with the "divine reason" of creation.[95] In view of such alienation, Friedrich Schiller proposes that we reconcile human beings to themselves and to the world as creatures of both mind and matter, possessing a corresponding "form-drive" and "sense-drive," which harmonize to apprehend beauty as "living form" (*lebende Gestalt*).[96] Schiller's notion accords with the dual formalistic and expressionistic impulses we find in the arts, each having their proper place.[97] It also accords with Aquinas's harmonizing of transcendent form with sensory experience to produce an aesthetically connected knowledge of God and the world.

If conflicts remain between classicists and Romantics, they could result from the overemphasis of beauty's subjective side (felt quality) at the expense of the objective (order), or vice versa. Conflicts could also remain over the extent to which mathematics illumines an unvitiated creation-order. But borrowing from both traditions, beauty could possess something of reason and order but also of a very different "felt quality," even awesomeness. Beauty sometimes may even be fearsome, but this also leads us into the category of the sublime. Though the term was used in the first century by Longinus to describe great literature, by the early eighteenth century, the Earl of Shaftesbury understood the sublime as the highest beauty, whereas Joseph Addison understood the sublime and beautiful as distinct and separate categories, arousing different emotions.[98] Differentiating myself from

---

93. Wordsworth, Thirteen-Book *Prelude*, 2.301–6. Gerard Manley Hopkins also emphasizes this subjective-objective interplay in his terms "inscape" (God's creative design in the world) and "instress" (humanity's creative working-out of God's design). See Devlin, *Hopkins*, 109, 283.

94. Beardsley, *Aesthetics*, 45.

95. See Beiser, "Romanticism, German," n. p.; Boethius, *Consolation* 1.6.

96. Schiller, *Aesthetic Education*, 100–101.

97. See Charlton, *Aesthetics*, 99.

98. Nicolson, *Mountain Gloom*, 322, discusses Shaftesbury's and Addison's views.

both of these positions, I understand beauty and sublimity to be distinct but overlapping categories. Neither category should be overly generalized, because each arises differently in different cases, as do pleasure and emotion. Hence, many beautiful objects may also be awesome and sublime to some degree, and many awesome and fearsome displays of nature exhibit a strange, nonhuman type of order that contributes to their beauty. We might usefully understand the natural sublime as that which overawes, or with Kant as a greatness that attracts and also repels,[99] or as the *mysterium tremendum et fascinans.* These understandings allow many instances of the natural sublime also to be beautiful, such as storm clouds, polar caps, and deadly predators. Wordsworth says that, in spite of the "obtrusive qualities" of some sublime objects, increasing maturity allowed him also to discover their beauty—"charms minute / that win their way into the heart by stealth."[100] But some instances of the natural sublime could fall outside the compass of beauty, such as natural disasters and their wake. I return to the sublime in my discussion of perceptual beauty in relation to natural evil and ugliness. For now, suffice it to say that beauty finds an intriguing context within creation's aesthetic and often sublime "text"—by which I mean a deeply significant reality in need of interpretation.

PERCEPTUAL BEAUTY: EXPRESSIONS OF THE DIVINE NATURE

Having described this notion of perceptual beauty, I now wish to maintain that it is *this* beauty that expresses aspects of God's nature and intentions. But could we go further and affirm that perceptual beauty is not just an expression of God but an essential attribute of God? I think not, and that is why I conclude this chapter with an examination of perceptual beauty's relationship to God. Osborne, however, dismisses such a relationship out of hand: he says that we cannot know whether the world's beauty relates to transcendent reality, because if we can only know ultimate "metaphysical beauty" through created beauty, which is an imitation, we have no independent way to know that created beauty is in fact an imitation or how closely

99. See Kant, *Critique of Judgment*, 23. Farley, *Faith and Beauty*, 37, describes the sublime, drawing on Edmund Burke, as "a way in which certain human emotions are seized by a dimension of things that human beings cannot control, predict, be secure with or even conceptualize."

100. Wordsworth, Fourteen-Book *Prelude* 14.238–42, and note. Storm clouds can be beautiful as a unique part of a landscape, although they may not be beautiful when one is in the middle of them. Storm clouds take on unique shapes and colors and display the sort of natural order discussed in chapter 5.

it imitates. Thus the imitation and the thing imitated must be known independently.[101] But Osborne does not consider that special revelation might offer independent knowledge of God, as well as the conviction that created beauty reflects God. Moreover, Osborne invokes metaphysical pictures of "metaphysical beauty" and "imitation" that do not necessarily apply to God or to perceptual beauty. Indeed, I am reluctant to posit an ultimate divine or metaphysical beauty in Osborne's sense. A better approach is to emphasize perceptual beauty (per my stipulative description) as expressive of various aspects of God's nature,[102] not merely of his "metaphysical beauty," whatever that might be. In fact, the only case in which perceptual beauty might be rightly ascribed to God himself would be a theophany or the physical body of Christ.[103] That is, perceptual beauty could not be an attribute of God's unchangeable and imperceptible essence, but would rather be an incarnation or perhaps some other "materialization" within creation. By a materialization of God I mean an entering into the laws of nature through which objects become sense-perceptible. In contrast, any view attributing an imperceptible or radically different sort of beauty to God, while tempting, is problematic given our understanding of perceptual beauty through the senses. So rather than argue that perceptual beauties reveal a different or analogous sort of divine beauty, I hold that perceptual beauties express God and his intentions for the world in other ways. It is this claim that becomes central to the remaining chapters, after the metaphysical quagmires of divine beauty have been circumnavigated.

Added to the difficulties surrounding divine beauty are the debates regarding Christ's bodily beauty. But rather than be detained by lengthy discussion of Christ's beauty, I would rather emphasize how Christ's entering into nature affirms the significance of all natural beauty. This is a reasonable application of the incarnation, since Christ's body in its pre-glorification state might have been perceptually beautiful (though not necessarily exceptionally beautiful), not by virtue of being divine, but by virtue of becoming subject to the laws of nature, much as the boy Jesus was subject to his parents. Christ would then have been beautiful not simply because he is Christ but because he has taken on a human nature. But such beauty of the ordinary human form may not occasion our most common or arresting experiences of "natural" beauty. On the contrary, many other aspects of

101. Osborne, *Theory of Beauty*, 60.

102. By God's nature I mean simply what God is like, how we can best describe him.

103. This is not to say that a theophany would have to be beautiful, or that the physical body of Christ would have to be exceptionally beautiful in its pre-glorification state. One might also question whether we can ever *perceive* God apart from the incarnate Christ, but we should not preclude the possibility of other perceptible manifestations of God.

a beautiful world might reveal God much more accessibly and eminently than Christ's pre-glorification beauty (or lack thereof). Therefore, although the incarnation is central to creational theology, we must look beyond the incarnate body of Christ to beauty wherever it is found in the creation to which Christ gave himself.

In the first section I present this view of perceptual beauty's relationship to God. In the second section I consider the difficulties with the historical emphasis on beauty as an essential divine attribute.

Perceptual Beauty's Relationship to God

A more modern approach to divine beauty is supported by Scripture's rather infrequent and ambiguous associations of perceptual beauty with God. The clearest instance of such association is perhaps the description of the figure on the throne in Revelation 4:3, where John describes God's appearance in terms of precious stones. But this image seems highly symbolic rather than a literal description of how God would actually present himself to human eyes. In Isaiah 35:1–2 there seems to be a direct comparison between the beauty of flowers and the glory and splendor of God:

> The desert and the parched land will be glad;
> the wilderness will rejoice and blossom.
> Like the crocus, it will burst into bloom;
> it will rejoice greatly and shout for joy.
> The glory (*kābôd*) of Lebanon will be given to it;
> the splendor (*hādār*) of Carmel and Sharon;
> they will see the glory (*kābôd*) of the Lord,
> the splendor (*hādār*) of our God (Is 35:1–2, NIV).

But in this context, glory and splendor have as much to do with the fruitfulness and renewal of life through flowers in the desert as with the idea of perceptual beauty, even though beauty and fruitfulness are linked. In Isaiah 4:2 and 33:17 the prophet ascribes beauty to someone who is likely the Messiah, but this speaks only to the beauty of God incarnate, or possibly to beautiful garments, or beauty as symbolic of glory. In Psalm 27:4 where David longs "to gaze upon the beauty (*nōʿam*) of the Lord" (NIV), given the context, the reference may be only to the beauty of the ark and the temple as symbolic of God's glory or pleasantness.[104] The word for God's glory, *kābôd*, comes from the root adjective "heavy" and is often translated as "honor" or "reverence"; it thus seems related to the sublime and the fear of God more so than

---

104. Davies, "Beauty," *IDB* 1:371–72.

to beauty. But the word is also used of "a queen in bridal array" (Ps 45:14) and a fine couch (Ezek 23:41) and does not necessarily exclude perceptual beauty.[105] According to M. Weinfeld, "*kābôd* represents the divine majesty in the broad sense," encompassing the ideas of God's face, goodness, power, and beauty.[106] There certainly could be connotations of perceptual beauty in glory (*kābôd*), splendor (*hādār, tiphāhrāh*), and beauty/delightfulness (*nōʾam*) when used of God, even if the precise Semitic nuance in a given passage is impossible to determine.[107]

In view of Scripture and my understanding of perceptual beauty, I maintain that if God presents himself as perceptually beautiful, this beauty is not an essential attribute or an aspect of God's unchangeable essence. Neither is perceptual beauty primarily a revelation of a different sort of divine beauty. Rather, perceptual beauty is an appropriate outworking of God's essence and activity within creation. So while affirming that God's perfections are essential to his being, I can affirm that perceptual beauty (as I have described it) is not a divine perfection, but a function of divine perfection as expressed within creation. And as an outworking of divine perfection, perceptual beauty is potentially revelatory.

This understanding follows from my description of perceptual beauty, because perceptual beauty cannot apply to God's essence without God being *necessarily* perceptible. That is, perceptual beauty, even in the case of God, requires at least the theoretical possibility of sense-perception.[108] But God as immaterial is essentially sense-imperceptible. For God to be perceptually beautiful, creaturely perception must contribute to what divine perceptual beauty is as a phenomenon. God's own "perception" could not contribute to this phenomenon, because although God certainly "perceives" or knows himself, God does not sense-perceive himself. God's perception is indistinguishable from his knowledge, because as omniscient, God does not *perceive* the contents of all opaque boxes but simply *knows* what these contents are. So to affirm that God "perceives beauty" is only to say that God understands beauty through the lens of creaturely perception. It seems better, then, to

---

105. *BDB* 653.

106. Weinfeld, "*kābôd*," *TDOT*, 7:22–38.

107. Nicholson, "General Revelation, 2, suggests aesthetic connotations in these words. Barth says that "the beautiful as such and *in abstracto* does not play any outstanding or autonomous part in the Bible," but "this does not mean that it is unimportant for the Bible or alien to it." He maintains that "glory" in its Hebrew and Greek forms "includes and expresses what we call beauty" (*CD* 2/1:653).

108. Or, it requires at least an integral connection to sense-perception, such as in the case of dreams and mental imaging, or the case of God knowing how creatures would perceive an object.

say that God knows himself to be perfect and glorious rather than to say that God perceives himself as beautiful. Still, God could certainly present himself as perceptually beautiful, and he would know what it is about his essence that makes this sort of presentation possible. So perceptual beauty, as an outworking of God's essence and creativity, would then be part of "God's knowledge of the consistency, plenitude and expanse of his own being and of the extent and implications of his own power and freedom."[109]

Of course God's presentation of himself through perceptual beauty would still arise out of his essential perfection; but this essential perfection of an essentially imperceptible God cannot be called perceptually beautiful. God can still be perfect and glorious while remaining incorporeal and imperceptible. And this imperceptible perfection relates to the broader understanding of divine majesty expressed by *kābôd*. This term highlights God's weightiness, his supreme importance, and depth of interest to us. This "weight" is an overflow of the divine nature; it is an experience that creates conceptual space to be filled with various descriptions. For example, God's triune harmony and interrelatedness is profoundly and intriguingly glorious and weighty, as are his infinitude and self-existent, uncreated being. But these attributes lack perceptual beauty, perhaps in a way parallel to mathematics. We can describe this essential perfection of God and its implications in a number of ways, but this divine perfection is a primal reality unenhanced by creation and creaturely perception. Still God could manifest this perfection within creation as perceptually beautiful when the right subjective, creaturely constituents of beauty, or the right conditions for personal experiencing, are present. This beauty need not be essential to

---

109. Richards, *Untamed God*, 243. So we could rightly call God supremely beautiful, but not "beauty itself." For if we can even talk about "perceptual beauty itself," we would only be referring to an aspect of divine creativity worked out in various ways within creation. This understanding of divine beauty accords with the biblical assertions that no one can see God (John 1:18; 1 Tim 6:16; 1 John 4:12). But this transcendent "distance" set between God and created eyes, according to Hart, *Beauty*, 18–20, 313–14, exists not for the sake of our isolation but partly for the sake of delight—our delight in God's transcendent mystery and his delight in the creation that exists for his pleasure (Rev 4:11). This "distance" is, in fact, God himself—the "absolute excess" of the Word who "infinitely comprises and outstrips all the finite utterances of being." Yet beauty traverses this distance separating "ideal from real, transcendent from immanent, supernatural from natural," and reveals a certain compatibility between the divine and the created. Furthermore, if the incarnation reveals both profoundly and materially, so then can material, perceptual beauty. To know God through beauty in this way does not diminish God but highlights his transcendent but expressible mystery, as well as the profundities of a creation that gives rise to the phenomenon of beauty. And since neither beauty nor Christ's humanity corresponds univocally to God's essence, along with any positive knowledge of God that they reveal, they also both speak of his ultimate mystery. Cf. Augustine, *Sermon* 3.12.

God, yet it is still an appropriate outworking of God's essence in the presence of percipients. God can choose to present himself beautifully, and so perceptual beauty then becomes an expression of the divine nature.

Thus, an experience of this perceptual beauty could orient one to God's nature: that is, by focusing our attention on what is perceptually desirable, valuable, and interesting for its own sake, we would also be orienting ourselves to what is ultimately most desirable, valuable, and interesting for its own sake, namely God. God is ultimately desirable even if he can also be terrible, because we are created to find fulfillment, our true identity, ultimately in God. In other words, we are created to participate in God, to experience him, to receive him as a gift in ways proper to our created nature, such as through beauty. Beauty could present God as desirable to us, and through our contribution to beauty as a phenomenon, our inclusion in beauty, we might even experience a forward-looking clarity about our place within God's shared life. That is, we might anticipate the overflow of God's goodness toward us. In addition to this desire for beauty and participation in beauty, we can also experience awe before beautiful wind-blown dunes or porpoises rising in formation (a different sort of awe than in the non-beautiful sublime). The beautiful can be awe-inspiring in its aesthetic power, in the way that it captivates us, and this awe is also proper to God's majestic importance. So for both Christian and non-Christian, by experiencing beauty we could be experiencing our orientation to a perfect God, whether we recognize this connection explicitly or not.[110]

Thus we might expect that perceptual beauty, in an artful way, offers us something of the character of God. And if God chooses to present himself to creatures through perceptual beauty, we would expect the properties of this beauty to be in keeping with the properties of creation. God could even be presenting his nature indirectly or symbolically through creation's existing beautiful forms.

Such revelation through perceptual beauty gives us more grist for the mill of contemplation of God: we are not forced to contemplate God as supreme paradox, like "the sound of one hand clapping," or as "we know not what." Neither are we limited to contemplating God's nature in strictly intellectual, non-sensory ways, since we believe that our eternal relationship with God, especially God incarnate, involves redeemed bodies and bodily senses as well as redeemed minds. Instead, we can contemplate God through the world's beauties rather than through some different, non-perceptual "Beauty." Nevertheless, the intermediate state prior to bodily

110. Cf. Viladesau, *Theology and the Arts*, 42; Hart, *Beauty*, 17; and Karl Rahner, Theology and the Arts," 17–29, on beauty orienting us to God. "

resurrection, due to the absence of sense-perception, might seem to make a sense-perceptual beauty irrelevant. But depending on how one understands the intermediate state, perceptual beauty could still be significant, as in the quasi-embodied world of mental images described by H. D. Lewis and H. H. Price.[111] In addition, perceptual beauty still seems relevant even if God is "radically other" than created beings, because God must still be at least somewhat familiar in the way that he reveals himself to such beings. This type of condescension seems in keeping with God's revelatory dealings with humankind, including the incarnation. And though human beings can "become partakers of the divine nature" (2 Pet 1:4, RSV), overall, God seems to have much more capability to become like created beings than created beings have to become like God. Apart from such condescension in revelation, God and humankind might be like two parallel lines that never intersect. As argued previously, God is knowable because he has embedded his revelation within an artful creation engaged by our aesthetic rationality. Thus we might also suspect that God has embedded revelation of himself within the world's perceptual beauty.

Problems with Essential Divine "Beauty"

But Navone takes a different approach to the relationship between God and beauty than the one I have proposed. Working with a Platonic and non-sensory concept of divine beauty, he cites Augustine, who responds to the biblical assertions that no one can see God by postulating a sense of the mind or heart that allows one to "see" God.[112] Navone takes Augustine to mean that one can "see" God's beauty in this way.[113] If Navone is correct, then we should re-describe divine beauty without reference to the physical senses. Perhaps God is essentially perceptible by spiritual senses and only imperceptible due to the lack of human capacity. Or God might be beautiful

111. Lewis, *Self and Immortality*, 147, says that departed souls might experience "an image world, very like the world of our dreams, consisting of tactual as well as visual images, auditory images and smell images too. There would be images of organic sensations, including somatic sensations connected with the images that would make up one's own body." Perceptual beauty would be as relevant to such a world as it is to our present world. Cf. Price, *Philosophy of Religion*, 98–117.

We should also consider making a distinction between the immaterial or bodiless and the spiritual. Spiritual natures might be compatibly coextensive with material or bodily natures. Thus, speculation about angels and deceased souls could hinge upon the question of whether these creatures possess spiritual or provisional bodies and what such bodies would entail.

112. Augustine, *Letters* 148.6.

113. Navone, *Theology of Beauty*, 18.

in the intellectual sense, like an idea or equation. He might possess order and splendor in strictly immaterial ways. Perceptual beauty would then be only analogous to, and derivative of, the spiritual or intellectual sense of beauty, much as we say that human love is the created reflection of intra-Trinitarian love. But difficulties plague this concept of divine "Beauty."

For God to be *essentially* beautiful, he must be beautiful in and by himself, without reference to creation. So created percipients and their (physical or spiritual) perception cannot factor into this divine attribute. God must understand himself as beautiful, and the question recurs as to how spiritual perception of beauty would differ substantively from knowledge of goodness or glory. It seems possible that God could understand his beauty as something distinct from his goodness or perfection; but, then again, if we are inclined at all toward the doctrine of divine simplicity, we would tend to say that God contemplates his perfections as a unity. So without perceivable properties, divine beauty seems indistinguishable from goodness or value—an essential, non-relational attribute. God's essential goodness could consist in his unity and harmonious integrity of being, which seem to encompass his moral perfection as well; and his glory could consist in his immaterial radiance and intensity of being. So someone might say that God is good or valuable in these immaterially fitting or "beautiful" ways, or that God's immaterial fittingness or "beauty" constitutes his goodness. In this way, one might place harmony "under the name of" beauty and thus attribute *essential* beauty to God, perhaps adopting Iris Murdoch's understanding of Platonic beauty: "good as harmony and proportion."[114] Similarly, Plotinus's reducing of ultimate beauty to oneness allows us to ascribe beauty directly to God.[115]

But with these understandings of beauty, we have now lost much of the human experience of beauty through the senses. And if Beardsley is correct that Plato "means beauty itself to be a single simple property, not analyzable at all," then we are no better off.[116] Inviting other difficulties, Bonaventure refers to beauty as a universal, attributable to all being by virtue of its inherent form.[117] But even if inherent beauty of form seems plausible in the building blocks of all matter, this approach breaks down at higher levels such as the human body, where form is very susceptible to corruption and ugliness. Thus, the Platonic tradition, says Beardsley, "comes close to exalting Beauty at the

---

114. Beardsley, *Aesthetics*, 180, suggests placing harmony "under the name" of beauty. See also Murdoch, *Fire and the Sun*, 59.

115. Plotinus, *Enneads* 1.6.2.

116. Beardsley, *Aesthetics*, 42.

117. See Bonaventure, *Commentaria* 2.12.1.1.

expense of beauty."[118] If we can call God's essence beautiful at all, even in an analogous way to perceptual beauty, we are still referring to a "Beauty" that is very different from our sensory experience of perceptual beauty in the world. This different Beauty might be like Brian Davies' understanding of God's essential goodness as different from human conceptions of moral goodness. That is, God might rightly be called good, but, from a human perspective, we would not always consider God to be a morally good agent or his actions to be morally good.[119] One might apply Davies' approach to both divine beauty and goodness, affirming that divine beauty and goodness coincide in the simplicity of God as an essence that is both beauty and goodness, but neither beautiful nor good as understood from a human perspective. Still, this approach amounts to an appeal to unreachable mystery, and offers no clear understanding of divine beauty or goodness.

One might also claim that beauty and goodness coincide in the simplicity of God, where they both reach full realization in a way that they cannot in creation. But surely we find it strange to say that divine essential "Beauty" is the *full realization* of beauty when there are so many particular aspects of created beauties that the immutable divine *essence* seems inherently *incapable* of realizing in terms of its being, manifestation, or becoming. The divine essence might fully realize all the objective constituents that make flowers beautiful, but it cannot realize or possess the beauty of *that* particular flower at *that* particular time for *that* particular person. The divine essence cannot realize a flower at all, cannot possess flowerness, because such a state of affairs as a flower is the contingent product of God's free choice and not solely a manifestation of his essence. In other words, the divine essence is a unity and can be beautiful as only one entity, whereas creatures can be beautiful as many different entities. The divine essence might be more beautiful than all creatures, but cannot be beautiful *in the same varied ways* as all creatures, and therefore it seems inadequate to call divine "Beauty" the full realization of all created beauty. Even a fully realized Beauty cannot realize the diverse scope of all beauties.

If we do wish to affirm divine essential beauty, it must be of a different order, and require a different mode of investigation, than created, perceptual beauty, even though I doubt that we can contemplate it without bringing in some conceptual tie to the sensory. And for this reason Patrick

118. Beardsley, *Aesthetics*, 86.

119. See Davies, *Philosophy of Religion*, 227–30. Barth, *CD* 2/1:650, 652, also calls God "beautiful . . . in a way that is His alone . . . as the unattainable primal beauty, yet really beautiful." But he describes divine beauty in terms of how God "enlightens and convinces and persuades us" and does not include beauty with the perfections of the divine essence.

Sherry says that theology leaves us ultimately dissatisfied, however skilful its arguments, when it attempts to correlate imperceptible divine attributes with beauty-properties perceived through the senses. We recognize that this imperceptible divine Beauty is something so far removed from our own experience of created beauties that we question the utility of the comparison. In addition, we sense the risk of merely extrapolating our own sensory perception of beauty into an immaterial or divine counterpart. Perhaps we derive the idea of an intellectual or spiritual sense of beauty purely from our physical perception of beauty, even if that perception does ultimately reflect God's essence in some way. In light of these difficulties, Navone (via Augustine) provides one of many examples of what Sherry calls the "spiritualization" of beauty, providing little help in determining what divine beauty might actually mean.[120]

As a result of such "spiritualization" of beauty, John of the Cross asserts that "all the beauty of creatures, compared with the infinite beauty of God, is the height of deformity."[121] But this assertion seems to call into question God's creative activity as a whole.[122] Similarly, Viladesau claims that "divine beauty . . . transcends . . . our natural desires and capacities."[123] But this suggests that God is beautiful in some radically other, discontinuous way from creation, necessitating different intellectual/spiritual mechanisms for apprehending this beauty, and forcing us to abandon the concept of perceptual beauty as we now understand it through the senses, at least in reference to God. But why should this be necessary? After all, perceptual beauty is part of the original good of creation, and while God might improve upon created beauty, vitiated as it may be, why should he drastically alter or spiritualize it in the process of glorification? Perhaps the new creation need only abolish corruption and intensify God's existing plan of beauty—a plan by which God could already be expressing himself through these created structures giving rise to perceptual beauty.

By such a plan, perceptual beauty could be a created framework of relations through which God chooses to present himself even in creation's everyday natural beauties. Beauty could present God in, around, and among us in creation. And this perceptual beauty could still be richly and artfully associated with God's nature even without being an essential divine attribute. Thus, the theoretical door remains open for natural beauty to function

120. Sherry, *Spirit and Beauty*, 65, 133.

121. John of the Cross, *Ascent* 1:25–26.

122. As Phillip Blond says, "we suddenly have a position where a God annihilates the visible world, as it represents an idolatrous failure to adequately resemble or capture the reality of which He apparently is the only measure" ("Levinas," 217).

123. Viladesau, *Theology and the Arts*, 146–47.

as a revelation of God. But we must consider whether this theoretical role for natural beauty matches human experience: we must look at how human beings make sense of natural beauty.

3

Making Sense of Natural Beauty
Tacit Knowledge and Saturated Phenomena

I HAVE SUGGESTED THE possibility that God is presented to human beings through the world's perceptual beauties. Yet theology has not sufficiently considered this possibility, and many would simply deny that God communicates in this way, apart from written or spoken words. But even the idea of verbal revelation should raise questions about the media of God's communication, since God as a non-physical being does not literally speak or write, at least not without entering into the laws of nature in some way. Moreover, written or spoken words do not account for much of our human communication and knowing—such as an infant communicating with her mother through vocal tones and facial expressions. Such communication might be said to function through an "aesthetic rationality" engaging "images" rather than words within the world's "artful" context. Given these sublinguistic modes of knowing and experiencing already at work, we might expect that God would also reveal himself by such modes, in uniquely personal and artistic ways. One significant way that God could reveal himself in creation would be by placing symbolic "images" within creation's artistic "text," and one significant category of such images would naturally be beautiful forms (including objects, creatures, actions, etc., under this heading of forms).

But to make such a claim, one must make this idea of symbolic beauty more plausible and thinkable: one must, in Paul Ricoeur's terms, "saturate" it with intelligibility.[1] I propose to do this by describing how beauty affects

1. Ricoeur, *Symbolism*, 355.

both religious and non-religious people at different "levels" of experience. These experiences of beauty contribute to patterns of experience—patterns that suggest revelatory values in nature often overlooked. And these patterns support the claim that beautiful forms function as revelation. Beautiful forms could be symbols to the extent that they evoke meanings beyond themselves, and this symbolic communication would support the development of a creational theology in dialogue with human experience of beauty. We can develop these claims, first, from the ideas and associations that beauty-experience intimates at a deep, existential level. And secondly, we can explore how such ideas and associations fit or resonate with human tendencies to make religious sense of beauty-experience.

This task of making sense of natural beauty spans two chapters. In this chapter, I describe the "saturated"[2] character of beauty-experience. In the next chapter, this beauty-experience receives further heuristic shaping as I consider beautiful forms as images. Artistic symbolism seems to be part of the very structure of the human experience of nature, as human beings apply symbolic thinking as an epistemic practice to make religious sense of beauty. This theological "sense-making" continues into the final chapter through an appropriation of John Ruskin's symbolic approach to natural beauty.

This chapter continues my largely phenomenological approach from the previous chapter, but moves beyond merely perceptual concerns to describe perceptual beauty's situation within creation at higher existential levels. Although it still builds upon perception, an existential focus draws out the total human response to beauty within a broad human context. This context encompasses past and present life-experience, training and tradition, and interpretation and personal formation. It is in the midst of these diverse personal connections that beauty becomes entangled with theology, and so this chapter also fits into the analogical, incarnational, epistemological framework of creational theology from chapter 1. Creational theology seeks to learn what it can from human experience of beauty, while integrating this experience into the wider context of Christian doctrine.

This approach to a beautiful world is a development of the notion that beauty, natural and artistic, could function as a theological "source" (such as Scripture, tradition, and religious experience), as it has traditionally been called.[3] Bonaventure suggests this idea, following Augustine, by describing the world as an artful "book reflecting, representing, and describing its Maker,

2. Here I am using the term *saturated* in a somewhat different sense than I use it in the preceding paragraph. The first usage relates to Ricoeur's understanding of descriptions. The second usage relates to Marion's understanding of experience.

3. Sherry, *Spirit and Beauty*, 69, suggests that beauty could be a theological source, and Viladesau, *Theology and the Arts*, 146, suggests that beauty is a natural revelation.

the Trinity," and in this book, he sees "in every creature . . . the refulgence of the divine Exemplar, but mixed with darkness."[4] Diverse theologians have held to this doctrine of God's "second book." Not only the medievals but the Reformed Belgic Confession also upholds the revelatory function of creation's "most elegant book"[5]—a book not of words or propositions but of artistic images with transcultural implications. This perspective on creation is also suggested more contemporarily by the "radically orthodox," who hold that "for phenomena really to be there they must be more than there" through participation in God, allowing "a depth of Being" to "'shine through' beings."[6] Such statements reflect a "sacramental ontology"—an ontology that allows embodied, experiential, and effectual participation in divine revelation through the world, especially through its beauty.[7]

Describing the world as a sacramental book invites further descriptions—of creation as a divine work of art, and of beauty as an artistic symbol. But these terms, like all descriptions, are the casting of a vision—an exercise in "seeing as"—an experiment that must be fitted into our broader understandings of the world and our experiential contact with it. Such an experiment will certainly require refinement under the ethos of epistemology in community, but all descriptive sense-making must begin somewhere. In my descriptions I am "wagering," as Ricoeur puts it,

> that I shall have a better understanding of man and of the bond between the being of man and the being of all beings if I follow the *indication* of symbolic thought. That wager then becomes the task of *verifying* my wager and saturating it, so to speak, with intelligibility. . . . I bet at the same time *that* my wager will be restored to me in power of reflection, in the element of coherent discourse. . . . The symbol, used as a means of detecting and deciphering human reality, will have been verified by its power to raise up, to illuminate, to give order to . . . human experience.[8]

The wager is that symbolic beauties can indeed detect and decipher human reality in relation to God, and I now turn to the task of "verifying" this wager. This involves "saturating" beauty-phenomena with intelligibility

---

4. Bonaventure, *Breviloquium* 2.12.1, 4; *Six Days* 12.14. Ernst Robert Curtius, *European Literature*, 319–25, surveys the extensive use of the *liber naturae* metaphor from the Middle Ages through the Romantic period.

5. "Belgic Confession," 190.

6. Milbank, Pickstock, and Ward, "Suspending the Material," 4, 12.

7. Muth, "Beastly Metaphysics," 242, connects "sacramental ontology" with radical orthodoxy.

8. Ricoeur, *Symbolism*, 355.

through various descriptions. Varied and overlapping descriptions have the best chance of attaining to accuracy of description, because beauty-phenomena are nonverbal in character and only limitedly describable. So in addition to Ricoeur's understanding of symbolic thought, I will enlist two other vocabularies to help describe how beauty affects us. The first of these vocabularies is Michael Polanyi's concept of personal, tacit knowledge; the second is Jean-Luc Marion's concept of "saturated phenomena." I will also intersperse texts by William Wordsworth and other poets, providing an overlapping layer of *poetic* description that is particularly relevant to our experience of nature. I further saturate the idea of revelatory beauty by considering how people make religious sense of beauty-experience. This involves drawing upon the resources of Christian doctrine and integrating this doctrine with the complexities of the world and its varied effects upon us, thus giving more theological shape to our experience.

Of course, beauty-experience is only one facet of the complex human experience of nature—one could also consider the sublime or other categories. But I will limit myself to a consideration of perceptual beauty as delineated previously. Despite this perceptual focus, however, it should become evident that our perceptual experience of beauty involves more than what we actually perceive.

APPROPRIATING POLANYI'S "PERSONAL KNOWLEDGE"

We make sense of a complex world, as Michael Polanyi observes, not by making tidy inferences from experience, but more realistically, by "indwelling" certain epistemic practices, skills, desires, and idioms within like-minded and practicing communities. We come to understand the world, not directly, but only through, and from within, these indwelt intermediaries, which are simply the epistemic conditions within which we find ourselves. These intermediary conditions are also the very tools of discovery and the factors that "shape our vision of the nature of things."[9] Polanyi offers this approach to "personal knowledge" as a physical chemist turned philosopher. His highly skilled experience in scientific research inspired an epistemology more faithful to the working realities of scientific practice. Polanyi observed human beings knowing and coming to know, and built his epistemological categories based on what he saw happening, rather than trying to fit what was happening into highly refined and abstract categories. This *a posteriori*, phenomenological engagement with scientific practice led Polanyi to reject the reigning Enlightenment epistemology of doubt and putative objectivity as untrue to science,

9. Polanyi, *Personal*, 203, 266.

and more generally, to human experience of reality. In its place, he developed a highly personal, yet realist and disciplined, approach to empirical investigation that can be applied in different ways to both science and the humanities.[10] With its emphasis on the emotional, embodied, and personal coefficients of knowing, Polanyi's epistemology is particularly suited to the development of a creational theology of natural beauty.

The indwelt practices, skills, desires, idioms, and communities mentioned above constitute what Polanyi calls "articulate systems." An articulate system can be anything from a scientific theory, to a religion, to a work of art, all of which "are validated by becoming happy dwelling places of the human mind."[11] "Articulate system," however, is a rather unhelpful term, because these diverse mental dwelling places are based on much that is inarticulate, and are not always very systematic. So a better term for many of these dwelling places, especially in the arts, might be "epistemic vision" or "framework." Through such visions or frameworks we come to know and to conceptualize (in part) certain aspects of reality. Such visions or frameworks must be *indwelt* personally and communally, which means to live, think, and work within and through them. Indwelling an epistemic vision requires entering into its specific practices and skills of knowing: for a chemist, learning to use laboratory equipment, for a composer, learning to play musical instruments. Such skills encompass a whole range of practical knowledge. Indwelling also requires observation, participation, and apprenticeship. Such training leads to conscious reflection upon a vision's "intellectual powers" in dialogue with others.

To truly indwell a vision, we must also acquire certain desires—desires that are specific to one's epistemic vision. These "intellectual desires" propel an epistemic vision forward, through a sort of perpetual dissatisfaction with its limitations and lack of knowledge. Such dissatisfaction becomes a pondering of how to satisfy one's desire, thus stimulating the imagination heuristically.[12] As part of this desire, an epistemic vision also explores new descriptions and descriptive idioms to deal more fittingly with the portion of reality with which it is concerned. All of these factors contribute to a distinctive way of viewing some aspect of reality. And from such an indwelt position, one can also, where appropriate, begin to develop, criticize, and modify an epistemic vision.

If we know the world only by indwelling such epistemic visions, then we present our truth claims, our "vision of the nature of things," not by courting

10. T. Clark, *Divine Revelation*, 77–83, discusses Polanyi's contribution.

11. Polanyi, *Personal*, 195, 280, 283–84.

12. Ibid., 127, 135, 143, 195.

a spurious objectivity. Instead, we invite others to enter into our vision and practices, and thereby, to see what we see. By virtue of this approach, our truth claims, our descriptions of the world, can seem alarmingly *personal* when viewed by someone inhabiting a very different vision. For example, two scientists indwelling conflicting scientific theories are likely to accuse each other of idiosyncratic assertions of personal belief, because they have not sufficiently indwelt, and therefore have not understood, the other's epistemic vision. Such assertions of personal belief seem idiosyncratic, because they arise out of a deep personal indwelling of a unique vision. But the disagreeing scientists can still understand one another, because of their shared humanity, and because of much shared ordinary and specialized knowledge. Therefore conversation and debate can still take place. Moreover, personal beliefs can still be checked rigorously by indwelling the vision from which they arise, according to its established practices, virtues, disciplines, background knowledge, and cultural heritage. Thus papers must still be refereed and experiments repeated, so that others can be persuaded to adopt a new vision of the world. And such persuasion is rooted in a firm submission to, and passionate striving after, "the universal status of the hidden reality" approached by the knower. This submission to reality "excludes randomness" and "suppresses egocentric arbitrariness."[13] Thus Polanyi's epistemology is decisively realist rather than relativistic or utilitarian.

But for Polanyi, it is also the *personal* nature of one's truth claims that is indispensable: personal knowing entails unique individual contributions to an epistemic vision. These individual contributions do not hinder but facilitate the discovery of truth by affording the mind greater powers than would an attenuated objectivism. We come to know the world, then, not by a putatively objective detachment, but through personal (yet publicly and communally shared) involvement in specific practices, desires, and idioms. In addition, we apply personally developed epistemic skills in original ways in "the art of knowing." Such an approach produces markedly personal and passionate understandings of reality, and because of these intellectual passions fundamental to all knowing, we recommend our personal understandings to others.[14] By such recommendation, we are claiming that our understandings are usable and that they point in appropriate directions. Thus our understandings become personally indwelt and manipulated "tools," with which we "probe" reality.[15] These epistemic tools are also usable by others, and by offering our understandings as tools, we extend the invita-

13. Ibid., 268, 310.
14. Ibid., 150, 311–12, 322–23. Polanyi and Prosch, *Meaning*, 63.
15. Polanyi, *Tacit*, 16–17.

tion to others to "try on" our personal understandings, and to see if they can in turn personally shape them to fit their own experience. But we must first offer our own initial understandings in order to invite the possibilities of different understandings, along with the possibility of being led by others into further, more accurate approximations of truth. This "being led" is part of the communally personal nature of knowing.

Such knowing is also irreducibly personal, because one cannot discover new understandings according to any prescribed, impersonal set of rules. Instead, discovery is always a fiduciary "plunge" across the "logical gap" between the known and the partially unknown.[16] This plunge involves personal commitment to the broad veridicality of our own heuristic understandings. Yet, at the same time, we are always making this commitment on "inadequate" grounds. In other words, we are committing ourselves largely based on our confidence in our own relevant epistemic skills, as well as those of our community. This confidence, in turn, is based not solely on universal criteria, but partly on a variable and unspecifiable set of our own *personal* criteria. So in this sense, our epistemic confidence and commitment are always a conquering of "self-doubt."[17] Nevertheless, these personal criteria are not the basis for a blind leap, because they are the result of a tacit, indwelt, and communally shared knowledge of one's discipline.

It is imperative to stress further this indwelt, tacit knowledge, because Polanyi declares that "all knowledge is . . . either tacit or rooted in tacit knowing."[18] Tacit knowledge is a matter of unspecifiable, and often unexplainable, human competencies, rooted in our mind-bodily adaptation to the world—competencies comparable to a rat's bodily and instinctual knowledge of how to run a maze. Such knowledge is more fundamental to our being-in-the-world than our linguistically described knowledge, and so we find, in every area of life, that *"we know more than we can tell."*[19] In fact, we rely heavily upon this unspecifiable knowledge to support and inform what we can and do verbalize. Thus words function as indispensable tools by which we describe and share understandings of reality, yet words can also sometimes mislead by reducing and/or distorting what we already know in more tacit, and more existentially robust, ways.[20] Such tacit knowledge becomes more robust according to the depth of our (often bodily) indwelling of the skills and practices fundamental to an epistemic vision. Through such

---

16. Polanyi, *Personal*, 123–24, 312.

17. Ibid., 90, 267.

18. Polanyi and Prosch, *Meaning*, 61.

19. Polanyi, *Personal*, 90; idem, *Tacit*, 4.

20. See Polanyi, *Personal*, 94.

indwelling, we increasingly access a vision of the world by absorbing its tacit knowledge stores, thus supporting our making of any specific truth claim.

We come to absorb and grasp this tacit dimension of reality, not directly or focally, but only *subsidiarily* as we employ it and *"look through"* it in order to focus on something else.[21] For example, a violinist focuses on a piece of music while attending subsidiarily to the musical notation and muscular movements of fingering and bowing that will produce the correct sounds. At the same time, while attending subsidiarily to all these factors, the violinist, at a higher level, actually "discovers," as well as shapes, the sound, feel, and pathos of a masterly performance. Similarly, tacit knowledge enables discovery by providing just enough of a hint of some reality that we can formulate a corresponding epistemic problem and look for its solution. It provides a "foreknowledge" of what we desire to discover—a foreknowledge of "not yet understood, perhaps as yet unthinkable consequences." Thus tacit knowledge undergirds the personal commitment essential to all knowledge.[22] Tacit knowledge allows the knower to venture out upon promising ideas with the intuition that resources will eventually become available to support these ideas. Imagination then "hammers away" in plausible directions to uncover the resources that will confirm one's guesses.[23] Imagination accesses and integrates tacit resources into new and meaningful configurations—new "focal centers" of meaning that contribute to "discoveries" of reality, such as the masterly performance of a musical piece.

So tacit knowledge helps to make so-called "inadequate" grounds for knowledge compelling. And indeed, living in the world demands epistemic commitment to reality based on tacit knowledge. Without such commitment, we shy away irresponsibly from contact with reality. But responsibility and commitment attend the scientist, as Polanyi observes, who "stakes bit by bit his whole professional life on a series of [creative] decisions and this day-to-day gamble represents his most *responsible* activity."[24] This creative gambling (cf. Ricoeur's wagering) is responsible, because, for Polanyi, "heuristic conjecture" is the very "function of philosophical reflection"—it is the "bringing to light, and affirming as my own, the beliefs implied in such of my thoughts and practices as I believe to be valid." The knower has the "right" and the "duty to declare such beliefs" based on an extensive network of practical, tacit knowledge. And though this personal declaration may appear too risky and error prone, especially to someone seeking an unattainable objectivity, it is

---

21. Ibid., 90.
22. Ibid., 312; idem, *Tacit*, 23.
23. Polanyi and Prosch, *Meaning*, 58.
24. Polanyi, *Personal*, 309–10, 315, 320, my emphasis.

checked further by intellectual virtues, communal disciplines, and submission to reality's universal status. Moreover, this risky personal knowledge is the only alternative to an even riskier objectivism—an objectivism that oscillates wildly between vaunted doubts and dogmas.[25]

A Polanyian Creational Theology

If this Polanyian approach to knowledge holds true for the scientific discoverer of physical realities, how much more so for the discoverer of spiritual realities, especially anyone who seeks God's revelation in nature. Unfortunately, Polanyi's own treatment of revelation may suffer from his insufficient indwelling of a religious community and religion as an epistemic practice. Nonetheless, his epistemology certainly applies to revelation.[26] After all, both the arts and sciences involve parallel indwellings of epistemic visions and practices, and both involve the "art" of integrating tacit elements. Both also require commitment to the presence of a partly mind-independent reality. But while a scientific vision requires *verification* by rigorous testing, the arts necessitate a less rigorous, experiential *validation*.[27] In the case of a theological validation, we must recognize that our vision is not the only one, and perhaps not even the best one, because it may be incomplete, require reform, and, of course, there will always be a range of different understandings from which we might learn. But we do claim that our theological understandings are valuable tools for putting us in touch with divine reality in particular ways that other visions of the world do not.

The religious practitioner, then, takes up these epistemic tools for approaching divine reality through nature. The religious person thus comes to indwell an epistemic vision held by a like-minded and intentioned religious community. This community's practices and cultural heritage discipline one's own personal conjectures. By indwelling this communal vision with its practices, the knower "consciously experiences its intellectual powers," and comes to reflect upon the "theoretic vision" and "passionate heuristic impulse" of knowing God through nature.[28] The religious knower thus experiences revelation only through this communal (Christian or non-Christian) vision. This vision's conceptual forms and epistemic practices shape inescapably even elements of religious experience that are common to humanity (such as beauty-experience, as I will argue). Furthermore, as knowers

25. Ibid., 208, 267–68, 270–71, 310.
26. See T. Clark, *Divine Revelation*, 125–44.
27. Polanyi, *Personal*, 202.
28. Ibid., 195, 280.

indwell this vision, they expand their tacit knowledge networks, enabling new, imaginative integrations of tacit knowledge toward new focal centers of heuristic attention. And the focal center of particular interest here is our experience of the world's beauty and meaning. Thus by indwelling a particular vision (e.g., Christianity), our "way of seeing" and interacting with a beautiful world is forever changed, and we come to experience and know what we could not through a different vision (e.g., Vedantic Hinduism).

Indwelling this communal vision also requires entering into its skills and desires, both intellectual and aesthetic. In this case of knowing God through nature, both kinds of desire draw upon, and overflow into, the aesthetic rationality of artistic reflection and communication. As opposed to an artificial and detached communication, artistic, symbolic presentations are the natural idioms of beauty-experience. And these idioms must be acquired and indwelt as beauty-skills—as necessary, discipline-specific ways of knowing and describing God through a beautiful creation. Regarding verbal idioms, Polanyi notes that "hidden meaning" lurks in the idiom of any discipline—meaning that is not yet fully apprehended by the hearer or even the speaker. This is because our words are "invested" with "a fund of unspecifiable connotations," of which we are only tacitly aware, and these meanings must be drawn out by imagination and desire.[29] Just as a poem's meaning cannot be reduced to prose, a poetic idiom evokes understandings that prose cannot access, and such understandings often correspond more faithfully to a realistic sense of "this is what it is like" to experience beauty. As Austin Farrer notes, whereas "exact prose abstracts from reality, symbol presents it. And for that very reason, symbols have some of the many-sidedness of wild nature."[30] Mark Wynn agrees that symbolic, poetic idiom captures affective and embodied "phenomenological complexes," thereby offering "existentially dense knowledge" of places and God through places.[31] Poetry facilitates the same sort of pause, reflection, and imagination that attend our experience of beauty, and so it can provide an apt verbal "rendering" of nature's non-verbal "language." Poetry can become a mouthpiece of ferns and wood thrushes, not so much possessing their meanings

---

29. Ibid., 112, 207–8. See Wordsworth: "Poetry is the breath and finer spirit of knowledge; it is the impassioned expression which is in the countenance of all Science" (Preface to *Lyrical Ballads*, 752–53). Rahner emphasizes the possibility that "the poet is basically giving expression to religious statements in this different set of analogous symbols. Such a situation calls for careful scrutiny of the language of the poet" ("Theology and the Arts," 17–29). Rahner also sees the lack of "poetic theology" as a theological defect.

30. Farrer, *Rebirth*, 20.

31. Wynn, *Faith and Place*, 104, 210.

as being "possessed by" them and speaking "according to" them.[32] For these reasons, the poets are skilled pillars of this epistemic community. As we will see, "primal" religion, biblical revelation, Romantic poetry, phenomenology, and Ruskin's symbolic practice in chapter 5, all adopt this poetic idiom to engage beauty; and indeed, even to participate in these discussions requires that this idiom be indwelt, desired, and understood. Therefore my own style of presentation is likewise adapted to the subject matter at hand. By these modes of poetic idiom, aesthetic skills and desires, personal and communal descriptions, a creational theology of natural beauty begins to emerge.

MEANINGFUL EXPERIENCE OF BEAUTY

Within this theological perspective, I propose the following sketch of the relationship between beauty-experience and religious experience: if all beautiful forms can be said to "image" God in some way, then God is "present" in this way in all human perception of beauty. That is, the immanent Creator is present and "experienced" tacitly in the form of other things, as long as beauty in nature or art presents God's nature in some symbolic way, regardless of one's recognition of, or response to, this presentation. So on this view, to experience the soaring, versicolored Sainte-Chapelle would be to experience the mediated character of God himself. And similarly, Ruskin believes that we should understand the biblical imagery of God in the clouds quite literally: that is, our experience of clouds is not just associated with our experience of God but is itself an experience of the God who is constantly at work in the clouds. We see God the artist in the beautiful shapes and colors of clouds, God the provider in the blessings of rain and shade, and the fearsome God in huge, dark, and destructive clouds. Otherwise, says Ruskin, "we refine and explain ourselves into dim and distant suspicion of an inactive God, inhabiting inconceivable places."[33] So with this approach, beauty-experience is not merely analogous to religious experience. Neither does it merely lead to religious experience by association. Rather, beauty-experience itself can be a form of tacitly "religious" experience.

But even if God is present and experienced tacitly in this way through all beauty, he is usually not experienced *as* God or even as a vague transcendence. On most occasions, beauty is experienced simply and casually *as* beauty or perhaps as a lesser "prettiness." This involves the heightened perceptual awareness common to all experiences of beauty and to all people. But often in our preoccupation with other matters, this is only a perfunctory

32. See Merleau-Ponty, *Visible and Invisible*, 118, on objects "possessing" language.
33. Ruskin, *Modern Painters*, 4:110.

experience. Sometimes beauty does "grab hold" of us, if only for an instant. But even in these cases the experience often provides no deeper, explicit meaning: it may be accompanied by emotion, but is simply a pause to appreciate or wonder at the beautiful object.

Yet it is in these brief pauses that "a something more," or a sense of specific meaning tied into the emotions, can sometimes intrude upon our experience. And this occurs especially as we have the time and willingness to pursue such threads of meaning.[34] This meaning, this "something," is often tacitly, sometimes explicitly, identified and interpreted as a "something," according to whatever background information and frameworks of understanding we possess, be they religious or non-religious, Christian or non-Christian.[35] So by this point we are already understanding beauty through a particular epistemic vision of the world. Such understandings accompany experience and are not imposed at a separate and higher experiential "level"; rather, the experience is interpreted as it is experienced.

But despite this inescapable interpretation, we might also usefully speak of an element in the experience that is common to humanity. This common element might be partly described in religiously "neutral" language, perhaps as a poignant or moving *significance* in the experience of beauty. This significance would also be experienced through various emotions, such as awe, admiration, or a grateful sense of contingency. This common experiential element lends itself to various religious interpretations, to such a degree that even non-religious people can acknowledge that such interpretations do suggest themselves. And consequently, *to this extent*, beauty-experience *itself* can be said to point toward God, regardless of which epistemic vision (religious or non-religious) one employs to make sense of the experience.

For non-religious people, the experience of beauty might not have any acknowledged religious meaning, but could have all sorts of associated meanings, varying with one's cultural and ideological visions (that is, one's indwelt epistemic conditions). From the Christian perspective, God would be "in" the experience simply by virtue of what beauty is as an operation within his creation, even if the percipient acknowledges no hint of transcendence in the experience. But non-religious people can be momentarily

---

34. We increasingly apprehend meaning in a place as we increasingly interact bodily with that place. For example, when we actually cook in another person's kitchen, we recognize how their kitchen is ordered differently from our own. And by experiencing that different order, we may also learn something about that person. See Wynn, "Towards a Broadening," 147–66.

35. Dulles notes "the need for a personal and communal framework of symbols and doctrines in order to give a determinate meaning to the otherwise vague experience of the transcendent" (*Models of Revelation*, 243).

"apprehended" by a prospect of "Lake, islands, promontories, gleaming bays / A universe of Nature's fairest forms."[36] And in this situation, the non-religious person might, for example, acquire a sense that the world is a wondrous and valuable place, and that life is worth living. But the non-religious person in this case could be a staunch atheist and therefore unwilling to entertain further religious associations beyond the world as good and life as valuable, even if further associations actually presented themselves in the experience. Much more could be in the experience but go unacknowledged because interpreted non-religiously or simply rejected; so the extent of the awareness could progress no farther.

But even at this point, a movement beyond the beautiful object has already begun. This movement, this "excess" of meaning in the beautiful, urges percipients beyond objects toward a sense of a profounder nature of reality (e.g., a valuable world and life).[37] In Jean-Luc Marion's terms, the "saturated" character of phenomena arises as intuition and idealizing thought outstrip sensation, concepts, and signification in our perception of beauty. In other words, more meaning arises out of the experience than can be perceived or inferred directly, or conceptualized and expressed straightforwardly. This excess of meaning is an object's "givenness outside the norm" and a "self-giving without self-showing." Givenness for Marion refers to an "unforeseen happening," an authentically lived experience that is not foreseen or constituted by a subject but happens to a subject. But this givenness does not always *show* itself perceptually, much like the three unseen but assumed sides of a cube, or like what a human face can "say" without showing, even to itself. It is this given but un-shown reality that the painter often shows by painting it—by transforming a given intuition about the world "into a distinct and constituted visible."[38] This un-shown givenness could account for our pause or second look at a photograph of a person or place: we are exceeding it; we are looking into its depths, much as a painter would do before deciding how to paint the scene. The scene's excess of meaning might also be compared to the "soul" or "feel" of a musical passage, which can supervene upon various alternative musical structures and performances, such that we can experience similar feelings (gravitas, for instance) from various unique melodies.[39] Thus we might also experience a similar depth or weightiness

36. Wordsworth, Fourteen-Book *Prelude* 4.8–9.

37. See Nicholson, "General Revelation," 7.

38. Marion, *In Excess*, xxi, 25, 43, 51, 61, 109.

39. Milbank, "Beauty and the Soul," 27, compares excess meaning to the "soul" of musical structures.

in seeing a beautiful human face or "the tall rock, / The mountain, and the deep and gloomy wood."[40]

This "sense" of excess flows partly with and through the affections, but involves more than just emotion.[41] It involves sublinguistic impressions that might also be described by the Heideggerian term *Befindlichkeit*, or a sense of "how one finds oneself" in relation to beautiful objects.[42] And this sense would also be a type of knowing or "know how"—a sensing of how to relate to a beautiful world, similar to one's sensing of how to drive a car. Such knowledge accords with Polanyi's emphasis on the tacit coefficient of all knowledge: we rely on tacit knowledge as we focus on something else. And as we focus on beauty, to use Marion's idiom, we "frame" it. We necessarily frame such experiences in order to "manage" the vast, unspecifiable amounts of information and associations that go along with the experiences. That is, outside this frame of our focus, we tacitly know a penumbra of unspecifiables that contribute to the very nature of our perception of beauty.[43] This tacit knowledge contributes to our skill in apprehending, appreciating, and understanding the beautiful. In another idiom, these tacit "clues" are, for Maurice Merleau-Ponty, the invisible stylings, axes, and forces that sustain the world and render it visible by "possessing us" in order that we may see the world.[44] Thus, we always perceive beauty through what Marion calls an "exploded frame." The frame is "exploded," because it encompasses much that is tacit though potentially meaning-laden.[45]

This knowing through an exploded frame of tacit knowledge— through an excess of meaning—could qualify as a minimal level of revelation. Much as tacit knowledge acquired through practice and skill tells us how to drive a car, tacit knowledge acquired through beauty-experience could give us partial but existentially rich understandings of how to relate to the world and to ourselves. Such experience might also stimulate our understanding of the transcendent nature of this excess's origin and end.

---

40. Wordsworth, "Tintern Abbey," 2:77–78.

41. There is reason to believe that emotions have intellectual content, and can be modes of meaning recognition, as opposed to being (on an older model) merely responses to some preceding thought. Thus we might suppose that God is sometimes made manifest in certain emotional responses to the world. That is, we apprehend the meaning that is God through the appropriate emotional responses to his creation, and only subsequently formulate this meaning discursively. See Wynn, "Phenomenology," n.p.

42. A parallel example is the way in which a very young child who cannot speak can still "find herself in relation to" a cow, and express this relationship by mooing.

43. Marion, *In Excess*, 57.

44. Merleau-Ponty, *Visible and Invisible*, 151.

45. Marion, *In Excess*, 72.

Such revelation would be, in Wordsworth's terms (which are not unlike Aquinas's), a "conformity to," or an aesthetic and epistemic harmony with, "the end and written spirit of God's works, / Whether held forth in Nature or in Man, / Through pregnant vision."[46]

Thus beauty's excess could consist in a tacit knowledge of the transcendent-in-the-immanent[47]—and this tacit knowledge may be simply a determinant part of how we often perceive beauty. Such knowledge might be tacit, not only because transcendence could be only partially present, but because it might be *too* present to be reductively framed and conceptualized. That is, God's presence in the world may be more than what we can handle. But while our limited grasp prevents our knowing from advancing too far, tacit knowledge also prevents our knowledge from resting content, by eliciting the intellectual desires fundamental to all knowing.[48] Through such desire, tacit knowing can spill over into *hope* for what is intimated but lies beyond our reach. In this sense, to reverse the cliché, hope *is* a method. We can enter into a dialogue of hope through beauty, or what Jean-Louis Chrétien describes as "call and response," in which beauty calls and we respond with hope and desire in a continuing dialogue.[49] In this way, tacit knowledge of transcendence, as it draws our knowledge along by hope and desire, could engender a temporary breaking through or suspension of our interpretive frameworks. And this temporary suspension might even contribute to "a change of our intellectual personality."[50] That is, due to an existential change in ourselves, we may find the need to modify our interpretations of our experience in order to account adequately for beauty's excess—in order to frame it, manage it, and perhaps eventually, to shape linguistically some of its intuitional content. But these existential changes of personality and interpretation are often not readily specifiable, because

---

46. Wordsworth, Fourteen-Book *Prelude*, 4.350–53. Wordsworth's approach here is strikingly similar to Aquinas's emphasis on the aesthetic, epistemic harmony between a divinely enlightened mind and a divinely ordered world.

47. Transcendence and immanence are spatial metaphors corresponding respectively to being beyond or within some object or space. But if God is omnipresent, he is neither beyond nor within objects spatially. So rather than understand these terms as predicating different modes of being to God, it seems better to understand them as predicating different modes of experiencing God to human subjects—that is, we experience God as being either beyond or within certain objects or spaces—as either coming from somewhere else or as being present in some special brilliance of the world.

48. See Marion, *In Excess*, 159, 162, on the non-conceptual and unsettling influence of a transcendent excess.

49. See Chrétien, *Call and Response*, 37.

50. Polanyi, *Personal*, 143, 196.

they are indwelt in tacit, subsidiary ways.[51] So we may know that something significant is occurring in our experience, but we may not be able to specify what that something is.

So tacit knowledge of divine things would obtain through our very perception of beautiful forms, such that to perceive beautiful, physical forms "pregnantly" would also be, in a tacit way, to "perceive" and "foreknow" (in Polanyi's sense) the invisible transcendent. As Phillip Blond proposes,

> to perception is given . . . the paradoxical and wondrous gift to see both immanence and transcendence, to discern in the heart of what is most material what is most transcendent; which is to say that perception always goes beyond its objects, because objects go beyond themselves. For immanence is founded on transcendence that is more intimate than itself. . . . But this transcendence does not stand above us as a transcendence hovering only in negation beyond a world that it cannot embrace. No—as soon as we open our eyes, as it were . . . we find the ideal already running over us, and the invisible already there streaming over our bodies. And all of the shapes that we see, all of the depth, perspective, color and form, are figures and contours that the invisible brings forth for the visible. It pulls visibility into attendance with its highest form and possibility, and in the end . . . we cannot see in this kenotic consort of the invisible and the visible where one ends and the other begins.[52]

Such an understanding of perception seems plausible in the moment of desire when the evening sun begins to light up hilly backdrops and sharpen every golden blade of grass, making the familiar strange, impossible, unreal. Blond's picture is based on Merleau-Ponty's phenomenology of perception, but is not far removed from Wordsworth's sensing of "a presence,"

> Whose dwelling is the light of setting suns,
> And the round ocean and the living air,
> And the blue sky . . .
> A motion and a spirit, that
> . . .
> . . . rolls through all things.[53]

---

51. Cf. Polanyi and Prosch, *Meaning*, 62, on existential changes.

52. Blond, "Perception," 239–40. Blond gives the impression that immanence and transcendence might be somehow opposed, but this need not be the case. See footnote 47 above.

53. Wordsworth, "Tintern Abbey," 2:152–53.

In such cases, the theologian might even call the experience a tacitly "religious" experience, because the intuition produced by a transcendent excess of meaning would still fascinate, even despite one's denying of transcendence, perhaps even provoking such a denial.[54] But of course the atheist would simply interpret such an intuition in some other way. Even for the atheist, however, a religious experience does not have to take on an acknowledged "religious" quality as distinct from its aesthetic or other qualities: we often cannot separate our religious experience from our life and background, because our experience of the transcendent is mediated through the immanent, and experienced in tacit, subsidiary ways. So it is the experience's setting and associations that often render it consciously "religious," rather than a certain "religious quality."[55] For example, someone might have many arresting experiences of the sky that only become consciously religious much later, perhaps after reading and reflecting upon Psalm 19:1–4.

Going beyond the atheist's tacitly (and in the broadest sense) "religious" movement toward a good world and a valuable life, a more open and ideologically uncommitted person might be carried even farther along this same path of excess. Many non-religious people would be more open at least to the possibilities of transcendence, and might be willing to entertain further associations. If the person is open, then beauty is also open to further associations, because if beauty does involve excess, there is no "mere" beauty or beauty by itself. Moreover, beauty never sufficiently explains or accounts for itself: it is always eluding exhaustive analysis and liminally suggesting realities beyond what it displays explicitly.[56] If this were not the case, we would find it much easier to dismiss or ignore beautiful "flash of fin, beat of wing."[57] But instead, beauty seems to demand explanations from both science and religion, from both theology and atheology; it is always raising questions of God's existence and nature. In Rahner's terminology, beauty calls attention to the "infinite horizon" of human experience, our orientation toward what is beyond the finite.[58] Perhaps this is why beautiful creatures—plants, humans, and animals—have always become symbols of divinity, and even atheist Richard Dawkins concedes that "when you consider the beauty of the world . . . you are naturally overwhelmed with a feeling of awe, a feeling of admiration, and you almost feel a desire to

54. See Marion, *In Excess*, 162, on the intuition of God.

55. Mircea Eliade holds that "man's becoming aware of his own mode of being and assuming his *presence* in the world together constitute a 'religious' experience," even if a radically secularized one. *The Quest*, 9.

56. See Nicholson, "General Revelation," 7, on beauty's liminality.

57. Raine, "Word Made Flesh," 45.

58. See Rahner, "Theology and the Arts," 21–22.

worship something. I feel this."[59] In this way, natural beauty might engender a mild sense of transcendence in the more open non-religious person who sits alone by a campfire in starlight, listening to wind in the trees, and sensing a wood's fey mystique. Apart from any explicitly religious associations, this person could gain, for example, an indescribable, visceral sense of the world's mystery, and even a curiously frustrating sense of alienation from nature's beauty—perhaps "Blank misgivings of a Creature / moving about in worlds not realised."[60] Many could identify with this experience and even find themselves at times participating in a sort of quasi-religious mysticism, being overwhelmed by experiences of beauty,

> when we were vaguely aware of something "beyond," of a presence in it, yet not of it, when we were stirred with a joy not far from tears. Stars and sea, great architecture and great music have the power to produce this mood in most of us—in each according to his temperament. . . . And common folks know it—gardeners and seamen, and young labourers, before the struggle of life dulls their sensibilities and binds them fast on the wheel of things, and nearly all women, especially mothers of little children, and all lovers. In intensity their perception will vary from a faint sense of wonder as at something not wholly of the earth, to the clear conviction that for a timeless moment they have been rapt into union with infinite reality.[61]

Sometimes if the sun dances at just the right angle through the trees, or the evening landscape takes on just the right color, scent, and stillness, it is almost as if the dark glass between us and God partly recedes, and we step into the outer reaches of heaven. Of course, by this point someone might be employing these religious concepts of God and heaven from a nominally Christian frame of reference. Or someone might be employing similar concepts from another religious frame of reference. The experience now includes a limited interpretation. But these religious interpretations do not impose concepts inappropriately upon the experience; rather, these concepts are already properly in the experience through the subjectivity of the experiencer, as well as through the objectivity of the divine operation of beauty in the world. So the same person who experienced the night in the wood without religious associations might later in life have learned something about Christianity. At this point in her life, she might have a similar visceral experience of natural beauty—she might walk through a mist that

59. Dawkins, "God Delusion Debate" with John Lennox, n.p.

60. Wordsworth, "Ode," 147–48.

61. Raven, *Creator Spirit*, 205.

suddenly lifts to unveil the Bernese Oberland peaks. But this time, associations of God, creation, paradise, and heaven flood into the experience, giving it a quite different character. She cannot help but make connections based on patterns and frameworks of thinking, and these are proper connections. These connections, as in a painting, are an interpretive sketching-in and showing of the given but not shown. But of course if the religious connections came from Zen Buddhism instead of Christianity, the connections made and the experience itself would be yet again quite different. And at this point, more extensive reflecting and associating will often mark a more conscious sense-making experience.

MAKING SENSE OF BEAUTY-EXPERIENCE

Sense-making experience of beauty moves subtly and seamlessly beyond tacit knowledge and interpretive experience, spilling over into religious and philosophical reflection. Such reflection is natural to human beings, because we are inveterate explainers and vision-makers—we seek to understand the causes and connections of our experiences. So the non-religious person may seek the grounds of her experience, and wonder why existence is meaningful in such a way as to produce such experiences of beauty.[62] As beauty evokes a view of the world as mysterious, and of potentially religious significance, it awakens and redoubles our awe at the mere fact of our contingent, personal existence. Thus beauty raises "those obstinate questionings / Of sense and outward things" that science cannot answer:[63] "Why existence? And given existence, why beauty?" Sense-making occurs from this minimal level all the way up to the most sophisticated discourses of metaphysics and theology.

Sense-making occurs in response to the continued movement of excess from the aesthetic, to the existential, to the properly religious. We can make theological sense of this experience and begin to develop a creational theology of natural beauty. But this is not simply to infer conclusions from these patterns of experience. Instead there is a simultaneous, two-way interchange of sense-making. The first movement of this interchange is from individual beauty-experiences toward larger patterns of experience—patterns that help to shape mythologies (as well as distinctively Christian theologies) engaging natural beauty. The second movement of the interchange proceeds in the opposite direction from these mythologies

62. Viladesau, *Theology and the Arts*, 45–46, suggests that beauty urges us to consider the meaning of existence.

63. Wordsworth, "Ode," 144–45.

93

and theologies back toward patterns of experience. In this movement we assess these patterns through and from within a religious vision of the world, and we explore "fits" and resonances between the shapes of experience and the shapes of our vision and practices. By working *through* these religious beliefs, traditions, and practices, we also deepen and enrich our experiences. And potentially, we enrich our understanding of what human beings experience in the beautiful. In fact, we enrich our understanding in ways that would be impossible if we only focused on experience's putatively "isolated" meanings, because with this narrower focus, we would miss the larger meanings that obtain only as experience interpenetrates and resonates with our broader visions of the world. Of course, it is very difficult to determine where interpretive experience ends and broader sense-making takes over: that is, it is difficult to differentiate experience's "original" shape (if such exists) from our further shapings of experience. But the aim is not to find elusive-but-exact boundaries between these two realities, but instead, workable "fits" and "harmonies." As Wynn observes, "in practice doctrine and experience are likely to be mutually informing, and it is reasonable to suppose that in some cases religious insight involves a kind of amalgam of a doctrinal scheme and associated experience, where these elements cannot in any simple way be separated out."[64]

This doctrinally informed sense-making is common to humanity but plays out in different ways as it is mediated through different religious worldviews. Since my approach is a Christian one, I emphasize how Christian doctrine makes sense of beauty-experience for Christians, but also for non-Christians who might be willing to consider Christianity's claims in relation to their experience. Christians can recommend their own sense-making to others, whose own experience might resonate with Christian ideas over time and reflection, such that revelation could be recognized more fully in hindsight. This community-specific sense-making is simply the process by which we come to understand much of the world. We come to understand through the communities in which we are already embedded.

By this process, the theologian can make sense of beauty's excess fairly easily. We might propose that beauty is transcendently grounded in divine reality beyond the physical and sensory. Thus our very delight in beauty's depths arises from the depths of God's nature revealed in the beautiful as something good and true, infinitely precious and fascinating.[65] And because of this relationship between beauty and God, beauty can impel the soul through the sensory and created, toward God—the soul "By sensible

64. Wynn, "Phenomenology," n.p.

65. See Balthasar, *Seeing the Form*, 118. on beauty revealing these aspects of God.

impressions not enthralled, / But, by their quickening impulse, made more prompt / To hold fit converse with the spiritual world."[66] We only experience God through the sensory and created in these forms of other things, but our joy in beauty's splendor is also an implicit delight in God as Creator and in our own existence: that is, because of beauty's universal appeal, everyone tacitly delights in God—there is an "anonymous reverence":[67]

> Here you stand,
> Adore, and worship, when you know it not;
> Pious beyond the intention of your thought;
> Devout above the meaning of your will.[68]

So by orienting us to its own valuable and fascinating nature, beauty at the same time orients us to an infinitely valuable and fascinating God, and invites us to take a personal stance toward him.[69] But as part of this invitation, beauty's excess entails that finite forms never satisfy us fully or permanently, and so longing besets us in the dialogue of "call and response." This longing is a proper response to, and proclamation of, the excess of beauty's origin over beautiful forms themselves, and without such longing, the dialogue between beauty and the soul could not continue. Through this very longing we come to hear beauty's invitation and recognize its message, as God is evoked as the object of the longing, and we are drawn implicitly toward him.[70] Our longing finds ultimate fulfillment only in an infinite God, its natural terminus. And because beauty as produced by this Infinity is also inexhaustibly diverse, it never ceases to be an object of our delight, fascination, and exploration.[71] Moreover, because beauty is produced by a personal God and is received by persons, it reflects the interpersonality of both creation and a triune ultimate reality. That is, God has in fact made the world beautiful for people—for us and for himself.

Similarly, in Blond's (and perhaps Wordsworth's) understanding of perception, God as *Logos* is in fact speaking through the beautiful structures of reality, as mediated not only through our emotion or reflection but

66. Wordsworth, Fourteen-Book *Prelude*, 14.106–8.

67. Cf. Viladesau on implicit delight in God. *Theology and the Arts*, 42. Rahner discusses "anonymous reverence." *Theology and the Arts*, 27. Simone Weil also speaks of love for beauty as implicit love for God. *Waiting on God*, 81.

68. Wordsworth, *Excursion*, 4.1141–44.

69. See Viladesau, *Theology and the Arts*, 149, 151, on our experience of beauty as a "reckoning with God."

70. See Ibid., 43, 145; Chrétien, *Call and Response*, 37; and Hart, *Beauty*, 20, on this longing caused by beauty.

71. See Hart, *Beauty*, 34, on the implications of beauty's source in an infinite God.

directly through our (pregnant) perception. Such is possible if transcendent form and intelligibility are always infused into the beautiful, making it what it is.[72] Thus beauty as perceived pregnantly could be its own form of communication and offer its own meaning tacitly, such that our perception of water-carved rock or sparkling icicles tells us something about the nature of transcendence, about God's nature, and of a perfected creation. Beautiful forms could actually "image" divine things artistically, by evoking ideas and feelings and thereby projecting an "affective world" that appropriately "represents" God.[73] Such imaging would be relevant even to the atheistic nature-enthusiast, who might be responding to this very aspect of beauty through hiking or environmental activism, while the Christian could develop this "mystical" perception of beauty in more conscious ways through religious guidance and training. In line with this understanding, Wynn's religious epistemology also involves tacit knowledge of God through places—knowledge rooted in bodily and affective interaction with the world, including religious practices. He understands God to be "revealed not as a specific item of experience, but rather as a meaning which infuses situations in general and which is made known representatively in a particular place."[74] Such an understanding certainly accords with beauty-experience as a representative or symbolic "operation."

This mode of revelation would lack verbal form but would nonetheless be "aesthetically rational." It would still involve the transfer of certain "information" and an existentially grounded knowledge. Such knowledge would be grounded in an excess of meaning that is known tacitly, in such a way that beauty functions symbolically in our experience. And we would enter into this knowledge as we develop certain beauty-skills, in a way akin to our learning to estimate speed or distance, and our learning to coordinate our movements in relation to the world. This skill development would not require formal, systematic instruction, but would be a matter of developing practices, borrowing from traditions, and sharing with one another. So, much as we develop the ability to skip stones or paint with perspective, we might also develop a spiritual aspect of human perception—spiritually oriented beauty-skills that deepen and enrich our experiences, and enable us to begin to see aspects of God's nature displayed in the world's beauties. And it seems that some poets, painters, and others have indeed developed their perception in this way. This development of beauty-skills would apply

---

72. See Blond, "Perception," 240.

73. See Wynn, "Representing the Gods," 315–31, on religious myths as artistic representations of God.

74. Wynn, *Faith and Place*, 35, 40, 231.

in similar ways to both Christians and non-Christians: it would be the engagement of an innate general capacity for the development of more specific aesthetic and religious capacities. And the implication is this: much as we grow into adulthood by learning how to perceive the world correctly, we might also grow spiritually into our full humanity by learning how to perceive the beautiful.

4

Making Sense of Natural Beauty
Nature as Text and Image

IF BEAUTY-EXPERIENCE IS INDEED saturated with meaning, then creation does take on the character of a "book." Or more adequately, creation takes on the character a work of art, in which beautiful structures reveal God apart from words.[1] "By a gracious art," then, God, for man, "Hid in these low things snares to gain his heart, / And layd surprizes in each Element."[2] In this chapter, I further "saturate" with intelligibility this belief, which Mircea Eliade observes throughout primal religion, namely that God reveals himself through nature in a "language" of mysterious symbols, speaking through nature's "mode of being," its structures and rhythms.[3] These structures and rhythms may also be beautiful, such that revelatory beauty functions through creation and humanity's shared aesthetic rationality, according to an artistic and symbolic structure. We can certainly test this

1. Throughout this chapter I include many different artistic and textual metaphors for creation, each trying to bring out some aspect of nature. "Sculpture" and "drama" are somewhat less metaphorical than "book," "story," or "text," because they involve visual perception directly; whereas books, stories, and texts, unlike nature, are verbal, and only involve perceptual images indirectly as they are formed mentally and described verbally. But all of these metaphors connect with perception and perceptual images.

2. Vaughan, "Tempest," 84. Cf. MacDonald: "If the world proceeded from the imagination of God, and man proceeded from the love of God, it is easy to believe that that which proceeded from the imagination of God should rouse the best thoughts in the mind of a being who proceeded from the love of God" (*Dish of Orts*, 254).

3. Eliade, *Myth and Reality*, 141–43.

possibility by considering our own experience of beauty as well as others' religious experiences. And, in fact, beauty's saturated character has already suggested a symbolic operation: symbolic thinking is a very appropriate response to a tacit knowledge of God through beauty—it is a reasonable way to "manage" or "frame" an excess of meaning that promises further knowledge while resisting "literal," verbal expression and conceptualization. In this sense, symbolic thinking "frames" an excess of meaning within certain recognizable and accepted images (and verbal descriptions of these images). These images are framed in the sense of being "dense or concentrated focal analogical representations" of reality.[4] This framing within an "exploded" (i.e., subsidiarily-connected) frame of tacit knowledge avoids conceptual and propositional distortion, but still allows communication of shareable experiences. After all, we need some way to present experiences that are often "larger than life and language" in order to share and understand them, and symbols enable this sharing and understanding.

Shareable, symbolic experiences also contribute to further discovery. Symbols facilitate our indwelling and our contributing to a communal epistemic vision—the vision of knowing God through nature. As part of this vision, artistic, symbolic thinking contributes to human sense-making in regard to a beautiful world. Symbolic thinking becomes a consciously indwelt epistemic practice, shaped by the aesthetic skills, desires, and idioms employed by (both Christian and non-Christian) communities seeking God and meaning through nature. As an indwelt epistemic practice, symbolic thinking becomes a heuristic "tool" with which we probe reality for deeper meanings: that is, by indwelling symbols, we expand ourselves and our epistemic vision, and explore a much wider range of tacit knowledge bound to symbols. So by focusing on symbolic beauties, additional meanings should become apparent, and consequently, we can wager that symbolic thinking about beauty will detect and decipher, illuminate and give order to, human reality in relation to God.

Taking up this ordering and illuminating tool from a Christian perspective, we can also engage certain structural parallels between divine and human art, as well as between beautiful images and the image of the incarnation. These parallels contribute to a religious, and ultimately Christian, epistemic vision of natural beauty's symbolism. And as primary elements of this vision, divine art and incarnation become hermeneutical keys to interpreting beautiful images within an ambivalent creation.

---

4. Brown, *Continental*, 179.

CREATION AS DIVINE ART

Creation, unlike a purposive work of human art, often seems wastefully, unexplainably, and needlessly beautiful. Yet this "needless" beauty suggests the gratuitousness of creation itself.[5] Creation is gratuitous, because God as the joyful and complete Trinity needs nothing and gains nothing by creating. Still God must have reasons for creating that go well beyond "needless ornamentation," and that account for the world's darker, less ornamental realities.[6] Creation would seem to be the natural, albeit unnecessary, expression of divine personality, and so we would also expect reasons beyond pure functionality for why God makes the world the way it is.[7] We might even see creation's aesthetic rationality or *logos*, not as needless ornament, nor as a stark product of God, barely and loosely connected to him, but as a purposive expression of God's vision, creativity, and personality—God's "future-directed" artwork,[8] perhaps even the archetypal *Gesamtkunstwerk*—a work of art with striking instances of beauty as a focal point amid ambivalence. As a work of art, creation might express the Creator, not simply through our dissonant experiences of the world as a whole, but more pointedly through the world's beauty.[9] Indeed, beauty could be a rubric (i.e., an interpretive guide) for the world.

Creation as "divine art," to use Augustine's phrase, would then be the context for all human art, which would be but a subset of that larger category.[10] And it is this relationship between divine and human art that should guide our understanding of creation and its beauty, by allowing us to apply some characteristics of human art to divine art. Notably, human art can communicate theological truths in ways complementary to the written texts of theology, which also include their own verbal images and artistry. Art with its surplus of meaning is especially appropriate as theology, because it uniquely mirrors the richness and messiness of reality, and can describe theological realities more aptly and powerfully than precise doctrinal for-

5. Jones, "Art and Sacrament," 153, suggests the connection between needless beauty and a gratuitous creation.

6. Hart, *Beauty*, 291, 309, refers to creation as "needless ornament."

7. D. Brown, *Continental*, 56–57, describes the natural, though unnecessary, character of creation.

8. Milbank, Pickstock, and Ward, "Suspending the Material," 9, see creation as "future-directed art."

9. Augustine implies something similar: "an artificer somehow suggests to the spectator of his work, through the very beauty of the work itself, not to be wholly content with that beauty alone, but to let his eye so scan the form of the material thing made that he may remember with affection him who made it" (*On Free Will* 2.16.43).

10. Augustine, *On the Trinity* 6.12.

mulations. For example, many worshippers have experienced how religious architecture, with its acoustics, dim "religious light," heavenward gesturing, and sense of lightness or stability, can communicate reverence better than many a sermon. Similarly, a painting of a biblical scene can suggest unique interpretations of Scripture, bringing out what goes unnoticed or unmentioned in the text. So alongside the spoken and written word, art becomes its own rightful *locus theologicus*.[11] Theology, therefore, must not limit itself to written texts, but embrace the total human response to revelation, including all art forms; and so a dialogue arises between theological images and written theological texts, with each informing the other.[12] Thus, if creation is God's art, we might also see creation as an artistic and theological "text"[13]— one that reveals God and informs theology. Creation certainly has more complex goals than human art, as well as a different Creator. But if God chooses to communicate in ways that humans find most powerful, and if humans are made in God's image, then the natural world could reveal divine ideas much as art reveals the human mind.[14] Creation's art, like human art, could be involved in "the process of interpretation, understanding, formulation, affirmation, and appropriation of the viewer's faith."[15]

Our understanding of art would then be a hermeneutical tool for dealing with the complexities of creation's text. But since creation as art would be "a symptom" of a God who expresses himself in various other symptoms, we must also bring our theology to creation as essential for its interpretation.[16] In the absence of any theological system or special revelation, human experience of nature might have to provide its own interpretive constraints. Still, one could question whether human beings ever existed *as* human beings without some sort of theological system—by which I mean the religious or metaphysical frameworks employed by the community.

One might object, however, that creation, even if seen as art, is the product of God's aims and ends and is not designed to communicate anything to us. After all, throughout most of human history, art has been more

---

11. Viladesau, *Theology and the Arts*, 127, 133, discusses how art communicates theological concepts more powerfully than prose. He also describes art as *locus theologicus*.

12. Rahner, "Theology and the Arts," 27, emphasizes art within the total human response to revelation.

13. For Ricoeur, a text can be "any set of signs that may be taken as a text to decipher, hence a dream or neurotic symptom, as well as a ritual, myth, a work of art, or a belief." This understanding of text involves "an enlarged concept of exegesis" (*Freud and Philosophy*, 26).

14. Carus, *Landscape Painting*, 86, makes this comparison between art and nature.

15. Viladesau, *Theology and the Arts*, 135, describes this role of human art.

16. Panofsky, *Meaning*, 31, describes art as "symptom."

concerned with religious themes and values than with any overt self-expression by the artist. For example, medieval patrons commissioned paintings that would communicate specific religious themes within a church, palace, or monastery, and even early landscape painters felt the need to justify their work through some sort of religious reference. Much later still did some art become concerned primarily with expressing the artist's own ideas or feelings. But despite vast differences between this overtly expressionistic art and earlier forms, in each case there is still a sense in which the artist expresses something of himself. Even art communicating religious themes and values can tell us much about an artist, and we should affirm as much regarding biblical art forms (narrative, drama, poetry) in their disclosure of the divine author. If every creator inescapably expresses something of himself in what he creates, then God's ends achieved in creation should also say something to us, even without requiring an unduly expressionistic theory of creation's art. Surely God means *something* by stark tundra, bleeding lava fields, wind-carved arches and mesas. Such forms might express God by being aesthetically complementary to his nature, in the way that works of art complement an artist's vision or personality.[17]

If we can understand creation as art, then we can adopt provisional interpretations of its meanings. And this provisionality does not frustrate revelation through creation; rather, it offers fruitful material for provisional analogies to divine truths. Analogies, like any representation, are provisional in the Polanyian sense, because they require continuous, imaginative refinement toward renewed approximations of truth. This *artistic* character of both knowledge and creation is the reason why theorists often call knowledge of reality "beautiful," and why scientists, theologians, and mythologists share an analogical, metaphorical engagement with reality. Without this sort of engagement, we could not begin to describe reality in any depth. It is this sort of artistic engagement with created forms—like the dance of flames or spindrift—that opens the door to an understanding of one reality as the symbolic expression of a greater and more mysterious reality. And if God reveals himself in this way, his self-expression is directed at those who, through an aesthetic rationality, can receive it and distinguish it from the hidden mystery

17. Wynn suggests the idea of the world as a necessary aesthetic complement to God's nature, much as one object in a painting complements another without strictly resembling it. We may even be able to guess the nature of this complementary object without seeing it beforehand, simply based on its aesthetic context. In such a model, "the world as an aesthetic whole will represent God in so far as its perfection presupposes the existence of a perceiver [and we might add, Creator] who grasps the world as a whole" ("From World to God," 379–94).

that is expressed.[18] Thus, it is worth indwelling and exploring the implications of this epistemic practice of knowing God through divine art.

Beauty, Natural Evil, and Creation's "Style"

Given the possibilities of artistic communication, one might, at first blush, think that creation's art would disclose God clearly in its eloquent artistic "style," or broad, overall, artistic pattern. But creation's overall style, like any artistic style or "mood," is certainly open to varieties of interpretation.[19] I must therefore make a few preliminary remarks about creation's natural evil and ugliness before returning to this topic more fully in the following chapter.

Many would interpret creation's style not as beautiful, eloquent, and corresponding to God, but as characterized by intense, apparently meaningless, and unequally distributed suffering of innocents. And this is in addition to nature's ordinary cycles of death and decay. Because of the world's pervasive natural evils, some people say that they can make no connection between the world's beauty and God. Indeed, if we claim that creation's style *as a whole* corresponds to God, we encounter the objection that such evils nullify any real correspondence. And if with David Bentley Hart we emphasize creation's style, rhetoric, and "needlessly ornamental" character, we, in effect, romanticize the world and gloss over horrific realities that make repugnant a creation that is merely "ornamental." Even so, we can perhaps see how creation's style takes up and deals with *some* of creation's evils. After all, art demands reckoning with evil in order to succeed as art, so we would expect this reckoning in divine art as well: natural cycles of death and rebirth seem to function along these lines. But because the world also operates through chance and contingency, disaster occurs, life is needlessly destroyed, and creation as art often becomes utter tragedy. Much natural evil seems excessive and irredeemable, and notwithstanding Wordsworth, nature does often "betray the heart that loved her."[20]

But if we restrict the revelation of God's character to certain aspects of the world, to beauty rather than ugliness or suffering, the notion of style retains more value; for in creation's style, goodness and beauty consort artistically with evil and ugliness. Beauty is often bound up inextricably

18. See Rahner, "Theology and the Arts," 29, on symbolic expression of a greater reality. Tillich, "Art and Ultimate Reality," 141, notes that such expression is directed at those who can receive it as such.

19. Hart, *Beauty*, 309, sees creation's revelation in its style, while Tillich emphasizes the need to interpret styles; Tillich, "Art and Ultimate Reality," 142.

20. Wordsworth, "Tintern Abbey," 2:153.

in what is naturally destructive, as in the "fearful symmetry" of Blake's tiger.[21] Natural evil and ugliness are also sometimes cases of indifference to human life and aesthetic sensibility, such that the raging sea may be beautiful to behold yet treacherous to navigate, and a weed may be a flower in the wrong place. In relation to humanity at least, creation can be seen as taking on more the character of *fallen* art, a magnificent ruin. Thus we might rather emphasize the contrasting styles of creation—of beauty and of ugliness, "The Marriage of Heaven and Hell"—and leave them in conflict, with each highlighting the other.[22]

In this way, beauty can still be fully integrated with, and implicated in, natural evil and ugliness in the created order—that is, according to a scientific understanding of order. Yet according to an aesthetic understanding of creation, this integrated beauty and ugliness, good and evil, can still be read as opposing themes in creation's drama. Such opposition means that creation's canvas is replete with shadow, and that beauty stands out in this ambivalent context. Nevertheless, it does not follow that evil increases the overall beauty or goodness of the world through chiaroscuro: surely the world's suffering outweighs in significance evil's highlighting of beauty. Yet overshadowing evil does not rob beauty of its eloquence or correspondence to God. On the contrary, in the midst of such darkness, beauty becomes like the polestar to a lost wayfarer. As in Job's theophany, the divine appeal to natural order and beauty points human beings beyond their own sorrows.[23] In this sense, beauty, like poetry for Seamus Heaney, can offer a reposeful "clarification, a fleeting glimpse of a potential order of things 'beyond confusion.'"[24] And to borrow Avery Dulles's words on symbols, beauty, like "the Kingdom of God in the preaching of Jesus," can be "an imaginative disclosure, under symbolic forms, of a world existing only in hope and promise"—a world lacking shape apart from symbols.[25]

This disclosive function of beauty should not be misunderstood as part of an attempted theodicy. Nonetheless, art has the strange power to incorporate evil and make the best of it without excusing it; for we require the tension of evil even to make "a good story." Art, as distinct from beauty, sometimes requires the evil and the ugly. Art thus provides a hermeneutical tool that can deal honestly with the text of creation in its commingled evil,

21. Blake, "Tyger," 24–25.

22. Blake, "Marriage of Heaven and Hell," 34.

23. Tyrwhitt, *Natural Beauty*, 43, notes the connection between suffering, natural beauty, and Job's theophany.

24. Heaney, introduction to *Redress of Poetry*, xv. Jüngel, "Even the Beautiful," 66, 81, also claims that beauty promises a wholeness that interrupts the world's scatteredness.

25. Dulles, *Models of Revelation*, 160. Cf. Farrer, *Rebirth*, 17.

ugliness, and beauty.[26] As a hermeneutic, art does not explain why God allows evil and ugliness, for we wonder if a good story really compensates for all the evil that went into its making. But art does provide an interpretive framework in which evil and ugliness still allow beauty to speak.

BEAUTIFUL IMAGES AND SYMBOLIC THINKING

Even taking into account creation's pervasive evils, we might still expect God to reveal himself through creation's artistry given the artistry of Scripture and Christian tradition. One cannot begin to understand the Bible without indwelling the artistic and symbolic communication that actuates biblical history as well as the teaching of Christ, the prophets, and apostles.[27] Christ also mandated this symbolic communication through the institutions of the Eucharist and baptism. And certainly, we are loath to say that Christ could have communicated better than through his "visual" images, such as the Johannine "I Am" statements. Christianity itself, says Farrer, is "a visible rebirth of images."[28]

Moreover, Scripture borrows images extensively from nature. Jonathan Edwards notes how Scripture employs natural objects (rock, sky, blood, water) as symbolic expressions of spiritual realities, and further, how natural objects like minerals, plants, animals, and humans resemble and correspond to each other artfully. He therefore finds it reasonable to assume that there are additional symbols in nature, as well as correspondences to God, that one can interpret as in any other work of art.[29] Similarly, for Tractarian John Keble, Scripture and the church fathers support the view that God "condescends" in the natural world, in a way parallel to Scripture, "to have a poetry of His own, a set of holy and divine associations and meanings."[30] If this view is correct,

26. Part of our making sense of creation as art may be our emotional valuing of a world that entails human vulnerability to both evil and ugliness. This sense of vulnerability is manifested in our emotions. In contrast, a world of human invulnerability strikes us as prosaic. Cf. Wynn, "Valuing the World," 97–113.

27. See Dulles, *Models of Revelation*, 135, on symbols in the teaching of Christ, the prophets, and apostles.

28. Farrer, *Rebirth*, 14.

29. Edwards, "True Virtue," 564. Wainwright, "Jonathan Edwards," 519–30, argues for the reasonableness of Edwards's approach.

30. This view is in keeping with the New Testament's fulfillment of the Old Testament through type and antitype, as well as Christ's fulfillment of natural images, as the "true vine" and "true light." Keble maintains that "if the Fathers were wrong in this matter, they were most perseveringly and obtrusively wrong"—"not as a local evil, but as a constitutional taint." Moreover, if this biblical and patristic symbolism had been intended merely as ornament or accommodation to culture, it would probably be more

then revelation in nature could function, much like Scripture, as a divine employment of symbolic communication.[31] But unfortunately, both Edwards's and Keble's applications of this approach are much too fanciful: for example, Edwards understands the sky's pale blue to typify the saints' humility and "holy pusilanimity" [sic], and he connects water to sin through its "flattering" and deceitful appearance. Keble links flying birds to "Powers in heaven above who watch our proceedings," and through Ambrose, he understands the moon reflecting the sun to typify the church.[32]

But by applying this approach in a much more disciplined way, we can still understand natural revelation to function, not like arguments or propositions, but like artistic images—"voiceless words" that "sound in the ear of an attentive reason" (cf. Ps 19:1–4).[33] And through such images, revelation could appeal much more directly to human senses, emotion, intuition, and imagination, and therefore to our personal, embodied, and temporal experience.[34] It is thus important to emphasize that such knowing through symbols is by no means unique to art and religion but has much in common with our everyday experience of the world. Many aspects of our subtle and multifaceted experience harmonize with this notion of images as a means to knowledge, even if our Enlightenment heritage encourages us to seek out simpler, more verbal, and less tacit ways of knowing. Verbal information is shaped and sometimes circumvented, for example, in our television broadcasts of politicians and other "authorities," who deliver messages via symbolisms of flag and podium. Human knowledge and communication in many cases bypass an artificially verbal knowledge, while the value of symbols lies in their artistic subtlety, poignancy, and disclosure. These qualities do not compete with reason but accord with our aesthetic rationality. Indeed, symbols are already built into the structure of human knowledge and communication: we cannot get beyond them to some purer grasp of metaphysical realities (for example, the relationship between mind and body, or between a knowing

---

fanciful and less constant than it is. If the intent had been merely to write good poetry, there would be a greater variety of images and more modification of metaphors; Keble, *Mysticism*, 147–48, 165–68, 176.

31. Dulles, *Models of Revelation*, 138, describes revelation as transcendent symbolic communication. Cf. Ricoeur: "Every symbol is . . . a hierophany, a manifestation of the bond between man and the sacred" *(Symbolism*, 356).

32. So I do not engage Edwards's and Keble's types further, even though their approach supports the idea of symbolic beauty and parallels Ruskin's typology. Ruskin, however, offers a much more restrained typology and a less spiritualized concept of beauty. See Edwards, "Images," 114, 117; Keble, *Mysticism*, 147–48, 156, 159.

33. Farrer, *Glass*, 79.

34. See Sayers, *Dante*, 93, on how artistic images affect us.

act and the object known). This is because symbols, drawing upon the concrete and spatial, are the only tools for describing or even thinking about such abstract referents.[35] Moreover, truths presented symbolically have greater power over us, says Augustine, than if we encounter them unadorned, without their mysterious symbolism.[36] As Eliade observes,

> Images, symbols and myths are not irresponsible creations of the psyche; they respond to a need and fulfil a function, that of bringing to light the most hidden modalities of being. . . . The most commonplace existence swarms with images, the most "realistic" man lives by them. . . . Modern man is free to despise mythologies and theologies, but that will not prevent his continuing to feed upon decayed myths and degraded images. . . . Archaic symbolisms reappear spontaneously, even in the works of "realist" authors who know nothing about such symbols.[37]

Indeed these "old" symbolisms connect directly with the "new," and communicate similar messages. Popular entertainment, advertising, and fashion rely on symbolic communication for their appeal, so much so that we might understand consumerism to be based not so much upon accumulation of "things" as upon the accumulation of symbols, or a quest to obtain the right symbolism. Who would buy outlandish clothes if they did not appear to *say* something important about the wearer? Who would become addicted to televised sports if they did not symbolically tap into certain basic human needs for meaning? In these images and in popular film and music, if we follow Carl Jung, the archetypes of the collective unconscious emerge as heroes and lovers, "gods" and "goddesses." These images communicate with mythological power and express metaphysical structures to such a degree that their interpretation even becomes a means by which secularism begins to "transcend itself."[38] Thus secularists as well

35. Ricoeur, *Symbolism*, 350, holds that symbols are built into language. Cf. Farrer, *Glass*, 67–74, on symbols as tools for describing and thinking. D. Brown notes the implications for religious language: "so far from religious language being an artificial construct, analogical language . . . is in fact built into the nature of things" (*Continental*, 179, 182).

36. See Augustine, *Letters* 55.21.

37. Eliade, *Images and Symbols*, 12, 16, 19, 25. This use of "myth" refers back to the broad understanding given in chapter one.

38. Ricoeur, *Symbolism*, 352, suggests that "hermeneutics, an acquisition of 'modernity,' is one of the modes by which modernity transcends itself, insofar as it is forgetfulness of the sacred."

For Jung, *Archetypes*, 44, 58, 66, archetypes are not inherited ideas but "inherited *possibilities* of ideas" resulting from "patterns of instinctual behaviour" in the unconscious of all humans. People of all cultures experience the world in similar ways due to

as Christians may have abandoned pagan myth as a means of salvation without thereby escaping the effects of religious myth upon the psyche.[39] This mythic and religious communication, rather than being a purely human construct, is more the function of a created order in which symbols impart so much meaning at a tacit level that people do not need to seek it consciously: that is, apart from a conscious search for meaning, the symbol has already addressed the "restlessness of heart and mind"—that inchoate but innate human search for meaning.[40] So in light of the ubiquity and effectiveness of symbolic communication, the presence of symbols within creation's art seems appropriate: to read nature as artistic text and image is simply to recognize and engage symbolic structures and mythological forces already in play in our experiencing of the world.

So symbolic thinking offers an epistemic access to reality that works properly through human perception, emotion, desire, and imagination. And these modes of access are all rationally structured, communally disciplined, aesthetically linked, and eminently human modes of knowing. Through this holistic engagement with human nature, images offer differently nuanced or even different kinds of knowings: images surpass discursive thought by integrating subjective and objective realities imaginatively, rather than by any "specifiable, explicit, or logically operative steps."[41] Images, as Farrer says, "continue to enter into fresh combinations, to elaborate themselves, to beget new applications" according to their own laws.[42] In fact, any attempt to reduce symbolic meaning to propositions disrupts these tacit, imaginative integrations, and therefore reduces the knowledge obtained through the symbol.[43] Knowledge depends upon this imaginative integration and association with other aspects of our experience, and the symbol acts like an integrative "net"

---

a common humanity. Consequently, we project unconscious patterns onto symbolic objects in imaginative but remarkably similar ways. This accounts for the "almost universal parallelism" among motifs in myths and dreams across cultures and individuals. Without following Jung in detail, Moltmann, *God in Creation*, 298, describes archetypes simply as "images which put a fundamental impress on the soul."

39. Eliade, *Images and Symbols*, 160–61. Eliade also points out that the early Christian apologists, Theophilus of Antioch and Clement of Rome, even employ cosmic nature symbolism (seeds, days, seasons) as an argument for resurrection. Thus, for Eliade, *Sacred and Profane*, 136–37, history adds new meanings to symbols, but does not modify the basic structure of certain archaic symbolisms.

40. Jung, *Archetypes*, 13.

41. Polanyi and Prosch, *Meaning*, 62. Cf. Dulles, *Models of Revelation*, 137, 142, on symbolic integrations.

42. Farrer, *Glass*, 45, 54.

43. Dulles, *Models of Revelation*, 142–43, emphasizes the impossibility of reducing symbolic meaning to propositions.

to capture these associations. Thus it does not merely "represent," but actually "operates a relation with that which it designates."[44] For example, a flag, a medal, or a pilgrimage site can effectively capture a range of interesting meanings. In the case of a flag, the entire history of a country, and one's life lived in that country, bear upon the meaning of the image. These meanings become integrated and *embodied* in the image, and since these meanings are connected to us, they also integrate us with the image, allowing it to "carry us away" emotionally.[45] But these are no "mere" associations: they are integrations of our tacit knowing, relying upon indistinct clues to discover new order and meaning in the assorted elements of experience.

Beauty-experience is also a skilful integration of this sort, involving human nature holistically, and relying upon many indistinct associations to bring new order and meaning to our experience. By thus integrating experiences, beautiful forms provide the sort of epistemic "node" or focal center that characterizes symbolic function. Polanyi and Harry Prosch describe this nodal characteristic of knowledge: "All empirical observation rests ultimately on the integration of subsidiaries to a focal center. All such integrations—from perception to creative discoveries—are impelled by the imagination and controlled by plausibility, which in turn depends upon our general view about the nature of things."[46] Through such symbolic integration, the beautiful image, as a center or node, draws together seemingly incompatible elements from life's great store —emotions, diffuse memories, diverse experiences—and fuses these into imaginative meanings. In similar language, Wynn describes places, including beautiful places, as integrative "organs of thought."[47]

The beautiful image is an organ of thought and a "package of clues" circumscribed by our perception. And, like any work of art, the image is experienced according to the artist's own prescribed laws. These laws for experiencing bring order to the vast, disorganized flux of sensations and irrelevancies of which everyday life is composed.[48] Beauty especially facilitates these unique moments of organizing experience, because beautiful forms are already framed or "set apart" by our heightened perceptual awareness. Beautiful forms can be so set apart that they are, in a sense, indifferent toward us in their perfection and "immortality:" as Keats says "A thing

---

44. Couch, "Religious Symbols," 119.
45. Polanyi and Prosch, *Meaning*, 72–73.
46. Ibid., 144.
47. Wynn, *Faith and Place*, 87–88.
48. Polanyi and Prosch, *Meaning*, 87–88.

of beauty is a joy forever."[49] Once the focal experience is concentrated and framed in this way, it achieves a "universal and yet personal significance" that is partly communicable symbolically.[50] As an example, a horizon in a landscape can do much more for us imaginatively in terms of meaning than simply fuse earth and sky. When we "solemnize" beautiful forms in this symbolic way, we affirm the value of, and our participation in, a world that surpasses us. On the other hand, without such solemnities, our lives become less integrated, more fragmented into details, and less meaningful. But beautiful images entwine the tethers bound to diverse aspects of our existence and situation in the world. Such integrations haul up before the consciousness depths of reality and a wonder of being that elude other modes of knowledge. By presenting these depths, images detect and decipher human reality in ways compatible with revelation.[51] Beautiful images thus fit well with Richard Niebuhr's understanding of revelation as the giving of an image that contributes to life's intelligibility.[52] Similarly, Wynn maintains that beautiful places can microcosmically embody the world's meaning, or *genius loci*, namely God—a meaning that imparts coherence to one's life-story.[53] Such understandings further suggest that beauty is a rubric for the world: Eberhard Jüngel affirms that "the beautiful gathers my existence out of its actual scattering and inner strife to a point that promises wholeness to scattered and torn life." Thus a ben mirrored in an evening loch, in all its brilliance, wholeness, and perfection can become in the moment of experience a "glimmer of truth that makes the torn world whole."[54]

So beautiful forms can contribute to life's intelligibility as focal points that integrate and embody our scattered lives. In addition, by fusing the seemingly incompatible spheres of the natural and the divine, beautiful images may contribute to the intelligibility of divine realities. Consider how an interesting poetic metaphor, when fused to a seemingly incompatible reality, can illuminate it. In a similar way, beauty, like a sort of metaphor, can express the divine in terms of seemingly incompatible, yet intrinsically interesting and illuminating, forms (much like bread and wine expressing Christ's body and blood). Such forms give divine things "new sharp and emotionally charged

49. Keats, *Endymion*, 3.

50. Polanyi and Prosch, *Meaning*, 109.

51. Eliade holds that images access depths of reality that elude other modes of knowledge. *Images and Symbols*, 12. Polanyi and Prosch suggest that myth reveals a wonder of being. *Meaning*, 128. Dulles maintains that symbols and revelation affect the soul similarly. *Models of Revelation*, 137.

52. Niebuhr, *Meaning of Revelation*, 109.

53. Wynn, *Faith and Place*, 82, 97.

54. Jüngel, "Even the Beautiful," 66, 81.

meaning."[55] For example, Ruskin understands beautiful colors in nature as a metaphor for divine love, while quiet valleys convey divine permanence. With this approach, we can bracket the question of to what extent such forms bear some deep ontological "resemblance" to a divine referent. Any cognizance of resemblance is secondary in importance to the way that beauty integrates diverse elements in our experience. And this integration might be said to aesthetically complement, rather than resemble, divine things.[56] Thus beauty can still point us toward God without us being conscious of any strict resemblance, between, say, color and divine love.

It is also important to emphasize that naturally beautiful forms have often been used symbolically to refer to divine things. For example, based on his surveys of the history of religions, Eliade observes that the most prevalent image in art across cultures and religions is that of a natural paradise lost.[57] Thus Chinese gardens are thought to symbolize and even mediate the regaining of an immortal paradise, and a similar function attaches to gardens in Christian monasteries, as well as Islamic paradise gardens in Spain and Iran.[58] Natural beauty, then, as one possibility, could function symbolically and even sacramentally by inaugurating our participation in an ideal world. Such experience might also call attention to the less than ideal character of the present world.[59]

Another widespread and archaic myth relating to natural beauty is the "earth mother." This image may involve an ontology and cultus that are problematic for Christians, especially in its contemporary revival of Gaia worship. But the image can also offer a sense of origin and participation in nature's creative fecundity, while contributing to the notion of sacred place.[60] In fact, even within contemporary culture, natural beauty's mythological pull could be a less personified expression of this same (perhaps archetypical) pattern. Such archetypical projections upon nature are by no means arbitrary, because it is the objective structure of natural objects that

55. Cf. Polanyi and Prosch, *Meaning*, 151–52, on metaphor and religion.

56. Wynn, "From World to God," 379–94.

57. Eliade, *Images and Symbols*, 16–17.

58. Eliade, *Sacred and Profane*, 153–54; idem, *Myths, Dreams and Mysteries*, 66.

59. Jüngel, "Even the Beautiful," 65–66, suggests beauty's "sacramental" function in relation to an ideal world or lack thereof.

60. Eliade, *Myths, Dreams and Mysteries*, 166. The ontology may not be so problematic, however, if, as Wynn, "Primal Religions," 88–110, argues, the language of "powers" or "deities" in primal religion is not so much a positing of individual entities as it is an artistic imaging of broad ranges of human experience of the world.

makes these projections possible.[61] It is the shape of the world that gives shape to our symbolic thinking.

Cultural plurality, however, might seem to pose a problem for beauty as a constant and transcultural symbol of the divine—that is, if symbolic forms change drastically from one culture to another. Yet beauty's diversity allows for different cultural appropriations, not to mention different appropriations among groups and individuals. No culture or individual can fail to perceive some beauty in its natural environment, and it is these diverse environments that primal religion finds sacred—that is, open to the operations of the transcendent.[62] Further, even if a culture (or group within it, such as atheists) lacks any explicit connection between beauty and deity, this does not mean that no connection exists; it may mean only that the connection has been overlooked in favor of other symbols or other frameworks of thought. But some symbols do recur transculturally, such as life in blood, cleansing/purification in water, and transcendence in the "height" of the sky, and these last two symbols are certainly conducive to a natural beauty of waters and heavens.[63] Regarding the heavens, Eliade notes that in primal religion, "simple contemplation of the celestial vault already provokes a religious experience." Simply through an awareness of its infinite height, the sky reveals "the 'wholly other' than the little represented by man and his environment. . . . For the sky, *by its own mode of being*, reveals transcendence."[64] By such modes, natural beauty's revelation could operate through the imaginative transformation of beauty as an inchoate category of symbols present in the human unconscious.[65] Beautiful forms would then image divine transcendence and promise through an interplay between the human psyche and the natural world.

Even so, this would not be a pure and uncomplicated relationship between humanity and natural beauty. Even if beautiful forms function archetypically, they always take on multiple, interconnected meanings according to a surrounding religious context. And we must draw upon this context's verbal and other resources, because we are confronted with the

61. Cf. Ricoeur: "the symbolic activity of thought and of language appears in the prolonging of a part of my power to dream—this is the oneiric side of the symbol—but it appears also outside of me, bound to the countenance of my universe, to the appearances of the universe such as water, fire, earth, wind, and sky" ("Language of Faith," 213–24).

62. Eliade, *Sacred and Profane*, 33–34, 116, emphasizes this sacred environment.

63. David Brown, "Symbolic Action," 114–15, discusses blood, water, and sky as symbols.

64. Eliade, *Sacred and Profane*, 117–20.

65. Cf. Brown, "Symbolic Action," 119, on revelation through symbols in the unconscious.

impossibility of reducing non-verbal revelation to words. Beautiful images suggest meanings that resist easy verbal formulation. Thus, beauty's revelation is appropriated differently by different cultures, groups, and individuals, and the result is different theological associations, even non-theistic ones, despite elements of beauty-experience that are common to humanity. So symbolic thinking about beauty cannot deliver a discrete and unambiguous meaning, yet beauty can deliver meaning, through interpretations that hold varying degrees of veridicality (or "validity" in Polanyi's terms). And this veridicality is not easily assessable in any single or general way. Beauty can still point to God irrespective of interpretations, but meaning always obtains in the resonance between interpretation and objectivity. Therefore we should make sense of revelatory beauty in distinctively Christian ways in order to give beauty its most appropriate associations and meanings. These meanings are shaped by our indwellings of a Christian vision of the world as it guides our sense-making. A Christian vision contributes unique conceptual "tools" and resources to the epistemic practice of knowing God through natural beauty. In this way, a Christian vision can further our knowing.

To sum up, I have addressed three main points in this chapter: (1) the general character of knowledge and revelation through images, (2) the epistemically nodal and integrative character of beautiful forms, and (3) the widespread symbolic and religious function of beautiful forms. Given the compatibility of these three factors, we can reasonably superimpose our understandings of *symbol, revelation,* and *beauty.* In so doing, we have bolstered the claim that the religious knower can reasonably indwell an epistemic practice engaging beauty as a category of revelatory symbols. To reiterate and apply Polanyi's principles, the knower must indwell aesthetic, symbolic, and religious thinking in order to achieve the most fruitful epistemic integrations. Indeed, such indwelling is the only means by which we can establish the workability of a symbolic beauty. This workability is established as symbolic beauties of sky, ocean, or woodland restore our "wager" through "coherent discourse" and "power of reflection."[66] We cannot establish this epistemic practice simply by showing that beauty or symbols in themselves point objectively to certain realities; instead, we establish it in practice, drawing on tacit judgments grounded in experience and commitments to certain views of the world. It is only by assuming and indwelling these practices and commitments, and by viewing the world *through* them, (rather than trying to specify or prove them), that integrative meanings arise in seashells, white beaches, or rocky torrents. And if there can be said to be any sort of "rules" for making these integrations, these rules are also indwelt

66. Ricoeur, *Symbolism,* 355.

and therefore largely assumed and unspecifiable as part of the deepest commitments of our lives and practices. Thus, symbolic thinking about beauty does not prove or demonstrate any correspondences between symbols and reality, but instead amounts to an "imaginative probing" of the "puzzling aggregate" of our experience of the world.[67]

Such probing would, however, be fruitless without the guidance of the knower's "anticipatory gifts," and the intuition of "hidden resources" in shared human experience. Only with such intuitive guidance can we step out in imaginative directions to integrate diverse experiential elements, and thereby to discover meanings in beautiful droplet, leaf, and sun ray.[68] With this guidance of the tacit, discovering symbolically captured meanings is not an entirely esoteric or mystical practice, but is comparable to a scientist guessing the presence of a hidden reality through certain signs, or a physician diagnosing an illness based on certain symptoms and other markers detected through laboratory tests. In turn, this skilled scientific perception is not unlike our everyday skilled perception of the world, in which we discover larger meanings through their relations to perceived objects: for example, we perceive certain facial expressions and vocal tones, and we thereby discover the larger meaning that a person is displeased by something we have said or done. This ordinary discovery of meaning through perception differs from discovery through symbols only in that we may be less skilled in symbolic thinking than we are in ordinary perception. We may be less skilled not least because symbolic thinking draws upon indwelt knowledge of such extensive cultural backgrounds and frameworks. But through symbolic practice, beautiful images begin to detect and decipher human reality, speaking to the image of God in humanity, and eliciting the aesthetic harmony of knowing God and the world of which Aquinas speaks—a knowing that often functions already through images.

As a way of knowing God, symbolic practice certainly risks vagueness and inaccuracy, but then, many of our ways of knowing are risky, provisional, and difficult in their own ways. In fact, most interpersonal exchanges, between humans or from God to humans, risk some misunderstanding. In the exchange from God to humanity, Carol Harrison observes how Augustine relates "parables and analogies, imagery and allegory . . . to the puzzling obscurity (*aenigmata*) of the mirror of 1 Corinthians 13:12." This obscurity is endemic to human knowledge yet "is in itself a way of seeing through the mirror."[69] Obscurities, but also riches, will accompany

67. Cf. Polanyi and Prosch, *Meaning*, 54, 61.

68. Ibid., 60.

69. Harrison, *Beauty and Revelation*, 266–67.

the interpretation of symbols, because all symbols are "lived" by complex human beings inhabiting varied epistemic visions and ranges of experience. Such obscurity, however, does not minimize the rationality of translatable and systematically connected symbols. These symbols convey their own metaphysical structures even if not in conceptual form, and it is the "lived" nature of these symbols that contributes to their epistemic possibilities as much as to their limitations.[70] Misinterpretation of symbols cannot always be prevented, even despite rational disciplines and genuine intent toward a hidden reality; but neither can we prevent all false justified beliefs of other kinds. Artistic symbols do offer us provisional meanings, yet we can engage art's rational ordering with an aesthetic rationality already attuned to images in our everyday experience.

We should therefore indwell the epistemic vision of symbolic beauty, because symbols contribute to knowledge by bringing into better focus a full range of tacit meanings and implications for human life. In fact, after only a brief focus on symbolic beauties, transcendence, paradise, and redemption have already begun to emerge from the peripheries. By funneling these meanings to us, symbols change us and our view of the world, making our lives more consciously meaningful. And even if we do not attach ourselves to religious symbols consciously, our human nature attaches us to symbols unconsciously through our immersion in certain lifestyles and forms of entertainment. Surely it is with this recognition that Jesus involved his disciples in symbolic institutions and forms of teaching by which they would "remember" him, but also come to know him better. In this sense, revelation through symbols (and sacrament) becomes God's "appeal to our imagination."[71]

Through such an appeal within the artistic fabric of the created order, it also becomes possible to know God better through nature. It becomes possible that within nature, as Blond says, "invisibility has a look" and "is not thinkable apart from visibility."[72] That is, only the image, verbally or physically presented, can begin to convey deity. Thus the Old Testament proscription against idolatry does not summon us away from images, but away from false images toward the true, as manifested in the temple worship and ultimately in the incarnation.[73] God is veiled inescapably in material and thought;[74] and since beauty is a prominent feature of divine art, it

70. Eliade *Images and Symbols*, 25, 37, 176, portrays symbols as "lived" but rational means of metaphysical communication.

71. See T. Clark, *Divine Revelation*, 181–82, 217, on revelation as an appeal to imagination, and Jesus' approach to participatory knowing.

72. Blond, "Perception," 236, 238.

73. van der Leeuw, *Sacred and Profane Beauty*, 305, 307.

74. See Ruskin, *Modern Painters*, 4:90.

may be especially through the visibility of natural beauty that God's invisible nature "has a look." Nature's beauties could function like the "outward and visible signs" of the other sacraments, expressing divine attributes and modes of action.[75] According to Harrison, Augustine would be in agreement, for whom "the beauty of creation bears witness to its Creator, the Word, because it assumes the nature of a sign; it points beyond itself, it is significatory, and, like Scripture, 'bears a kind of testimony' and 'proclaims' its inspirer and Creator."[76] This vision of revelation through natural beauty certainly harmonizes with human experience, and everything that follows is intended to fill in and substantiate this proposed epistemic practice. We substantiate this practice of knowing God through beauty as we indwell it and find it true to our own experience, such that our "know-that" depends inescapably upon our "know-how."[77] That is, insofar as we know how to experience something in the beautiful that we believe to be genuine, just so far also can we validate beauty's imagery.[78]

GOD EMBODIED IN CREATION

Nothing contributes more to the validation of beauty's imagery than the image of the incarnation—invisibility's most complex and profound "look." The incarnation profoundly extends the notion of image across the broad spectrum of Christ's living and working in the world, making the revelation of Christ more accessible to living and working people. And in the incarnation, God subjects himself to "material classification"—to a human life that can be described partly in material terms within the veils of human thought and flesh.[79] It is in this flesh that the incarnate Word also becomes a paradigmatic image that is rationality (*Logos*) itself, and thus establishes the veridicality of images: Christ as God-man spans not only the conceptual gulf between human and divine realities but also the skeptical gulf between image and referent, being at once both the image of God and the God imaged.[80] And through this aesthetic rationality of

75. Dowden, *Beauty of Nature*, 17–18, compares natural beauty to the sacraments.

76. Harrison, *Beauty and Revelation*, 116.

77. See T. Clark, *Divine Revelation*, 223, on this relationship between "know-that" and "know-how." Wynn similarly describes a kind of know-how: "to see in full what it is for God to be present, one needs to have some experiential knowledge of the contexts in which the concept of divine presence originates" ("Phenomenology," n.p.).

78. See Polanyi and Prosch, *Meaning*, 146, on validating myths and works of art.

79. Ruskin, *Modern Painters*, 4:90, notes the "veils" of thought and flesh, although *veil* should not be understood docetically.

80. Dulles, *Models of Revelation*, 257, notes the spanning of this conceptual gulf.

incarnation and symbolic communication, Christ informs our interpretation of creation as art, which is a specific application of the creational epistemology outlined in the first chapter: the analogically inclined, transcendent-but-incarnate, limited-but-God-ordained process by which we come to know the world and that which is beyond it.

As embodied image and *Logos*, Christ offers, and is himself, an aesthetic rationality and symbolic communication that becomes a hermeneutical key to the artful book of the world. As Christ images God via the physical-sensory, perceptual beauty can do likewise, albeit with different emphasis: whereas Christ is, in some respects, a "stumbling block," beauty is a smoother path to tread. Yet the ascended body of Christ establishes a place for perceptual beauty—the "natural" beauty of the human form—within the divine fellowship. This perceptual beauty of Christ's human form is a corollary of the incarnation as well as of Christ's resurrected, glorified humanity. That is, beauty is a corollary of glorification especially if glorification is the enhancement of existing reality, and particularly, the exaltation of humanity.

Furthermore, Christ's beauty, like other aspects of his humanity, could express something of the divine. If Christ's glorified body images the glorification of all creation, then perceptual beauty, now at home in the Godhead through Christ's body, in tandem with Christ, can likewise portend a "resurrection" or glorification of the natural world. This glorification entails human integration with divine glory, made possible by the representative integration of Christ's humanity (created, beautiful form) into the Godhead. But in addition to the beauty of the human form, if "all nature" is in Christ through Mary, as Anselm holds, then Christ can be understood to represent and redeem all created beauty.[81] And if this is so, then all beauty, viewed christologically, can be "read" within creation's text as revealing a destination for both nature and humanity that is bound up in Christ's glorified body. That is, beauty is a created end (like love, joy, peace, etc.) that is anchored in Christ's body. And Christ's natural body becomes the theological fulcrum that moves the entire natural world, especially the beauty of the world, through Christ's participation in that beauty. This participation makes the beauty of the world, as a category of images, redemptive christologically. In this way, the incarnation contributes to the "storied identity" of the world's beauty, allowing us to return more plausibly to Simone Weil's claim that all beauty is "as it were an incarnation of God in the world."[82] Thus Christology points to beauty

---

Bauerschmidt, "Aesthetics," 214, notes the spanning of the skeptical gulf.

81. Anselm, "Prayer to St. Mary," 120–21.

82. Wynn, *Faith and Place*, 249; Weil, *Gravity and Grace*, 137. Cf. Farrer: "To naturalize

much as Christ the image pointed to beautiful images of vines, lilies, sparrows, and lambs to instruct the crowds. And just as the incarnation instructs us on how to read so many aspects of the world, the incarnation also instructs us in beauty-skills by giving us guidance on how we should read beauty. So our christological reflection can allow us to see something of God's nature presented to us, not merely through our contemplation of Christ's human form, but through our experience of everyday beauties—the same beauties that reflect God's giving of himself to the world and the world's consequent redemption. If we can see all beauty as reflecting Christ and redeemed through him, we can find "present good in life's familiar face," building thereupon "hopes of good to come,"[83] and we will need only walk a common footpath to see present and future glory welling out of every damp lichen and stone. Through such reflection, we may begin to indwell more fully the epistemic practice of seeing the invisible in the visibly beautiful.

OBJECTIONS TO REVELATION THROUGH ART, SYMBOL, AND BEAUTY

So the notion of a symbolic "beauty-practice" is bolstered not only by the structure of human and biblical communication through artistic images, but also by the incarnation as paradigmatic image. Although Christ as image does not argue conclusively for beauty as image, the incarnation does present a challenge to those who object to revelatory images in general. Furthermore, this developing theological and epistemological vision implies that percipients access "information" and receive tacit knowledge through beauty's excess and imaging of God within creation's art. But in opposition to this vision are several theologians inhabiting different aesthetic, theological, and epistemological visions. These differing visions of course lead to different conclusions about what art and beauty are and do, and consequently, to certain objections to the idea of revelatory beauty. But these alternative visions also harbor certain weaknesses that undermine their correlative objections. I consider three relevant categories of objections under the three subheadings below.

God is idolatry: for God to supernaturalize his instrument is incarnation" (*Glass*, 106).

83. Wordsworth, Fourteen-Book *Prelude*, 13.61–63. Adherents of other religions might be able to experience something similar through similar religious interpretations.

Objections to "Information" Delivery through Art

In potential opposition to the possibility of knowing God through creation's art, two theologians, one Catholic and one Protestant, question what can be known through art. Aidan Nichols denies that art offers any "information about the artist."[84] Neither can art, for Nichols, offer individual "facts" or "truths," or any "detachable conclusion . . . used apart from the work itself." Rather, he maintains that art reveals by placing us "in communion with" the artist. But we are left wondering what form this communion would take, since it would be a rather trivial communion that does not enable us to know something about the artist or what the artist wishes to communicate. Such communion sounds less like revelation and more like a supposedly "pure experience" devoid of knowledge, even though it is doubtful that there is such a thing as pure experience that does not contribute to knowledge in some way. Aesthetic experience may not concern propositional information or detachable conclusions as Nichols seems to understand them; not much of life does. Nonetheless, we are constantly receiving "information" through the senses as we perceive art, and as we do things like drive a car. We can know how to drive a car without being able to specify or "detach" all the information that enables us to drive, because the information is bound up in the flow of activity. Similarly, apart from information or conclusions in Nichols' sense, our aesthetic perception can still lead to knowledge. This knowledge may be a "know how" or "know who"—a knowledge of a skill, a person, or a place (like a home or garden), and certainly these latter two knowings are relevant to the beauty of people and places. We might also have a "know how" or beauty-skill that spills over into a "know who" regarding God.

Interestingly, Nichols does claim that aesthetic experience "shifts our whole way of reading the significance of the world."[85] But if I have only an "information-less" experience without interpretation, I acquire no new beliefs, and my worldview does not change: I read the significance of the world no differently than before. If, however, my aesthetic apperception leads me to some new belief, then I might read the world differently in light of that belief. But this would seem to be a conclusion upon which I focus, at least partially, "apart from the work itself," which is what Nichols seems to disallow. Of course, in the case of creation as divine art, it would be impossible to "detach" a conclusion and use it "apart from the work" that is creation as a whole.

Nichols would also seem to have difficulty affirming as he does that aesthetic experience can be a "rich source of meaning" that bears "evident

84. Nichols, *Art of God*, 99–100.
85. Ibid., 99–100.

truth," and "proves able to place us in touch with an absolutely satisfying and complete hold on the reality that blesses us with its own truth."[86] Nichols is content to attribute this acquiring of truth and meaning to mystery rather than epistemology; but any apprehension of truth and meaning, even in art, requires something along the lines of information and belief involved in some kind of knowing. Even if we acquire no discrete propositional information or conscious belief, we must at least acquire some new "know how," "know who," or some other experiential knowledge. Otherwise when Nichols tells us that God's "style" of artwork displayed in the incarnation "simply is the disclosure of the artist, the Father of Christ," we are left wondering how the incarnation can disclose the artist without offering any sort of knowledge about him.[87] But disclosure of knowledge through art does take place, although it obtains neither through nebulous communion with the artist nor through discrete information delivery. Nichols draws too sharp a dichotomy between aesthetic experience as *either* communion *or* individual "facts" and "truths," and the result is that he neglects other fruitful possibilities.

Perhaps Nichols means to emphasize quite rightly that art does not always excel in clarifying precise theological concepts; rather, its gift is to employ form, symbol, and fiction to engage us experientially in a way that systematic theology cannot.[88] But such experiential engagement is also a kind of knowing and can be a clarification in its own right. Against such clarification, however, Emil Brunner asserts that "the message of what God has done for our redemption certainly cannot be expressed as music, and what God wills to say to us in Jesus Christ cannot be painted. In this respect the human word is not simply one method among others, for human speech alone can indicate quite unambiguously God's thought, Will, and Work."[89] But Brunner should rather say that words may indicate God's thought *less* ambiguously, provided that they are in contexts where we know what the words mean, since we require words, and life-contexts in which words are used, to explain words as much as to explain works of art. In the right context, non-verbal art may communicate as well as, or better than, a theological treatise. Otherwise Brunner must downplay the communicative role of centuries of religious music and visual art.

---

86. Ibid., 113.

87. Ibid., 115–16.

88. See F. B. Brown, *Religious Aesthetics*, 167, on the contrast between theology and art's experiential engagement.

89. Brunner, *Divine Imperative*, 502.

Objections to Revelation through Beauty and Symbol

Eberhard Jüngel objects to beauty as revelation, because he sees revelation primarily in terms of the Christ event. Jüngel's concept of revelation embraces the ugliness of the cross, and therefore seems contrary to beauty. He also reacts against the identification of goodness with beauty, seeing beauty as "essentially finite and transient" rather than a transcendental.[90]

My treatment of perceptual beauty in the preceding chapter alleviates some of Jüngel's concerns, because it draws a distinction between beauty and moral goodness and does not require beauty to be a transcendental. In addition, I have begun to describe a conceptual framework for understanding creation's art that contextualizes beauty alongside creation's evil and ugliness. And the intermingled good and evil, beauty and ugliness of the Christ event is a pointed instance of the world's strange mixture of the same. Jüngel, then, only really succeeds in arguing that *some* aspects of the complex totality of revelation are not beautiful, and most would not deny this. On the other hand, he does not mention the category of natural revelation. But he speaks of beauty in terms that are highly conducive to revelation by calling beauty a "pre-appearance of the truth."[91] He distinguishes this mere earthly "*appearance*" from the actual "*being in glory*" that occurs in heaven.[92] But this understanding of earthly beauty as the "appearance" of heavenly glory, however scant and fleeting, seems to affirm rather than deny revelation through beauty. We are, after all, human and earthly, and in our present state can only receive glimpses and "appearances" rather than "being in glory." Moreover, Jüngel's stress on the Christ event reaffirms Christ's human and earthly imaging of God. Christ's humanity and actions in the world communicate existentially and dramatically what cannot be stated succinctly in doctrinal precepts. Thus, Christ as revelatory image lends support for similar images in the beautiful. In addition, Jüngel describes beauty as a symbol and sacrament, and this description fits well with the idea of symbolic revelation through beauty.[93] Jüngel's "objections" to revelatory beauty, then, seem to be more a case of different emphasis than a totally different framework.

Raising more serious objections, and indwelling a much different theological/epistemological framework, Hans Rookmaaker and Abraham Kuyper both carry out sustained polemics against the idea of revelation

90. Jüngel, "Even the Beautiful," 69, 79–80.

91. Ibid., 79.

92. Ibid., 81.

93. Ibid., 65–66.

through artistic symbolism. Rookmaaker's and Kuyper's ideas on art are influential in Reformed circles in their own right, as well as through their influence on the work of Francis Schaeffer. The Dutch Neo-Calvinists are responsible in part for the negative Reformed stance toward creational theology. But their criticisms of revelatory symbolism are leveled at human rather than divine art, and particularly at a version of neoplatonic art theory. Their criticisms depend upon what they understand artistic symbolism to be and how they see it functioning. Thus, these criticisms can be taken into account without excluding the notion of revelation through art, human or divine.

Rookmaaker maintains that some late nineteenth-century artists understood art as a means of knowing the Platonic Ideas, equivalent to revelation.[94] Apparently steeped in "Plotinian Swedenborgian theories about the 'correspondences,'" this particular group of artists was, in Rookmaaker's view, "making art to take the place of divine revelation and thus elevating it to religion." Charles Morice, for instance, asserts that "art is but the revealer of the Infinite . . . . By nature, then, art is in essence religious."[95] Baudelaire describes the artist as "king, priest, and god";[96] and for Thomas Carlyle, the artist is a "Messias of Nature" delivering natural revelation through creativity.[97] Like Rookmaaker, Kuyper sees artistic symbolism as "a new religion" opposed to Christianity and biblical revelation, because art becomes the new locus of revelation displacing the Bible.[98] But Rookmaaker and Kuyper are dealing, not with a christocentric creational theology engaging images, but with a mystical Romanticism that does sometimes disguise pantheism in Christian terminology.[99] Rookmaaker argues that the spirit of this new religion is a desire for total self-determination, complete freedom from God's laws.[100] Kuyper adds, "Their constant endeavour is not to fear, to serve and to love the living God . . . but to enjoy fully the mystical titillations of a delightful religious feeling." Thus, symbolism is an intoxicating "passion" that is "indulged in."[101]

Rookmaaker and Kuyper can be seen as offering a legitimate criticism of one particular use of artistic symbolism. But the artists they mention are also confronting the church with its own failure to deal effectively with the

---

94. Rookmaaker, *Art, Artists and Gauguin*, 28, 34.

95. "L'Art n'est pas que le révélateur de l'Infini. . . . De nature donc, d'essence l'Art est religieux" (Morice, *Littérature*, 34–35).

96. Baudelaire, "Exposition Universelle," 127.

97. Carlyle, *Sartor Resartus*, 213.

98. Kuyper, *Antithesis*, 11, 17.

99. Rookmaaker, *Art, Artists and Gauguin*, 164.

100. Ibid., 63.

101. Kuyper, *Antithesis*, 7, 11.

nineteenth century's social and intellectual upheaval. Notably, Van Gogh and Ruskin also reacted against a cold and anti-intellectual orthodoxy—an orthodoxy that failed to address and encompass all of human experience in its theology. Through his experience of art and natural beauty, Ruskin eventually became convinced that he had been misled by evangelical frameworks similar to Rookmaaker and Kuyper's.

Furthermore, the problems and overreactions that Rookmaaker and Kuyper cite do not necessarily render all neoplatonic thought, still less all symbolic revelation, inherently incompatible with Christianity. And Kuyper's criticisms even go so far as to call into question the biblical doctrine of natural revelation. For him the situation is very clear-cut:

> Everyone who, moving in the finite, becomes aware of the existence of something Infinite, has to form a conception *of the relation that exists between both*. . . . Either the Infinite reveals itself to man, and by this revelation unveils the *really existing relation*, or the Infinite remains mute and silent and man himself has to guess, to conjecture, and to represent to himself this relation *by means of his imagination*; that is, in an artificial way. Now the first line is the Christian one. . . . Paganism . . . wants the symbol and creates it in its idols. . . . *Symbol* means a fictitious link between the invisible Infinite and the visible finite.[102]

Kuyper assumes that symbolism is a "*fictitious* link," and seems to take a pejorative and reductive view of all "fiction" and myth. Therefore, for Rookmaaker, who accepts Kuyper's analysis, "the conclusion is obvious: 'Revelation and Symbolism are in principle opposed, one to the other.'"[103] And this opposition, says Kuyper, "must lead necessarily to opposite conclusions and issues, both for our social and political, our moral and scientific views." He believes that symbolism leads ultimately to relativism, because it is inherently fictitious.[104] But it is certainly not obvious that no symbol could be a God-ordained and designed link between the Infinite and the visible, nor does the Bible's status as a revelatory norm preclude this possibility. The Bible could not cohere or function without its symbolism, and if its symbols are revealed, then the Bible also raises the possibility of revealed symbols in creation. Symbolic images in creation's art could be supplemental and complementary to biblical ones.

But Rookmaaker does not allow space for an aesthetic rationality already attuned to such images. Instead, he sees the "revelation" of art, as

102. Ibid., 15.
103. Rookmaaker, *Art, Artists and Gauguin*, 166; Kuyper, *Antithesis*, 16.
104. Kuyper, *Antithesis*, 17.

inherently mystical and non-rational.[105] He also believes that those who seek revelation in art are asking art to do something that is fundamentally non-artistic: that is, he believes that appeals to revelation through art are misplaced efforts to secure art's significance in a scientific age in which that significance is questioned. This effort is misplaced, according to Rookmaaker, not least because art already has many important functions apart from revelation. Thus any view of art as revelation actually diminishes art by misunderstanding its nature and function. Revelation is handled in a better way than by art, says Rookmaaker: "If you want to prophesy, become a preacher."[106] But this seems a reductive view of both art and preaching, which can also be artistic.

Rookmaaker concedes that there may be "'glimpses' of ultimate reality" in art. Here he parallels Jüngel's language of "appearances." But for Rookmaaker, "the difference between 'glimpses' . . . and 'revelation' speaks volumes."[107] This distinction, however, is an unnecessary bifurcation that contrasts with biblical accounts of natural revelation. Ironically, Rookmaaker blames Aquinas for a similar distinction between nature and grace, which, he believes, led people to see the truths of special revelation as in some sense unreal because not based on reason.[108] But it is actually Rookmaaker himself who suffers from a separation of revelation from other modes of knowledge, including the artistic—a separation that has the effect of making biblical revelation seem unreal, because it is supposed to function so differently from our aesthetic engagement with the world. Despite Rookmaaker's assessment of scholasticism as "one of the most subtle and dangerous enemies of true biblical thinking,"[109] Aquinas achieves an admirable synthesis of nature and grace, aesthetic rationality and revelation, whereas Rookmaaker cordons off the reasonableness of revelation from any sort of aesthetic rationality: "In the one case the acceptance of Revelation by faith will be the way to gain fundamental knowledge of the basic principles of reality; in the other, art will be the medium: 'art, by the wonderful power of its imaginative gifts, creating the corresponding symbols.'"[110] Again, this is an unnecessary "either-or" posed between art and revelation, faith and imagination, which excludes the possibility that faith can accept aspects of natural revelation that are mediated imaginatively through artistic images. Rookmaaker and

105. Rookmaaker, *New Orleans Jazz*, 120.

106. Rookmaaker, *Western Art*, 239.

107. Rookmaaker, *Art, Artists and Gauguin*, 29.

108. Rookmaaker, *Western Art*, 297.

109. Rookmaaker, *Modern Art*, 21.

110. Rookmaaker, *Art, Artists and Gauguin*, 166; Kuyper, *Antithesis*, 16.

Kuyper do not consider that imagination's creation of symbols in no way precludes revelation through those symbols, especially since imagination is integral to human knowledge and to human nature made in God's image. Kuyper calls imagination's work "artificial," but imaginative symbols are especially at work in biblical revelation. Neglecting this aspect of the Bible, Rookmaaker's dilemma between "Revelation by faith" and art's "imaginative gifts" would also seem to deny any "imaginative gifts" or artistic creativity to the biblical writers. And similarly, in the case of symbols in nature, God could imaginatively create the potential for symbols, while humans imaginatively actualize this potential. Without such allowances, we limit not only the religious significance of human creativity but also God's prerogative to reveal himself in various ways, as he pleases. Thus, given the limitedness of Kuyper and Rookmaaker's view, it is not surprising that Kuyper notes the attraction of artists to Roman Catholicism, since this attraction probably reflects a preference for religion that takes seriously worship through sacrament and the mediation of revelation through symbols.[111]

Rookmaaker and Kuyper's objections to revelation through art are epistemological, in the spirit of Reformed objections against creational theology in general. Rookmaaker believes that "in starting from the human, from *human* sense-perception, *human* thinking," secular philosophy and art have "automatically closed the world" and "shut off any possibility of a transcendental, truly living God."[112] But if as humans we cannot start from human perception and thinking, one wonders where else Rookmaaker would have us humans start. Revelation must reach humanity if it is to be revelation, and God even reaches out to humanity *in* humanity, in the incarnation. So one can, with less strain, assert against Rookmaaker that our human sense-perception and thinking, our art and symbol-making, actually open God's world and put us in touch with the possibility of a transcendent, truly living God. This is certainly more plausible epistemologically, and more observable in human experience, than Kuyper's animadversion: "Symbolism . . . stuns, blunts and stultifies the organs of understanding, and checks their function agnostically."[113]

Rookmaaker is also concerned that in symbolic revelation "reality is deprived of its proper character and remains merely as a metaphor of the authentic absolute "reality"—where the term "reality" is meant in a Platonic (Greek) sense."[114] But it is ironic that Rookmaaker raises this

---

111. Ibid., 7.
112. Rookmaaker, *Modern Art*, 68.
113. Kuyper, *Antithesis*, 21.
114. Rookmaaker, *Modern Art*, 185.

concern when Kuyper's own assumptions contribute to this very problem. Kuyper assumes dilemmas "of feeling or faith" and "between sensation and understanding." These dilemmas actually have the effect of depriving felt and sensed reality of its proper character in favor of Kuyper's own "authentic absolute 'reality,'" namely that of faith and putatively "non-sensory" understanding. As a result he believes that sensuous, "high-church" worship leads inexorably to disregard for God's Word, and that Calvinism must rescue the church from "that *lower* stage of religious development," presumably through "non-sensuous" preaching.[115] But unlike Kuyper's "non-sensuous" religion, symbolic revelation does not require any devaluing of material reality. On the contrary, I have maintained that we should see beauty primarily *as* beauty, as a created end in itself, and only in view of its created, physical nature, as a revelatory image.

Despite his extensive critique of symbolic revelation, Rookmaaker, interestingly, is not opposed to what he calls the "iconic" representation of an artist's ideas by means of lines, colors, and forms—he champions this sort of symbolism; and really this is all that is needed for divine art to be revelatory.[116] Rookmaaker also acknowledges revelation in the created order.[117] He says that things in the world "are so full of meaning that words fall far short to express it all. This reality is there and is given to us, and our task is to open it up and to realize its possibilities."[118] And even Kuyper adjures us to repent of our "lack of obedience to the law of the Sublime and the Beautiful."[119] Given such statements, perhaps Rookmaaker and Kuyper could have accepted a more cautious and nuanced revelatory symbolism—one that does not look for symbolism in every natural or artistic form, and that allows biblical revelation to inform and govern natural revelation.

Beauty and Idolatry

But Rookmaaker and Kuyper seem to be exercised in part by the fear of idolatry: if beautiful forms present God symbolically, and if we enjoy God *through* this presentation, are we then in effect squandering on beauty the adoration that belongs to God alone? And are we distorting God idolatrously by refracting him through beauty's earthly lens?

115. Kuyper, *Antithesis*, 19–21.

116. Rookmaaker, *Modern Art*, 171.

117. Rookmaaker, *New Orleans Jazz*, 19

118. Hans Rookmaaker, *Our Calling*, 246.

119. Kuyper, *Antithesis*, 24.

Jaroslav Pelikan, writing in his Protestant period, raises objections along these lines by opposing the human category of the beautiful to the severity of the God who would abandon his Son to the cross. In fact Pelikan sees the Holy, including Christ, the "rock of offence," as a contrast to all human concepts of the good, the true, and the beautiful.[120] He argues that in identifying God with beauty, the will-to-power of fallen humanity takes up "the Beautiful as a shield for its demonic urgings."[121] This amounts to a "drive for control over the Holy" by reinventing God idolatrously in the image of humanity's "fondest dreams" and "tenderest longings." Because of beauty's defacement of God in this regard, it fails to speak of him.[122] In a similar vein, Søren Kierkegaard fears that aesthetic enjoyment in religion becomes an idolatrous substitute for decision, commitment, and action: we enjoy beauty and use it to avoid attending to the more important matters of who we ought to be and what we ought to do.[123] Surely Pelikan and Kierkegaard are right to draw attention to possible misuses of beauty, but they are wrong not to entertain the possibility that beauty might reveal God despite human misuse and corruption of beauty. It seems that they are forced into the odd conclusion that simply because the beauty of the tree of knowledge of good and evil became a distraction, or was sought in an act of will-to-power, therefore beauty says nothing about God. Yet the beauty of the forbidden fruit is not unlike the beauty of all other fruit created and given freely for enjoyment. The problem, then, is not with a beautiful creation or its message but with human misappropriation and misuse of beauty, along with the misuse of so many other good things, such as knowledge, power, and freedom. If Pelikan and Kierkegaard would protect us from all that is good, their religion must remove us from the world itself. Pelikan concludes that any search for God in beauty "ends in the maddening realization that the Holy refuses to be taken captive in the Beautiful."[124] But this is only to state what is true of all revelation: God is never exhausted or taken captive by it. So if beauty indeed proceeds from God and is redeemed by him, as Pelikan affirms, there is no reason why it cannot also function as revelation.[125]

Nonetheless, this much asserted, beauty does often seem to function idolatrously. The apostle Paul suggests that when human beings worship

120. Pelikan moved toward Eastern Orthodoxy later in life. See Pelikan, *Human Culture*, 141.

121. Ibid., 142.

122. Ibid., 144.

123. See Kierkegaard, *Journals*, 829.

124. Pelikan, *Human Culture*, 145.

125. Ibid., 172.

created beauties, we make evident our estrangement from the Creator (Rom 1:21–25). We must consider the possibility that beautiful people, places, works of art, etc., could be worshipped idolatrously, since every grace, including the operation of beauty, is affected to some degree by a fallen human context. We might then expect difficulty in ascertaining when we have crossed over from knowing or worshipping God through orchids or arias to idolatry. Idolatry could offer a false and truncated repose in beauty's misuse, rather than in beauty's proper depth and reference to God. And indeed Ruskin was criticized for propounding an idolatrous natural theology of beauty.[126] Yet if beauty in some way presents God, how then can one fall into idolatry by worshipping God through beauty any more than Moses could by kneeling before the burning bush?

In response to this question, we can affirm that we do not ultimately lose God among the objects of the world, because every object participates in him and expresses him to the extent that it remains uncorrupted by sin or fallenness. It is therefore inappropriate to place God and the world, as Hart says, in a relationship of total opposition, "an oscillation between wealth and impoverishment, ideal and shadow, truth and falsehood."[127] Giving full attention to worldly beauty is not idolatry, because not only is God implicitly present in moonlight and snowfall, but a desultory outlook on God's world is no virtue. Moreover, beauty affirms the value of our aesthetic desire toward the world by reminding us of creation's present goodness and by foreshadowing its impending consummation. Beauty cannot of itself lead one away from God, especially if God is its ultimate meaning. It is rather our broader patterns of life and frameworks of thought that create idols, not the character of objects themselves: only sin distorting beauty toward its own egoistic ends brings disorder to the world's beauty and draws it away from the God whom it properly declares. This corrupt desire is not for a lesser, earthly beauty as opposed to the spiritual; it is rather to fall out of harmony with what material beauty is as a divine operation within creation. We lose beauty *as* beauty when we put it into the service of unduly selfish ends rather than enjoying it for its own sake and for God's.[128] We are often so turned in upon ourselves that we cannot even enjoy beauty—this is to see beauty only through the lens of an improper sort of self-love. We then value beautiful people, places, works of art, etc., merely for what they can do for us, rather than for what they are in themselves and for others. We substitute an egoistic pleasure for beauty's proper pleasure, and in the process

---

126. See Wheeler, *Ruskin's God*, 34.

127. Hart, *Beauty*, 255.

128. See ibid., 255, on egoistic distortion of beauty.

our pleasure is diminished.[129] Beauty becomes dull and eludes us if we seek it too intently, but finds and surprises us when we are not questing for it. So there is still an appropriate kind of self-love and love of beauty, such that "whoever truly serves beauty, serves God."[130]

But this merely implicit service to God, such as might be performed by a non-religious person, might still leave beauty an idol according to Graham Ward, who argues that one must not ignore beauty's transcendent aspect and reduce it to sensible properties.[131] Yet I have focused on sense-perceptual beauty in order to protect it as a distinctive phenomenon that exists apart from explicitly religious experience. I have not, however, focused on the perceptual to the exclusion of God. God does participate in the world's beauty; yet at a lower stratum of reality, beauty need not forfeit its integrity as a perceptual phenomenon. On the other hand, if we insist that canyons and rainforests are only valuable when we recognize their relationship to God, beauty begins to disappear into a religious and metaphysical haze: we begin to replace beauty with an aesthetic-religious phenomenon that is something other than, or in addition to, beauty. Jonathan Edwards makes this mistake by reducing perceptual beauty to a mere stepping stone to moral goodness. According to his very different aesthetic and metaphysical vision, Edwards sees physical objects as "but the shadow of beings," their value being in the moral and spiritual beauty that they typify, which is true being.[132]

Despite the danger of idolatry, we need not relegate created beauty to the status of shadow or "untrue being." Our aesthetic desire and rationality are too persistent and God-given to be suppressed rightly, or to permit the neglect of the valuable in creation—let alone that which presents God to us. Moreover, the triune God is not lacking or unfulfilled, that he should demand an absolute sacrifice of every earthly love. In fact, God, rather than being an individual in competition with every earthly love, is the supra-individual reality through whom alone we can properly understand every earthly love. So while both the sacrifice and the affirmation of earthly loves can feed egocentrism, neither can add to the glory of a superabounding Godhead.[133] In contrast to the simplistic affirmation or denial of beauty,

129. Tyrwhitt, *Natural Beauty*, 88, notes the diminished enjoyment of egoistic pleasure in beauty.

130. van der Leeuw, *Sacred and Profane Beauty*, 335.

131. Ward, "Beauty of God," 63.

132. Jonathan Edwards, "Beauty of the World," 305–6. Edwards also sees beauty as the symbol of charity and "mental beauty," which he connects with God's original moral and spiritual beauty; "True Virtue," 564–65. "Excellency of Christ," 278.

133. Hart, *Beauty*, 255, makes a similar point about God not requiring the sacrifice of earthly love. See Wynn, "Knowledge of God," 152, on God's supra-individuality.

Dietrich Bonhoeffer casts a better vision, describing the ideal love for God as a *cantus firmus* around which the love of beauty and all other human loves find their proper place as contrapuntal melodies in "the polyphony of life."[134] When beauty finds this proper place in the created order as a perceptual phenomenon, it actually guards against idolatry through the longing of beauty's excess: this longing is a recognition that although beauty reveals God, it certainly cannot reveal him exhaustively. Therefore we direct our worship beyond beauty toward its inexhaustible and ultimately mysterious referent. For although the commandment prohibits us from making any image of the ineffable God, it does not say that no image is given to us, for instance, in Christ, or, for that matter, in the beautiful.[135]

CONCLUSION

The objections against revelatory beauty just considered seem either misplaced or based on very different theological/epistemological visions, but they do highlight potential pitfalls, and help set boundaries for a creational theology of natural beauty. But my artistic, symbolic vision is not the only one that maps onto the world or illuminates human experience of beauty. The sciences also offer their own ways to make sense of beauty, just as different types of maps (political, geographical, topographical) can describe the same landscape in different ways without exhausting its complexity. But in a world so complex and mysterious—perhaps more mysterious than we can imagine—we would do well not to exclude the aesthetic heuristic from our ordinary attempts to know the world. We would do well not to exclude it, especially because primal reality (i.e., God) is personal, making it likely that aesthetic interchange between persons is more essential to reality than matter, science, laws, or any other phenomenon viewed as impersonal or prosaic fact. In light of the irreducibly personal nature of reality in a theistic cosmos, we should not view beauty as impersonal fact but as artifact of divine personality. And as such, beauty as a category of revelatory images begins to give a certain unity to the disparate elements of the world's story, just as any momentous event, such as the birth of a child, or the enfleshing of a God, can help set the drama of life in order.[136] As momentous events and images, beautiful forms illuminate a distinctive aesthetic rationality within

---

134. Bonhoeffer, *Letters*, 303.

135. van der Leeuw, *Sacred and Profane Beauty*, 323, 333, speaks of beauty as an image given to us.

136. Cf. Niebuhr, *Meaning of Revelation*, 109–10, on momentous events as ordering influences.

ourselves and the world—a rationality engendering, for Wordsworth, pregnant perception and enduring "spots of time," "In which the heavy and the weary weight / Of all this unintelligible world, / Is lightened" and "We see into the life of things."[137] The following chapter explores this symbolic disclosure of *natural* beauty more specifically. The natural world is a locus of beauty that no one who looks out a window can escape entirely. I continue to "saturate" this beauty with intelligibility by incorporating Ruskin's "typical beauty" into the epistemic vision of creation's art.

---

137. Wordsworth, Thirteen-Book *Prelude* 11.258; "Tintern Abbey," 2:151.

5

Re-envisaging Ruskin's Types
Toward a Creational Theology of Natural Beauty

IN THE EIGHTEENTH CENTURY, the poet James Thomson remarked, "I know no subject more elevating . . . more ready to awake the poetical enthusiasm, the philosophical reflection, and the moral sentiment, than the works of Nature. Where can we meet with such variety, such beauty, such magnificence? All that enlarges and transports the soul!"[1] But three hundred years later, the environmental aesthetician, J. Douglas Porteous, believed that modern aesthetics engages natural landscapes only with difficulty, because landscapes lack an author or authorial aesthetic.[2] Under such tacit atheism, natural beauty lacks the context necessary for meaning, even though our experience of beauty actually cries out for meaning.

One thinker, however, who contributes significantly to the theological context for making sense of natural beauty is John Ruskin. Seen as the profoundest art critic of the nineteenth century, and perhaps of all time, Ruskin is also an interesting figure for Protestant theology in that, at least in the early part of his life, he upheld a commitment to biblical revelation alongside emphasis on the revelatory function of natural beauty.[3] Regrettably,

1. Thomson, preface to *Winter*, 15; more accessible in *Seasons*, 305.

2. Porteous, *Environmental Aesthetics*, 23.

3. Ruskin was raised as an evangelical, but eventually moved away from his conservative view of the Bible. In Letter 35 of the *Fors Clavigera*, he denies that the Bible is the "Word of God"; however, in Letter 42 he calls his childhood learning of the Bible "the most precious, and, on the whole, the one essential part, of all my education." At the

however, he has rarely been taken seriously as a theologian or as a stimulus for theology. Ruskin's understanding of beauty differs in some respects from mine, and the "types" of God that he sees in natural beauty are certainly open to question and refinement. But his use of *type* connects with my use of *image* and *symbol*, functioning as a more definite symbolism. And his "typical beauty," or the beauty of types, fits well within creation's artistic text as a multifaceted image of the divine. "Typical" beauty for Ruskin means that, within a certain theological framework, beautiful things in general typify God, while aspects of beautiful things typify aspects of God. These aspects of beauty are phenomena, such as order, repose, and boundlessness, which Ruskin perceives through his personal epistemic vision and symbolic practice. Ruskin's vision and practice can be established by working with and through them to detect and decipher, illuminate and give order to common human experiences of beauty. Moreover, his vision and practice can be fruitfully indwelt and extended toward a wider creational theology. I propose in line with Ruskin that his typology contributes to an understanding of how natural beauty reveals God's nature.

In addition, building upon some of Ruskin's undeveloped allusions, I propose that natural beauty reveals not only God's nature but also something about human nature and destiny: human beings can experience God through beauty and, in the same process, we can see ourselves in a different light. Through the vague human longing to integrate with natural beauty, we are actually seeking to integrate ourselves with images of God's nature. And this aesthetic integration foreshadows our intended eschatological integration with God. These more extensive referents of beauty are not mere accretions but natural connections, consistent with the operation of our knowledge through images, and consistent with beauty's inherent associative power. These are appropriate "indwellings" and extensions of Ruskin's epistemic vision of knowing God through natural beauty, and as such, they explore new possibilities and further understandings.

The chapter is divided into four parts. In part one I describe and begin to reformulate Ruskin's approach to natural beauty's symbolism. In part two I take up *order* in natural beauty as revelatory of divine harmonies, both within the Godhead and relative to creation. Within this discussion of order, I first critique classical understandings of order that would deny beauty to much of nature. I then rework a number of Ruskin's types that relate in some way to natural order, while dealing with his types of repose, color, and infinity separately. In the third part I expand upon Ruskin's idea of repose

---

time of his writing on typical beauty, Ruskin seems to have held to biblical inspiration in the traditional sense, and his understanding of revelatory beauty is tenable for those holding higher views of Scripture; *Fors Clavigera*, 1:650, 2:102.

as the type of divine permanence, contextualizing repose within nature's flux, and arguing against the Augustinian tendency to reconcile beauty with decay. Within nature's unsettled and destructive context, a reposeful beauty shows forth the divine permanence. This emphasis on repose continues the previous chapter's introductory response to natural evil and ugliness as potential confutations of revelatory beauty. Also under this heading of repose, I describe revelatory beauty in living forms (biotic beauty) as a "living repose." As life contributes to beauty, and beauty to life, biotic beauty reflects God's life and life-giving. It is in this connection with life and fecundity that color, Ruskin's type of divine love, fits most appropriately. In the final part of the chapter, I expand upon Ruskin's type of infinity in the context of the human desire to integrate with a boundless creation imaging an infinite God. In the desire for harmony with, and repose in, a boundless creation, the types of order, repose, and infinity converge, illuminating an eschatological *telos* for both nature and humanity. This *telos* is experienced in the form of a "frontier"—an endlessly expansive interface between nature and humanity—where beauty and knowledge unfold with the landscape, unveiling the divine mystery that is displayed aptly in the beautiful.

RE-ENVISAGING RUSKIN'S TYPES

In the second volume of *Modern Painters*, Ruskin presents a unique view of beauty as a primarily theological and even revelatory phenomenon. In the manuscript of this volume, he states, "all which is the type of God's attributes—which in any way or any degree—can . . . fix the spirit . . . on the types of that which is to be its food for eternity;—this and only this is in the pure and right sense of the word BEAUTIFUL" (2:365).[4] Ruskin sees in creation "expressions" of God's nature that are found to be beautiful (2:91). These types of the Godhead, rather than being "stamped upon matter for our teaching or enjoyment only," are "the necessary perfection of God's working, and the inevitable stamp of His image on what He creates" (2:143). The types, then, are artistic outworkings of God's nature rather than Platonic types or forms existing apart from God. Through this typological vision, beauty promises "a communion ultimately deep, close, and conscious, with the Being whose darkened manifestations we here feebly and unthinkingly delight in." Seeing this revelation of God in creation is

---

4. Ruskin, *Modern Painters*, 2:365, capitalization original. All parenthetical volume and page numbers refer to this work and edition. Here Ruskin seems to be not so much narrowing the scope of what is beautiful as he is claiming that all beauty is already typological in character.

"cause for thankfulness, ground for hope, anchor for faith" (2:144–45). This is Ruskin's development of Wordsworth's "pregnant vision."[5]

While maintaining a position similar to Ruskin's, I seek to improve upon his formulation of types, as well as his understanding of beauty. Based on my understanding of perceptual beauty, I differ with Ruskin on how we respond to beauty. According to Ruskin, we respond to typical beauty primarily through our feelings and our moral sense (2:49). He distinguishes this moral and theological pleasure, which he calls "theoria," from the pleasure of the physical senses, or simple aesthetic pleasure, which he calls "aesthesis." But this distinction is somewhat unclear, since he denies that theoria is intellectual while implying that it depends upon reflection (2:42, 211). He also denies that theoria is sensuous, yet he believes that any sense pleasure can become theoretic if received with proper feeling or heart, which for him is a moral quality (2:42, 51). Ruskin may intend to contrast the value of sensory pleasure with the value of recognizing the significance of one's pleasure. But if this is his aim, he expresses himself oddly by saying that theoria is not a matter of the senses or the intellect, for surely it must involve both. He probably means that theoria does not depend on the senses or intellect *alone*. Perhaps Ruskin was grasping toward a more holistic view of perception that integrates the moral, affective, sensory, intellectual, and imaginative. But unfortunately his language continues to give the impression of an artificial separation of these aspects of experience. Ruskin does involve the imagination in the perception of beauty, and he understands imagination to penetrate to the heart (i.e., the true meaning) of beautiful objects, grasping what the senses miss (2:251). But even this "penetrative imagination," if it is to apprehend the truths about God that Ruskin intends for it, would also involve the intellect. Ruskin devalues the intellect and the senses unnecessarily in the perception of beauty, perhaps because of an evangelical moral emphasis on the "sense of the heart." But his concern also seems to be that aesthetics not be reduced to a matter of psychology or philosophy—beauty must instead be a matter of religion and morality.

Still, Ruskin overstates the importance of morality and affections in apprehending revelation through beauty. He does not consider that we experience beauty through diverse metaphysical systems and epistemic visions of the world. We also evaluate and reflect upon our beauty-experience through these visions. Of course, this evaluation and reflection does not occur separately from affections, morals, and imagination—on the contrary, these aspects of our knowing are intertwined inseparably. So Ruskin is correct that our heart response to God affects our theology and therefore our

5. Wordsworth, Fourteen-Book *Prelude*, 4.353.

understanding of aesthetic experience: purity of heart does enable one to recognize beauty *as revelation* and to be thankful to God for his gifts. In this sense, it is quite true that only "the pure in heart . . . shall see God" (Matt 5:8, RSV; 2:49–50). So I can concede to Ruskin that the ideal Christian, with the right theological outlook on nature, can "see" God through the world much more readily. And to this extent, Ruskin's emphasis on moral, affective, and reverent beauty-perception is comparable to my own emphasis on the need to understand beauty ultimately through a Christian epistemic vision (with its own morality, affections, and reverence) in order to understand beauty as fully as possible. In contrast, attempts to understand beauty through a neutral vision only impoverish experience.

But despite Ruskin's emphasis on morality and reverence, many people have no access to a Christian vision of the world. And many people also have profound experiences of beauty without the purity of heart that Ruskin requires, and without making any explicit connection between beauty and God. So beauty's excess of meaning is still at work without a moral or doctrinal prerequisite. Non-theists, vaguely religious people, or lapsed Christians could still experience God tacitly through beauty while hiking or gardening, but be less able or willing to connect their experience explicitly with God's influence or claim upon their lives. Even the atheist could apprehend revelatory beauty displayed in glacial ice or panda bear cubs, but act upon this revelation only in apparently non-religious ways, such as by becoming an artist or environmental activist. The non-believing environmentalist could still be living out a response to natural beauty's revelation, as it imparts an implicitly eschatological hope for a redeemed order between nature and humanity. Similarly, the artist in painting a landscape could be replying in kind implicitly to creation's revelatory artwork, much as a theologian draws up more prosaic descriptions of the world. These "non-religious" responses to revelation may not benefit from conscious recognition or acceptance of God's self-disclosure, but this does not make them less important in their own right for being only implicitly moral or theological, as Ruskin seems to think, probably here again due to his evangelical background. Ruskin even claims that one can always recognize the work of a moral artist as superior to that of an immoral one, owing to the latter's merely aesthetic rather than theoretic perception (2:211–12). But I do not follow Ruskin here in giving primacy to the moral and affective over the sensory and cognitive in beauty-experience, except insofar as morality and affections influence one's theological understanding of beauty.

Still Ruskin may well be correct in his central claim that it is beauty's artistic and microcosmic presentation of deity that produces pleasure in the viewer (cf. 2:144). Ruskin emphasizes six types of the Godhead in the constituents of beauty: unity, the type of divine comprehensiveness; symmetry, the type of divine justice; moderation, of divine government by law; purity, of divine energy; repose, of divine permanence; and infinity, of divine incomprehensibility (2:76–145). In volume five of *Modern Painters* he adds to his list color, the type of divine love (5:417–19).

Ruskin's typology is noteworthy in that it permits no superficial reading of God off the face of nature but requires thought and reflection (often theologically informed reflection) upon natural forms. It is not obvious, for instance, how purity of matter could relate to divine energy, even though Ruskin makes a good case that it does. And perhaps we require even more thought and reflection on nature than Ruskin did, because our culture is more alienated from nature than his: urbanites today know less about birds and wildflowers than did city-dwellers of the past, when economies were more agriculturally based.[6] Ruskin's typology also requires a poetic sensibility toward nature that is nurtured by theism but squelched by modern naturalistic science. Ruskin himself was especially gifted with poetic imagination, but he also lived in an age that was more gifted with sight toward creation. The nineteenth century was more concerned to find God in nature, especially through the influence of natural theology and literary figures such as Wordsworth. And Wordsworth may have inspired Ruskin's concept of types with his "types and symbols of Eternity."[7] Such readings of nature were encouraged by a more pervasively religious zeitgeist, since only religion can legitimately extract poetry from, and attribute art to, the natural world, while naturalistic science must smuggle art into nature as the work of human subjectivity apart from God.

But in interpreting creation's art, as with the work of any human artist, we must be cautious in affirming that a particular flourish of divine style reveals God in a way that we can apprehend. Although Ruskin's typology is quite restrained in comparison to Jonathan Edwards's and John Keble's, Ruskin's affirmations can still be overly ambitious, and he criticizes this tendency in himself in his 1883 commentary on *Modern Painters* (e.g., 2:112n). Ruskin's ambition stems partly from his belief that beautiful

6. Adams, Introduction to *Pilgrim*, 8, makes this connection between agricultural economies and knowledge of nature.

7. Wordsworth, Fourteen-Book *Prelude*, 6.640. Ruskin says that he "used Wordsworth as a daily text-book from youth to age" and "lived . . . in all essential points according to the tenor of his teaching" (*Old Road*, 349). Finley, *Nature's Covenant*, 13–40, notes other influences on Ruskin's typology in John Bunyan and Ruskin's professor of poetry at Oxford, John Keble. Ruskin's typology resembles Keble's understanding of typology in his *On the Mysticism Attributed to the Early Fathers of the Church*, 147–48, 165–68, 176. Ruskin also cast himself in the role of Bunyan's character, "Interpreter," in reference to nature's images. See Ruskin, *Love's Meinie*, 112.

forms reveal a fairly extensive range of monotheistic attributes. He also assumes that his readers possess some prior understanding of these divine attributes, and so he tends to read attributes *into* nature even where they do not seem readily apparent *from* nature.[8] But despite this tendency, Ruskin's types are significant, because they highlight vague elements of religious experience through natural beauty—elements that all religious (and perhaps non-religious) people can share, even if they share them only through very diverse symbolic practices. Non-monotheists, with no doctrinal understanding of divine attributes, might still have an awareness that something deeper is occurring in their experience of an aurora or a sea eagle in flight. This is a differently-skilled[9] experience of significance in the beautiful, and this experience of significance can still be common to humanity without the experiencer always being able to describe it in terms of Ruskin's chosen divine attributes. Such common experience could still intimate something *like* divine order, permanence, and infinity, but take on somewhat different conceptual "shapes." This is because these shareable elements of experience are only shareable in more or less symbolized and conceptualized ways, and people symbolize and conceptualize experience in more or less skilled ways, according to different metaphysical visions of the world. But in many cases the lack of monotheistic conceptualization is to be expected, because Ruskin's typology describes a more general, universal aspect of human experience—our perception of a beautiful world. In this broader life-context, lack of monotheistic conceptualization does not speak against God's designing beauty to point to him, because beauty's revelation is non-verbal and difficult to describe, perhaps impossible to describe without drawing on whatever concepts are ready to hand. People draw on very different conceptual frameworks to describe their experience, and owing to these different frameworks, their descriptions are veridical to varying degrees and often in need of refinement, especially in light of monotheistic and Christian truth.[10]

8. But Ruskin does give this disclaimer: "Let . . . the reader bear constantly in mind that I insist not on his accepting any interpretation of mine, but only on his dwelling so long on those objects which he perceives to be beautiful, as to determine whether the qualities to which I trace their beauty be necessarily there or not" (2:91).

9. That is, non-monotheistic—utilizing the skills of the non-theistic religions according to their own unique metaphysical and epistemic visions, but not skilled in the theological resources of the monotheistic religions or the specifically Christian epistemic vision of the world (e.g., Trinity and Christology).

10. All of this is compatible with Ruskin's qualification: "I have, throughout the examination of Typical beauty, asserted our instinctive sense of it; the moral *meaning* of it being only discoverable by reflection" (2:211).

So because experience is always conceptualized according to different frameworks, and because there is need for refinement according to a Christian framework, we should not wholly or artificially disentangle Ruskin's Christian framework from the vaguer elements of experience common to humanity. We should not force such a separation, because a Christian epistemic vision and practice could be the heuristic that unlocks better understandings of these common elements. In other words, Ruskin's vision becomes a tool that we indwell and use to probe the non-conceptual reality of human experience. And with such a tool we may discover more than we would otherwise. So Christian truth need not be something imposed inappropriately upon the world, but can be part of the heuristic vision through which the world is "discovered," becomes intelligible, and is understood correctly.[11] In this sense, experience and religious understandings of experience are not so separable or distinguishable, because our religious understandings are also part of our experience. Moreover, there is no "pure" experience uncolored by our prior visions. There is rather a complex, mutual interchange of meaning between experience and religious vision, with each shaping the other. But by recognizing the importance of human experience of the world, and by engaging it theologically, albeit through a Christian vision, creational theology is distinct from a theology of nature built solely upon Scripture and tradition. And at the other end of the spectrum, creational theology is also distinct from a putatively neutral natural theology, since, in the interests of neutrality, natural theology forfeits the richness and resources of the Christian vision. The result is that natural theology merely constitutes its own attenuated epistemic vision.

But despite the contribution of a Christian vision, non-Christian understandings of the world are not categorically untrue for being made without the light of Christian truth, because they can be seen as less skilled, or often just differently skilled, understandings of the same revelation. All such understandings, including Christian ones, are by nature indefinite: they are like the different understandings given by different instructors as to the correct way to swing a golf club, and such "instruction" relates to the development of our skills and practices. We require this sort of instruction or guidance on how to perceive and understand the beautiful, and in this respect Ruskin's typology (or a modification thereof) becomes important as an instructional "pointer." As we indwell Ruskin's epistemic vision and symbolic practice, his types give general form and direction to our more particular, nonverbal beauty-experiences. This typological form and direction

---

11. Nevertheless, I do not attempt to prove, but only saturate with intelligibility, this possibility that Christian theism allows us to know more than do other worldviews.

help to shape our own beauty-skills and symbolic practice, which contribute to a larger whole than our recognition of individual types alone. This larger whole of our aesthetic apperception is like the mastery of a painter, which comprises a wide range of brushstrokes, shading techniques, and thematic knowledge, but surpasses each of these by integrating techniques with unconscious ease. The painter's mastery gives rise to the overall excellence of the painting, while our understanding and integration of specific elements in the painting allow us to recognize its aesthetic power. In a similar way, we can learn to see better the brushstrokes within creation from aesthetic, scientific, and religious angles and thereby to understand better the divine artist. These brushstrokes may not always take on the character of distinct types in our experience, since, as we walk outdoors on a particular day, we may only take note of, say, strikingly bright planes amid bold lines and shadows. Yet this clean strikingness may also speak of God in its own way.

Due to this complexity and variability in our beauty-experience, we can move beyond types of divine attributes to include a broader symbolic "beauty-practice" within creation's art. Such symbolic practice integrates a wider range of meanings than does a strict typology, and Ruskin seems to leave this possibility intentionally open. Ruskin says that his types are only the most "palpable and powerful" of the ways that matter may "put us in mind" of divine perfections (2:76, 91, 211). Ruskin's vision, then, can instruct us not just in a typology but in spiritually oriented beauty-skills, as in the previous examples of paintings and golf-swings. Although these beauty-skills comprise specific aspects of instruction and technique, they are complex and partly unanalyzable abilities—they are abilities to perceive God's nature or intentions as imaged in a beautiful world. These beauty-skills apply not only to types but also to experiences that elude such formulations, and ultimately to future realizations of these types and experiences, whatever forms these realizations might take. In this respect, imagination factors prominently into our beauty-practice. But if we try to force beauty's revelation too rigidly into a typological or other abstract conceptual mould, we risk imposing artificial structures upon our less systematizable experience of reality.

So while I seek to indwell Ruskin's epistemic vision of knowing God through natural beauty, I do not hesitate at the same time to reshape it in an effort to make it more plausible and widely applicable. Because Ruskin's typology is ambitious, it is difficult to discern all the nuances of the Godhead in beautiful forms that he discerns, especially for those indwelling very different religious visions. Thus natural beauty may not reveal in as many distinctly different ways as Ruskin claims, although it may reveal most of what he claims in less distinct ways. Ruskin probably included his full list of types in an effort to give a fairly extensive picture of God from nature, perhaps in the spirit of a formerly more ambitious natural theology. Nonetheless, some of his types are problematic, and probably too conceptualized to describe accurately our more nebulous experience. For example, the types of unity and moderation, rather than showing distinct aspects of God or his relationship with creation, seem to highlight the same divine order in slightly different ways. Symmetry seems to be another aspect of this same order, although Ruskin links symmetry to divine justice in a rather tenuous way.[12] In addition, the type of infinity seems implausible insofar as Ruskin tries to derive it from our experience of order; but he does provide a better approach to infinity through experience of the sky. So to reshape Ruskin's types, I combine unity, symmetry, and moderation into a broader type of order, and I retain but modify the types of purity, repose, color, and infinity.

But despite my reshaping of Ruskin's types, I retain his general approach to typical beauty as symbolic of the divine. And it is an approach that Ruskin himself does not overturn despite all his later hedges and revisions to *Modern Painters*, implying that he found it compatible with Darwinism and his own later, less evangelical outlook on Christianity. Even so, in light of Darwinism, I believe that Ruskin's vision requires a more extensive consideration of natural evil. I seek to address beauty's context amid natural evil more adequately by broadening Ruskin's notion of repose into a sort of artistic leitmotiv in opposition to natural evil.

Through similar broadening and reshaping in different contexts, the other types, as artistic motifs, also suggest more than what Ruskin describes. Such reshaping reflects Polanyi's contention that we must indwell, but also extend or depart from, any epistemic vision by "a passionate pouring of oneself into untried forms of existence."[13] As we indwell this symbolic beauty-practice, we indwell a new range of skills, working assumptions, and tacit "principles" through which we look at the world, and we apply these tools in unforeseeable ways in different contexts. Each new application requires acts of creative imagination leading to newly integrated meanings. These are new "discoveries" of reality's continued unveiling that cannot be fully predicted before we in fact discover them.[14] By this indwelling and heuristic extending of Ruskin's symbolic practice, we move toward a more fully-orbed creational theology. And thereby we say something not only about God, but in the very process of knowing God through nature, we also

---

12. Though it might be defended through appeal to a retributive theory of justice ("an eye or an eye")—an appeal that I will consider shortly.

13. Polanyi, *Personal Knowledge*, 208.

14. See Polanyi and Prosch, *Meaning*, 62–63.

come to say something about humanity in relation to God and creation. In this way, a personal and communal reshaping of Ruskin's vision opens up new epistemic vistas and horizons, potentially deepening and enriching our understanding of divine revelation.

From Ruskin's typology, it appears that beauty reveals nothing inconsistent with, or drastically different from, special revelation. But by revealing in a different way—through creation's art, through the senses—beauty furthers our understanding, our overall picture of God, much as human art furthers our understanding of doctrine, and reveals something about our humanity that cannot be translated fully into words.[15] And though God's artwork in natural beauty cannot resemble God himself as "wholly other," we are not thereby forced onto the other horn of an unpleasant "either-or" dilemma: we need not plunge into the apophatic abyss of God as *je ne sais quoi* (I know not what). Rather, God's artwork might at least give us an aesthetically complementary picture of his nature—an artistic image that "fits along with" his nature, and in that sense reveals the divine. And if natural beauty does communicate something in this way that is irreducible and not fully translatable, how much less can we afford to ignore its message? If beauty images what cannot be fully verbalized, then beauty's revelations, in a profound sense, can only be accessed through beauty.

BEAUTIFUL ORDER AS REVELATION

In addition to this need to access beauty's revelation through beauty, a further constraint is that beauty's symbolisms are not fully separable into constituents. Beauty as a whole images God in ways that aspects of beauty cannot, much as a myth analyzed and demythologized cannot bear the same meaning as the myth itself, and the divine essence cannot be rightly divided.[16] But despite this caution, we must somehow obtain greater purchase on beauty's symbolisms. Ruskin does this by examining perceived aspects of beauty, and one such aspect to consider is order.

The Psalmists' view of nature emphasizes order through God's immanence, his abiding and ordering presence within his creation.[17] Such divine presence in nature is consistent with violent change and cataclysm, but

15. Rahner, "Theology and the Arts," 17–29, emphasizes how art communicates what cannot be put into words.

16. D. Brown, "Symbolic Action," 120–21, notes that demythologization is a reduction or change in meaning.

17. Pss 1; 8; 19:1–6; 24:1–2; 33:6–9; 50:9–11; 65:5–13; 74:13–17; 104; 133:3; 135:5–7; 136:4–9, 25; 147:4–9, 15–18; 148.

Ruskin holds that natural beauties also manifest "a holy reference, beyond and out of their own nature, to great harmonies by which they are governed, and in obedience to which is their glory" (2:140). Certainly there is a profound order to creation, a unified complexity at every conceivable level of reality: cosmological, geological, ecological, physiological, cellular, chemical, and physical, to say nothing of mind- or spirit-matter interrelations. Even at the apparently chaotic level of molecular and subatomic motion, the axiom "from nothing, nothing comes" seems applicable, in that order cannot arise mysteriously from an absolute disorder. Whatever chaos there is in creation is bounded and checked by order.

A strong connection between natural order and beauty is also made by the environmental philosopher and "father of environmental ethics" Holmes Rolston. An ordained minister and son and grandson of Presbyterian ministers, Rolston began his academic career by seeking out scientific and ethical principles to support his theological perspective on creation.[18] Rolston examines the scientific complexities of life in diverse ecosystems such as swamps and alpine regions, and he suggests that beauty arises out of this ecological complexity. He observes that nature at the extreme ends of the size continuum (subatomic and cosmological) displays the least complexity, while the mid-levels of scale occupied by humans (e.g., ecosystems and the psyche) display the most. Thus human beings do not live at the level of the mysteriously large or small but at the level of the mysteriously complex.[19] It is precisely at this human level of reality that beauty becomes significant as a combined subjective-objective phenomenon. Beauty, personality, and ordered complexity are allied in the created order.

Critiquing Classical Views of Natural Order

As a prolegomena to understanding Ruskin's and my own accounts of beautiful natural order, I will briefly consider the history of attitudes to natural order and beauty. The Christian tradition has always emphasized created order, as characterized by Augustine, who claimed with Plato that beauty is reducible to number.[20] So in adapting this traditional emphasis on or-

18. Weir, "Rolston," 260–61.

19. See Rolston, "Celestial Aesthetics," 18–19, on size, complexity, and humanity.

20. Augustine, *On Order*, 2.11.34, 2.15.42. Augustine and Plato stand in the tradition of the Pythagorean "golden section" or "divine proportion," which is approximated by the ratio 8:13. In his *Divina Proportione* (1509), the mathematician Luca Pacioli, close friend of Leonardo da Vinci and Piero della Francesca, linked the ratio to the Trinity and to God's incomprehensibility, in that it cannot be expressed exactly as a finite number. Extensive empirical studies appear to demonstrate that people prefer

der, I am saying nothing new. But created order has meant different things to different thinkers, and Ruskin's view of order and beauty takes its place in a long history of diverse thought on nature. After all, the injunction to "follow nature" was issued by the neoclassicist long before it was adopted by the Romantic, and long after it had been a way of life for many before them both.[21] Ruskin became convinced of the need to "follow nature" and of the revelatory power of natural beauty in a way that has not always been accepted—namely, by contemplating the precipitous scenery of the valley of Chamonix in the French Alps (2:363). Such appreciation of mountain beauty was not common until the eighteenth century; moreover, beauty is denied to mountains by certain classical views of order. But notwithstanding these views, the natural order displayed in mountains and other natural landscapes demands a special appreciation.

In contrast to Ruskin's sense of mountain beauty is Thomas Burnet's seventeenth century cosmogony, *Sacred Theory of the Earth*. Burnet was a clergyman from Yorkshire who served as clerk of the closet to William III until he fell out of favor due to his allegorical understanding of the fall.[22] In his *Sacred Theory*, Burnet presented a spiritualized geology that lamented the lack of geometric order in Ruskin's beloved Alps. He believed that God had, in line with classical notions of order, designed the earth "in Measure and Proportion by the Line and by the Plummet."[23] Mountains, however, were traditionally seen by many theologians at this time as a curse, resulting either from Adam's sin or the earth's receiving of Abel's blood.[24] Similarly, Augustine had speculated that the original earth consisted of mostly flat plains, allowing subterranean springs to water the earth rather than rain (cf. Gen 2:5–6).[25] This arrangement left rugged mountains and valleys to be carved out later after the fall of humanity, perhaps in part by the Noahic flood. In addition to Augustine's speculation, Isaiah 40:3–5 speaks of all mountains being lowered and all valleys raised to form a plain. This leveling activity is associated with the revealing of God's glory (or salvation in Luke 3:4–6). Such theology could easily earn mountains the labels of "Nature's shames and Ills" or "Warts, Wens, Blisters," and "'Imposthumes' upon the

---

proportions approximating the golden section in both nature and art. But such proportion may not be as relevant to irregular natural forms such as mountains and coastlines. See Osborne, "Golden Section," n.p.

21. Nicolson, *Mountain Gloom*, 22, notes this widespread injunction to follow nature.

22. Thorne and Collocot, "Burnet," 198–99.

23. Burnet, *Sacred Theory*, 1:125, 137–38.

24. Nicolson, *Mountain Gloom*, 82–83, cites these theological explanations of topography.

25. Augustine, *Literal Meaning* 5.25.

otherwise fair face of Nature."[26] With such doctrinal history and the authority of Augustine behind him, Burnet concluded not surprisingly that mountains are "the ruins of a broken world."[27]

Beyond such theological reflections, mountains also posed a very real threat to survival and basic human needs. Not only did mountainous regions provide refuge for bandits and dangerous animals, they were also largely inaccessible and unsuitable for cultivation or civilization. Mountains and wilderness, as a realm beyond the structures of society, thus came to symbolize chaos and evil.[28] Mountains also became literary symbols of the socially or politically lofty and corrupt (4:427; cf. Isa 2:12–17).

Marjorie Nicolson points out how such negative symbolism could easily suppress any sense of beauty in mountains or wilderness. Yet from a theological standpoint the matter is a bit more complex than Nicolson allows in her emphasis on a culturally determined, negative view of mountains. Notwithstanding our modern acceptance of mountain beauty, the negative symbolisms of the past are also quite appropriate to the extent that natural evil pervades all of life, even the beautiful parts. Alongside the beautiful in nature, within the category of the sublime, there is room for repulsion as well as attraction. The natural sublime intertwines beauty with evil and danger, and Greek poetry understands nature in just this way.[29] Thus we should not entirely separate negative and positive views of nature along historical and cultural lines as Nicolson does. We can hold together in appropriate tension the good and bad in nature, the overlapping beautiful and sublime, if we understand creation as a divine work of art integrating both good and evil.

Hebraic poetry evokes this intermingled outlook on nature by treating the destructive sublime along with hints of appreciation for beautiful hills and mountains. Isaiah and the Psalmists have the mountains bursting into song, perhaps through their beauty and fruitfulness (Isa 44:23; 55:12; Ps 98:8; Dan 11:45). The Old Testament writers value the mountains of Lebanon especially as a water source and habitat for trees and wild animals (2 Kgs 19:23; Ps 104:10–13, 16–18; Song 4:15; Jer 22:6). Still, we must look further than the Bible for an explanation of our contemporary sense of natural beauty. The biblical writers are far from Romantic nature worship,

---

26. Nicolson, *Mountain Gloom*, 2, lists these unattributed epithets for mountains.

27. Burnet, *Sacred Theory*, 1:144.

28. Porteous, *Environmental Aesthetics*, 54, notes this connection between wilderness and social chaos.

29. See Nicolson, *Mountain Gloom*, 39, on culturally determined views and the Greek understanding of nature.

and it is difficult to see how the modern sense of mountain beauty could have emerged out of negative prevailing attitudes such as those of Burnet.

In addition to his concerns about mountains, Burnet also wished for more order in the location of stars. At the time, he could not see or conceive of spiral galaxies with their strange orderliness. But despite nature's apparent disorder, its vastness gave Burnet a pleasurable feeling: mountains, stars, and ocean still demonstrated the greatness of nature and therefore of God.[30] Burnet's classical aesthetic, however, demanded a distinction between vastness and a more tightly-ordered, geometric beauty.[31] Burnet's judgments lay not only in his theology and classical aesthetic but in another questionable distinction between "two Sorts of Opinions in all Men, *Inclination-opinions*, and *Reason'd-opinions*; Opinions that grow upon Men's Complexions, and Opinions that are the results of their Reason."[32] Beauty belonged to the latter category of reason, while any pleasant feelings for vast nature belonged to the former category of emotion. If Burnet had held a less Cartesian epistemology that could integrate reason and emotion, he might have given beauty further admission into the vast reaches of nature. But tradition's curbing of aesthetic experience is not unique to Burnet's ideological constraints. Petrarch in 1335 also recounted an aesthetic experience of Mount Ventoux, although his appreciation of the mountain scenery was curtailed by the redoubtable Augustine when Petrarch remembered the saint's warning against too much admiration for things in the world.[33] But by the early eighteenth century, the Earl of Shaftesbury had begun to warn his readers of classical tradition's ability to squelch legitimate, God-given feeling toward nature.[34]

The leading factor in this shift from a classical to a Romantic aesthetic may well have been seventeenth century science. Galileo's astronomy forced theologians to reckon with a larger universe that did not conform to classical ideals of order.[35] Thus the Cambridge Platonist Henry More began to praise irregularity and diversity as consonant with the doctrine of creation.[36] Scientists, or "physicotheologists," marveled at their new knowledge of a vast and only partially comprehensible universe, which, with the development of microscopes, also now encompassed the infinitesimally small. This

30. See Burnet, *Sacred Theory*, 1:129, 309.

31. Nicolson, *Mountain Gloom*, 215, suggests this point about Burnet's aesthetic.

32. Burnet, *Sacred Theory*, 1:292.

33. Petrarca, "To Dionigi," 177–78.

34. Shaftesbury, *Moralists*, 61–62, 100.

35. Nicolson, *Mountain Gloom*, 299, emphasizes this influence of Galileo and seventeenth-century science.

36. See More, *Divine dialogues*, 2:146.

philosophic wonder at a vast cosmos spilled over into aesthetic appreciation, which the poets of this new science also transferred to vast objects on
the earth: "the greatness of God, reflected in 'the sightless realms of space'
and 'the planetary way,' they found again in 'the mighty prospects . . . the
mountain's brow, the long-extended wood, Or the rude rock that threatens
o'er the flood.'"[37] Moreover, Isaac Newton described natural laws that for the
first time encouraged theorists to seek complex principles of order *in* nature
itself rather than in more abstract and a priori mathematical theorems.[38] In
addition to these scientific developments, Nicolson mentions the possibility
that Eastern philosophy contributed to the development of a Romantic aesthetic through emphasis on the Tao of nature.[39] But this Eastern influence
seems unlikely and, in any case, insignificant compared to the pervasive
cultural influence of science. Prior to this scientific explosion, neoclassicists
may have acknowledged a "grace beyond the reach of art," or a divine order
outside their own categories of order.[40] But even so, John Dryden noted a
decisive change in thought: "Is it not evident in these last hundred years
(when the study of philosophy has been the business of all the Virtuosi in
Christendom) that almost a new Nature has been revealed to us?"[41] A science of sublimity now inspired the Pre-Romantic English poets.[42]

Burnet stands in this scientific tradition of seeing nature as sublime but
not necessarily beautiful. But the science of sublimity had also prepared the
way for a new aesthetic of the naturally beautiful. In reaction to Burnet, and
possibly influenced by Locke, Richard Bentley was perhaps the first to give
voice to the new aesthetic in terms of beauty rather than vastness or sublimity.[43] Bentley was an English classical scholar, apologist, and Master of Trinity
College, Cambridge.[44] His observations mark the beginning of a new stage
in aesthetic development—a move from vast nature as merely sublime, as
Burnet had seen it, to nature as sublime *and* beautiful. Criticizing the artificial
imposition of a classical aesthetic upon nature, Bentley states,

37. Nicolson, *Mountain Gloom*, 143, 331, quotes unnamed eighteenth-century
poets.

38. See ibid., 272.

39. Ibid., 24.

40. Ibid., 317.

41. Dryden, *Belles Lettres*, 19.

42. Nicolson, *Mountain Gloom*, 340, notes how science influenced the poets' ideas
on sublimity.

43. Nicolson, ibid., 262–63, discusses Bentley's contribution.

44. Cross and Livingstone, "Bentley," 191.

> There is no Universal Reason that a Figure by us called Regular, which hath equal Sides and Angles, is absolutely more beautiful than any irregular one. . . . We ought not then to believe that the banks of the Ocean are *really* deformed, because they have not the form of a regular pyramid; nor that the mountains are out of shape, because they were not exact pyramids or cones; nor that the stars are unskilfully placed, because they are not all situated at uniform distance. . . . This objected Deformity is in our Imaginations only, and not really in the things themselves.[45]

This is also the view of Ruskin, who holds that there is "scarcely anything in pure, undiseased nature like positive deformity, but only degrees of beauty, or such slight and rare points of permitted contrast as may render all around them more valuable by their opposition" (1:111). In light of this new perspective on nature, people could now recognize that mountain formations are in no way deformed, even if they might appear at first quite disordered. Indeed, the more people recognized natural order going on its mysterious way, indifferent to their preconceived notions of order, the more mountains could even be seen as presenting beautiful pictures incidentally. After all, natural order seems in no way obliged to provide aesthetic opportunities; so beautiful landscapes could now be understood as perceptually framed by a subject, and for that reason, their beauty could be quite extraneous to nature's functions.[46] In this way, nature's ordered indifference opens up an understanding of (perceptual) natural beauty as conceptually distinct from the sublime, as well as from the naturally good, fitting, or useful.

Such an understanding of beauty places new emphasis on the subject's perception; nonetheless, Ruskin does not relegate order or beauty to the subjective realm. He points out that although mountains appear jarring in form, especially due to their great size and height, their curvature when measured is very similar to that of animal and plant forms (4:224–27, 240). This similarity suggests continuity between geophysical and biological order. And along with this continuity comes the recognition that natural order is not an immutable and atemporal Platonic form; rather, natural order, like music, plays out through time in processes such as mountain formation. Thus nature's lack of spatial and temporal fixity in no way implies disorder.[47]

Natural order is also compatible with certain levels of disorder and indeterminacy, which contribute aesthetically to nature's diversity and wildness.

45. Bentley, *Folly*, 273.

46. Tyrwhitt, *Natural Beauty*, 20, suggests this point about nature being unobliged to offer us beautiful pictures.

47. Begbie, *Voicing Creation's Praise*, 226, suggests the link between time, music, and order. See Milbank, Pickstock, and Ward, "Suspending the Material," 19.

This is especially true in geological and meteorological processes, which are governed by chance to a greater extent than physical and chemical process-es.[48] A meteorological example of chaos and order in concert is the snowflake. All snowflakes form according to a hexagonal pattern that can be subdivided into about a hundred different sub-patterns. At the chemical level, water molecules crystallize into snow according to strict order. Yet no two snowflakes are the same, because at the meteorological level, molecules collide randomly at various temperatures, producing an infinite variation of structure within preset limits. In the formation of mountains too, there are many variables resulting in diverse forms, and yet there are constants in the geophysical forces that uplift and erode land. This mixture of constants and variables suggests that "simple beauty" or "beautiful simplicity" cannot produce the most interesting or the most beautiful natural forms. Only complexity, spontaneity, and broken symmetries can give rise to the inimitable beauty of nature.[49] This scientifically informed view of natural order accommodates Romantic intuitions about natural beauty and wildness, even if science does not factor prominently into Romantic accounts of beauty.

Thus Ruskin commits himself rightly to natural order, to *logos* or divine wisdom, "submissively acknowledging the great laws by which the earth and all that it bears are ruled throughout their being."[50] In this respect, Ruskin agrees with Augustine, for whom order is central to God's revelation through beauty. In Augustine's aesthetic, order belongs to God primordially and there-fore functions as an image of God that is manifested in created beauty.[51] But Ruskin also leaves room for the artistic element in natural beauty, noting that "love of order" is not "love of art." He acknowledges that order is necessary to art just as time is necessary to music, but some types of order have nothing to do with art, like routine and punctuality, "an ordered room, or a skilled piece of manufacture." "Rules and models" result in manufacture not art, but the merit of art "consists in its saying new and different things" or the same things in different ways.[52] Ruskin makes these statements in reference to architecture, but I extend their application to his typology of natural beauty: Ruskin allows natural beauty also to say new and different things through God's cre-

48. Rolston, "Celestial Aesthetics," 9, discusses this relationship between wildness and science.

49. Rolston, ibid., 10–11, makes this contrast between "simple" beauty and natural beauty's interesting, complex, and spontaneous forms.

50. Ruskin, *Sea Stories*, 155. Wheeler, *Ruskin's God*, 33, links Ruskin's view of natural order to the wisdom personified in Proverbs 8:27–30.

51. God's "traces appear in creation in a way that is fitting. In that supreme triad is the source of all things, and the most perfect beauty" (Augustine, *On the Trinity* 6.12).

52. Ruskin, *Sea Stories*, 170–72.

ative production and our creative reception of beauty. In other words, beauty is able to function within the context of creation's art. Natural beauty can say different things through its different configurations of order, such that a stag, a mountain, and a daffodil will display somewhat different natural orders and therefore communicate differently as art.

Ruskin's artistic outlook on creation, however, stands in marked contrast to Rolston's. Overlooking the artistic communication of nature, Rolston not only links beauty to scientific complexity, he also suggests that our aesthetic appreciation of nature *depends* upon our scientific knowledge of this order and complexity.[53] Surely order and complexity contribute to beauty, and scientific advances such as those of the seventeenth century can help awaken an aesthetic sense toward nature. But the natural sciences by themselves do not provide a sufficient explanation for our experience of natural beauty. We do not need to become scientists, conscious of nature's every mechanism, in order to appreciate beautiful mangrove islands set above translucent waters. Rather, natural beauty appeals to our aesthetic rationality more than our discursive reason, and it excites an admiration of the Creator above and beyond our appreciation of intricate mechanisms—mechanisms that may or may not in themselves be beautiful.[54] In this respect, Ruskin's artistic approach to nature fairs better than Rolston's reduction of natural beauty to science; for, as George MacDonald notes, natural beauty is "the impassioned expression, for the sake of which the science of God has thought and laboured."[55] Rolston's scientific approach also suggests an overly objective understanding of beauty—one that overlooks the style of the divine artist in favor of mechanism, and minimizes the felt quality of the percept in favor of objective order. Rolston also blurs the distinction between beauty and intricacy, and this blurring eventuates in his calling the ugly, but elaborate, aspects of nature "beautiful."[56]

But even Ruskin is nearly led into a similar belittling of art at the feet of nature, leaving his view of order in relation to art still lacking. Due to his strong commitment to strictly natural order (meaning for him order that is observable in and derivable from nature), he adopts the antithesis of the classical aesthetic. In the name of "obedience to nature," he rejects classical architecture in favor of the Gothic.[57] Ruskin may be correct in highlighting

53. Rolston, "Aesthetic Appreciation," 374–86.

54. Tyrwhitt, *Natural Beauty*, 33, points out that our aesthetic appreciation involves more than appreciation of design.

55. MacDonald, *Dish of Orts*, 258–59.

56. Rolston, "Swamps," 584–97.

57. Ruskin, *Sea Stories*, 173.

the merits of the Gothic, but he pushes the point too far. There is room for beauty in the geometrically ordered as well as in the freer natural order, and there is revelatory potential in both. For surely God can speak in different ways through different historic styles, communicating his stability in the Romanesque columns and arches or his freedom and extravagance in the Gothic vaults and spires.[58]

Like architecture, the natural world must be allowed a similar freedom of expression as a divine work of art. Even mountains, once symbols of evil, can communicate something about God through the beauty of their free natural order. This is not to say that all natural order is beautiful, or that no beauty-skills are required to see mountainous landscapes as ordered beauty rather than merely sublime or threatening. And mountains need not be either wholly positive or wholly negative aspects of creation. In their size, height, and danger they can be destructively sublime as easily as they are beautiful. Along with forests, they can also be nature's beautiful cathedrals, while manmade cathedrals can be seen as variations on their structure (cf. 4:425). But there is still a common element in the human experience of natural beauty that people symbolize and partly conceptualize in different ways. Given this common experience, it is not surprising that many ancient cultures besides Israel symbolize the meeting place between the human and divine by a sacred mountain (manmade in the case of the ziggurat), the ascent of which is an ascent toward the divine.[59] Indeed our experience of natural beauty suggests that God "does not live in temples built by hands" (Acts 17:24, NIV). And if God's dwelling place cannot be thus confined, neither can his creation of beauty be constrained by human conceptions of order. If the earth itself is his temple "with its font of waters, and mountain pillars, and vaults of clouds" (5:114), then no less than sacred architecture, the earth in its ordered beauty also speaks of God.

Reformulating Ruskin's Types Dealing with Order

With special relevance to natural order, Paul Tillich draws attention to "the inexhaustible richness" of objects in "sober, objective, quasi-scientifically observed reality." Tillich holds that this rich givenness of reality when expressed in art reveals ultimate reality even without displaying an overt numinousness.[60] Similarly, when artists, such as Dutch landscape painters,

---

58. See D. Brown, *Enchantment*, 153, on the differing messages of the Gothic and the Romanesque.

59. Eliade, *Images and Symbols*, 42–43, notes this prevalent symbolism of mountains.

60. Tillich, "Art and Ultimate Reality," 147.

celebrate the beauty of objects as they are, their work can be read as an affirmation of God's providential care for the world.[61] These observations regarding art also apply fittingly to Ruskin's locus of revelation in natural beauty, because beauty manifests ultimate reality as we observe soberly "the inexhaustible richness" of material order. This richness of order is a matter of perceiving the transcendent depth of objects through their immanent form, such that, for Jacques Maritain, like Augustine, ordered forms are "a vestige or ray of the creative Intelligence imprinted at the heart of created being."[62] This understanding of ordered form is also conducive to Ruskin's typology, since he is seeking the "vestige or ray of the creative Intelligence imprinted" in beautiful floes or moors, sand dollars or golden trout. Of course, non-religious people might deny such creative intelligence, and interpret beautiful order only in terms of the aesthetic richness of an ordered cosmos. But theists can experience beautiful order as the revelation of God's rich and ordered inner life, which also upholds and interacts closely with creation. And by entering further into a Christian epistemic vision, Christians can make sense of beautiful order in terms of the harmonious interrelation and interdependency of the divine persons. Thus, although beauty does not reveal threefoldness, it can reflect God's triune harmony within himself and toward creation.

Ruskin discusses order under the headings of no less than five separate types or qualities displayed in natural beauty: unity, symmetry, moderation, purity, and infinity. But despite Ruskin's categories, we seem to experience the first three of these qualities in nature not so much individually, but more generally and less conceptually in terms of a complex natural order.[63] Therefore, in contrast to Ruskin, I maintain that unity, symmetry, and moderation do not reveal distinctly different aspects of God so much as they bring to light the harmony of the divine nature and its implications in slightly different ways. So in my revising of Ruskin I subsume these three qualities under the broader heading of natural order. Purity and infinity, however, though Ruskin relates them to order, are experienced somewhat differently, and while both may be attributable to natural order, neither is experienced in terms of order. Therefore, they both function better as separate types. But

---

61. See D. Brown, *Enchantment*, 112, on this reading of landscape painters.

62. Maritain expresses the idea in terms of *splendor formae*: "that is to say, the principle which constitutes the proper perfection of all that is . . . the ontological secret that they bear within them, their spiritual being, their operating mystery" (*Art and Scholasticism*, 24–25).

63. But this experience need not be conceptualized exactly as I have conceptualized natural order, for example, by someone with no scientific knowledge.

first I will consider Ruskin's three types that I do believe are reducible to natural order: unity, symmetry, and moderation.

Not all natural order is beautiful, but in the beautiful, all "connection and brotherhood" among elements strike us as both "pleasant and right," reflecting Ruskin's understanding of *unity*: the aspect of order that contributes to beauty by joining various parts (2:92). Without such unity among parts, newness and variety alone cannot produce beauty; for even a kaleidoscope does not produce totally new things, but only ordered re-combinations that must display a certain unity.[64] This unity is present even in the great diversity of natural forms, which do not weary the mind or senses, as do too much change or repetition in human work or leisure. Nature's diverse unities hold our attention, supporting Ruskin's contempt for rigid models in art, and demonstrating that "complexity need not involve the loss of grace, nor richness that of repose."[65]

An example of this natural unity is the central theme uniting many variations, like the basic order of a tree uniting many different species of tree, such that beauty obtains in both similarities and differences among species. Similarly, Ruskin notes the "unity of membership" among parts of the body or notes in a harmony, as well as the "original unity" of objects originating from the same source, such as petals of a flower or branches of a tree. There is also a "sequential unity" in the progression of musical notes in a melody, and a "subjectional unity" among many objects subjected to the same force, such as waves or clouds ordered by the same wind. (2:94–95).

Symmetry also is a kind of unity of parts, although Ruskin distinguishes it from unity, describing symmetry as a separate type of divine justice (2:125 ff). Ruskin was probably eager to find a trace of God's moral nature in creation; nevertheless, the similarity between equal lines or masses and equitable dealings with humankind seems coincidental or superficial at best. Moreover, the God of the Bible seems to deal with human beings in peculiarly unequal ways, lavishing favor with inequality, and suspending his just judgments in ways that pose an inequality between what is deserved and what is received. One might defend Ruskin's link between justice and symmetry by saying that justice excludes mercy: he may be thinking of justice at the most basic level of an eye for an eye. But this exclusion is still somewhat artificial and does not factor extenuating circumstances into the concept of justice, as divine justice surely must. In any event, these complexities seem well beyond the reach of physical symmetry. Given a fuller account of justice, one might suppose that the freedom and complexity of

64. This, however, is in contrast to Ruskin's notion of kaleidoscopes (2:96).

65. Ruskin, *Sea Stories*, 197–98, 205.

natural order could image justice better than a simple, bilateral symmetry. Even so, it seems very difficult to *experience* a sense of justice through order or symmetry. Therefore symmetry as a type, like symmetry as a beauty-property, fits more appropriately within the broader categories of unity and order. Both symmetry and other kinds of unity seem to be experienced in beautiful forms in roughly the same way.

Ruskin describes another aspect of unified order under the heading of *moderation*—that is, the aesthetic moderation of form and color in the beautiful, without which forms become ungraceful, movement violent, and colors glaring in comparison to nature's subtle and almost unnoticeable curves and colors (2:139). This aesthetic moderation forms the unified backdrop that makes peacock feathers and swallowtail butterflies aesthetic extravagances by comparison. Ruskin understands this aesthetic moderation as the type of divine governance by law, bringing into focus another facet of God's ordered relationship with creation. In this relationship, moderation expresses what Ruskin calls divine self-governance: the divine nature that is in no way above God and thus able to constrain him, but that flows freely from his being into the physical and moral order of creation (2:139). Because of this self-governance, God is not capricious or arbitrary but committed to governance through laws flowing from his being. These divine laws are expressed in a natural beauty displaying an ordered and appropriate moderation.

Ruskin believes that this aesthetic moderation also explains the degrees and absences of beauty in creation: he believes that there are absences of beauty for the purpose of highlighting the types by contrast with their absence (2:144). But a better explanation for these absences is that all cannot be equally beautiful simply as the result of an intricate and free created order. Freedom in the created order involves constants working together with variables, and only this arrangement can produce so many diverse and complex natural beauties, carving out braided rivers instead of canals and growing gnarled tree trunks instead of pillars. This natural diversity requires so much freedom that we can rightly wonder at how nature allows for so many beauties without producing more monsters.[66] Yet even the forms that lack beauty are not usually monstrous: they are often odd or interesting. If God takes pleasure in the odd and interesting in nature as well as the beautiful, then an equal distribution of beauty might have proved undesirable by excluding giraffes, dinosaurs, and hippopotami, the delights of all children.

66. Dillard, *Pilgrim*, 133, expresses surprise that nature does not produce more monsters.

Whether we consider this free natural order in terms of unity, sym-metry, or moderation, creation is full of harmonious rapports, both among objects, and between objects and subjects. These rapports include the interrelated orderings of days, months, seasons, and ecological rhythms, as well as the interdependent ordering of elements in beautiful wholes. Elements such as color, pitch, curve, size, and location have an "insepa-rable dependency on each other's being" within a beautiful whole (2:93). This beautiful interdependency as Ruskin notes, often "has no reference to ultimate ends" but "is itself, seemingly, the end of operation to many of the forces of nature" (2:107–8). But this end in nature is also a beginning for religion of a movement toward God: Mircea Eliade notes the wide-spread religious consciousness of sacred natural order—a consciousness of human work, construction, or any form-giving as a *conforming* to "the pre-eminently harmonious organism," the divinely created cosmos.[67] For the religious person, nature's beautiful harmony can be experienced as an expression of God's intimate harmony with creation, as well as God's own inner unity and harmonious life.[68] And just as created harmony is expe-rienced as a proper end, so also this divine harmony has no reference to ultimate ends but is itself the end of all existence. The Christian can then go further in connecting this experience with biblical revelation: the in-terdependency of beauty-constituents (color, pitch, curve, size, location) corresponds to creation's dependency upon God and the interdependency of the divine persons (cf. 2:93). God in essence is harmony, not a terrible monotony, and his eternal harmony overflows into the beautiful through various created mediums, such as sound in the case of music or birdsong.[69] The non-Christian apprehends this divine harmony without being able to relate it to Trinitarian doctrine; so the Christian's perception is privileged in this regard. Yet through the new interrelations that perception brings to the beautiful, both Christian and non-Christian can begin to understand and enter into this divine harmony and presentation of God for us.

67. Eliade, *Myth and Reality*, 32–33.

68. Ruskin understands material unity to typify "divine comprehensiveness," which means God's immanent and all-encompassing relationship with creation, rather than God's own inner being (2:92). But it is difficult to separate God's inner being from his comprehensive relationship with creation, because this relationship is but the outwork-ing of God's inner comprehensiveness of being.

69. Dowden, *Beauty of Nature*, 36, sees music as an overflowing of divine harmony.

Purity: The Type of Spiritual Energy

Ruskin also holds order to be fundamental to another of his types, that of material purity. But purity seems most valuable and plausible as a type when experienced apart from Ruskin's rather technical linking of the idea to order. Ruskin notes how a pure appearance in matter arises from a higher degree of order among particles, and so purity is also a unity or consistency of form. Along with this consistency comes a sense of greater energy in the object, because purity results from a high degree of order and energy among particles. Ruskin gives the examples of crystals as more pure (i.e., highly organized and energized) than rocks, which are also more pure than the random and passive connection of particles in dust or mud. He also describes the more orderly and energized fluid dynamics of "pure" water in deep lakes and flowing waters as opposed to stagnant pools (2:132–33). Ruskin's connection of energy to order is perhaps attributable to his knowledge of the chemical relationship between increased energy and increased molecular organization. Ruskin is also probably indebted to Plato, who in *Parmenides* questions whether there can be a Form of mud.[70]

But although purity does arise from order, it is not readily experienced in terms of order, except perhaps by someone with Ruskin's scientific knowledge. And it is the experience of purity itself, rather than the order from which it arises, that typifies God's spiritual energy. Throughout most of his discussion of purity, Ruskin links the concept somewhat unhelpfully to order. But in the final paragraph, he notes that matter is characterized by its inertia, its lifelessness, but by energizing this inert matter, and thereby purifying it, "we may in some measure spiritualize even matter itself" (2:134). Ruskin is here addressing the religious problem of how matter can relate to spirit. But whereas Plato would answer that we occupy the material and spiritual worlds at once, Ruskin's solution is somewhat different: he sees matter's energy as ultimately a spiritual affair (not unlike Newton's take on gravity). After all, it is God's Spirit that gives life and energy to inert matter (Gen 2:7). Thus energetically *pure* matter produces the greatest sense of *spiritual* energy. Such experience explains the purity of materials described in the heavenly Jerusalem of Revelation 21–22 (cf. Zec 9:16–17). The more that such materials reflect the input of divine or human energy, the more likely they are to be beautiful (2:134).[71] In a similar way, a pure white sheep implies a more energetic animal life than one sitting in the mud, and it is for

---

70. See Plato, *Parmenides*, 130–31.
71. See Ruskin, *Seven Lamps*, 271.

this reason that material *purity* (i.e., whiteness) is used to illustrate the ideal *spiritual* condition of righteousness (2:131–34).

The non-religious person, however, would experience this material purity, not as spiritual, but only as reflecting the cosmic energy that happens to produce many compelling forms. But the religious experience of purity relates to the energy "by which all things live and move, and have their being" (Acts 17:28), and this energy reflects God's self-existent being (2:133). Of course this self-existent energy is inseparable from God's ordered and omnipotent tri-unity; and similarly, pure matter is a function of harmonious ordering of particles. But rather than emphasizing divine harmony, the unique *oneness* of pure forms speaks especially to the indivisibility of the one God.[72]

Infinity

Ruskin's most problematic type dealing with order is infinity, the type of divine incomprehensibility (2:76). He holds that variety and complexity in beautiful forms, though finite, suggests the infinite, because we can imagine a potentially infinite number of variations, combinations, and gradations of curve and color (2:89). This endless possibility for variation might even be a source of frustration for the landscape painter, who might agonize over how exactly to shape and arrange every line and mass in a landscape. As we experience beautiful landscape, perhaps we can intuit potential infinitude insofar as we contemplate how each form might be slightly different than it is, and insofar as we contemplate a simple source from which all variety and complexity derive, or an incomprehensible mind that comprehends the infinite possibilities. But Ruskin's approach here seems too abstract rather than based on our actual perception of beauty, because beauty for us is always composed of particular curves and particular shades. We do not experience beauty by contemplating infinite possibilities, even if infinite possibilities contribute to what beauty is. Infinitude seems to be part of the anatomy rather than the experience of beauty. So even if we do connect infinitude to God in this way, it probably only relates to beauty incidentally. But Ruskin offers a better approach to divine infinitude through experience of the sky, and I return to this idea in the final section.

72. Compare Mark Rothko's use of single colors to express transcendence in the Rothko Chapel.

REPOSE IN THE BEAUTIFUL

In addition to his types relating to order, Ruskin draws attention to a sense of "repose" in our experience of beautiful forms. He understands this reposeful beauty to typify the divine permanence and immutability. Here I concur with Ruskin and indeed go further. I expand upon his notion of repose as a way of grappling with the natural evil in creation's text. For it will not go unnoticed that beautiful order, as it images God, stands in opposition to the entropy of a self-disorganizing creation, in which death, decay, and disaster produce much ugliness. As Ruskin says, "Foulness is painful as the accompaniment of disorder and decay, and always indicative of the withdrawal of divine support" (2:133). In addition to this disorder, there are some forms of natural order that either produce ugliness destructively (e.g., tornados and predation) or are ugly themselves (e.g., some decomposition processes). Still, within this ambivalent creation, natural beauty flourishes wildly. What Ruskin does not consider sufficiently is how beauty is intertwined naturally with ugliness and natural evil. Natural beauty can even be said to pose a stern dialectic between the powerful and destructive on one hand and the delicate and vulnerable on the other: the powerful lion is not more or less beautiful than the elegant gazelle, and so beauty applies equally to the destroyer and the destroyed. Beauty has a certain indifference to life, in that the beautiful forms contributing to one animal's survival lead to another's destruction. This is not to say that destruction itself is beautiful but that the lion's form is beautiful in its strength and motion even as it kills. Beauty is self-destructive and at home with death, and nature is still "red in tooth and claw" despite Ralph Waldo Emerson's belief that "nature never wears a mean appearance."[73] Natural beauty is often hostile or indifferent toward life, yet it still nourishes us aesthetically: it is fully integrated with evil and ugliness, but is still an ordered reality that is profoundly "right" in the world, and can therefore be "read" as opposing evil artistically. In other words, we can read beauty as being in thematic tension with evil and ugliness within creation's artistic text. Through such artistic opposition, beautiful "repose" reveals not only divine permanence amid creation's vicissitudes, but also the hope of a new reposeful order for creation.

In the current order, natural beauty, natural evil, and ugliness often commingle in what might be called the natural sublime, in the sense of that which is powerful or dangerous. But beauty does not equal the sublime; rather, that which is vastly or threateningly sublime is often also beautiful. As Byron observes, "Oh night, / And storm, and blackness, ye are wondrous

73. Tennyson, *In Memoriam*, 1087. Emerson, *Nature*, 22.

strong, / Yet lovely in your strength."[74] An avid reader of Byron, Ruskin understands beauty and the sublime similarly. He observes in the clouds the "passings to and fro of fruitful shower and grateful shade, and all those visions of silver palaces built about the horizon, and voices of moaning winds and threatening thunders, and glories of coloured robe and cloven ray," all of which display in the heavens the commingled beauty and awesomeness of God (4:114). Ruskin also says of the sublime, "with every manifestation of destruction or overwhelming power, there are addressed to the senses such accompanying phenomena of sublime form and sound and colour that the mind instantly traces some *ruling sympathy* that conquers the *apathy of the elements*, and feels through the inanimation of nature the supernatural unity of God" (2:370–71, emphasis mine).

Ruskin allows natural beauty to contrast with the sublime, yet it is beauty that can also partially bridge this contrast, serving as the "ruling sympathy," that if not conquers, at least mitigates, "the apathy of the elements." For if beauty is present in the storm and the deep—symbols and instruments of God's power—and the mountains movable only by God and faith in him, as well as in the lily and the sparrow, then beauty could indeed be a rubric or ruling sympathy. If beauty is a common thread running through the expanses of the galaxies as well as through the ephemeral rainbow and snowflake, then beauty connects human awe before the sublime with our grief before beauty's frailty and evanescence. Human delight in the sublime reflects our delight in unmanageable strength, which is a divine quality for the religious percipient. But beauty's fragility heightens the desire for a similar strength to be applied to the fragile—a longing for the powerfully and incorruptibly delicate. C. S. Lewis captures the idea in the image of heavenly grass that is so substantial as to be painful and unyielding to the feet of those not yet fit for heaven.[75] We can hope for such firmer establishment of beauty, while still enjoying it presently in its frailty. This is not to say that some beauties (e.g., music and sunsets) do not have a proper progression and termination over time, but that beauty is often subject to corruption and destruction.

Beauty as a rubric amid the fragile and the destructive accords well with Ruskin's concept of repose in the beautiful. Repose in material forms is an appearance of rest, calmness, or fixity in "things in which there is vitality or capability of motion actual or imagined." Examples include mountains, boulders, great trees, and "the lulling effect of all mighty sight and sound" (2:114). "Repose demands for its expression the implied capability of its

74. Byron, *Childe Harold's Pilgrimage*, 3.859–61.

75. Lewis, *Great Divorce*, 25.

opposite, Energy" (2:116). For example, a mountain has no actual capability of motion, but if we imagine the great energy required to toss it into the sea, then we sense the opposite magnitude of its repose. Yet some rugged mountains convey such a sense of violence and changeableness in their rockfalls, avalanches, and dizzying heights that they lack repose. Wordsworth says that the smoother and more rounded English mountains give "a sense of stability and permanence that is, to many minds, more grateful" than Alpine extremes.[76] The same could be said for the undulating ridges of the Appalachians with their soft hardwood-covered forms. Repose is also present in calm and quiet scenery in general:

> Not a breath of air
> Ruffles the bosom of this leafy glen.
> From the brook's margin, wide around, the trees
> Are steadfast as the rocks; the brook itself,
> Old as the hills that feed it from afar,
> Doth rather deepen than disturb the calm
> Where all things else are still and motionless.[77]

We experience repose in being led beside still waters and made to lie down in green pastures, thus restoring the soul (Ps 23:1–3).

The non-religious person, however, might experience reposeful beauty only as a human projection upon nature, or perhaps as tied to a sense of nature's intrinsic value. But for Ruskin and religious perception, repose in beautiful forms typifies divine permanence. Reposeful beauty can be experienced as "the 'I am' of the Creator opposed to the 'I become' of all creatures," and this sense of divine permanence is addressed to the human longing for peace and rest: "The universal instinct of repose, / The longing for confirmed tranquillity / . . . The life where hope and memory are as one" (2:113, 117).[78] By addressing our need for tranquility and restoration, repose evokes our "hope and memory," which is to say, our longing for a paradise that was lost or that will be gained. Such longing also characterizes the widespread primal religious belief that the earth and its inhabitants are worn out and require rebirth.[79] Ruskin alludes clearly to this human rebirth or redemption foreshadowed by repose (2:113–14, 117), and this foreshadowing accords with the idea of symbolic revelation as an intimation of a more complete unveiling to come. That is, the symbol implicates both

---

76. Wordsworth, *Guide to the Lakes*, 99.

77. Wordsworth, "Airey-Force Valley," 1–6.

78. Wordsworth, *Excursion*, 3.404–5, 407.

79. Eliade, *Quest*, 106.

time and eternity in disclosing hints of a new creation.[80] In view of this new creation, images of repose can integrate a broader range of meanings, including not just rest but shalom, a dynamic flourishing. Repose can describe not just fixity but continuity of character relating to God's own active stability and continuity—that is, the "central peace, subsisting at the heart / Of endless agitation."[81] Such could be beauty's central message even as it pervades the sublime or less tranquil aspects of creation's "endless agitation." In this sense, to expand upon Ruskin, not just calming beauty but all beauty offers a deeper repose.

But why does this message of repose have power and evoke longing for a redeemed creation if the current natural order is entirely good and beautiful as it is? The message of repose has power only because we perceive it to be somewhat incongruous with nature. As a rubric, reposeful beauty jars against the destructively sublime, against death and decay, and therefore implies a "fallenness" in nature. Human beings experience fallenness insofar as we experience ugliness or suffering, or see it in other creatures. We also sense the fallenness of the world as we experience hope or memory of a better world. But in opposition to this view, one could argue that nature only appears "fallen" for other reasons: natural evils and ugliness could be bound up in the order and material chosen by God to achieve his ends in creating.[82] Nature's fallenness would then have nothing to do with a fall but with human anxiety in the face of nature. And beauty as a "ruling sympathy" would be unnecessary, because there would be no true "apathy of the elements." But this approach belies our human "felt response" to nature—a response that is especially important if creation is indeed art—an activity directed by mind for mind. Moreover, such emotional response to creation's art may in fact be a veridical and indispensable mode of apprehending the value or meaning of some state of affairs, even the world as a whole.[83] And if this is the case, then these emotional responses are actually invaluable components of our epistemic and aesthetic skill sets. So an anthropomorphic sense of "revolt" against nature's evil and ugliness is significant even if we recognize that pain and death can play important ecological roles within nature[84]—that is, even if pain and death are interwoven into creation's art.

80. See Dulles, *Models of Revelation*, 229, 238, 243, on symbolic revelation.

81. Wordsworth, *Excursion*, 4.1140–41. God's nature is not statically inactive but is always at work, interacting with the world and being expressed through the world.

82. Farrer, *Love Almighty*, 71, maintains that evils result not from a fall but from God's aims in creating.

83. See Wynn, "Valuing the World," 97–113.

84. See Wynn, "Natural Theology," 27–42.

Of course, to make further sense of this experience of fallenness, we re-sort to more speculative theological systems.[85] But at the level of experience, creation's evil and ugliness both imply fallenness, suggesting that natural evil and ugliness are somehow linked. The problem of ugliness, however, is not the problem of evil, since evil can be beautiful while the good, ugly. For example, beautiful storm clouds and lightning over a landscape can wreak natural evil, while unsightly lice and grubs can sustain beautiful birds. But we usually experience death, at least to some extent, as an evil, and much ugliness results from death and decay, including the loss of unique, irre-placeable beauties. Given such loss, both evil and ugliness seem to require redemption on an eschatological scale—a redemption encompassing not only humanity but all of creation.[86]

85. If creation is fundamentally artistic, we might expect not only creaturely per-ception to be integral to beauty, but created wills might also be linked to natural order and beauty more closely than is readily apparent. Perhaps human action as well as per-ception is bound up in the fall and redemption of nature, so that nature's fate is tied to our own. So even if a destructive kind of disorder, such as death, preceded the entry of human sin into creation, God might have incorporated that destructiveness into the created order in anticipation of sin, not because of any inherent value in destructive-ness. As Phillip Blond asserts, "nothing is created so that it might die," at least not as a final cause ("Theology before Philosophy," 28). Creation, then, might have always been fallen in the sense of possessing unrealized potential, and humans might have always been prone to sin as a result of evolved selfishness. Yet the fallenness of creation could still be the theological anticipation, if not the historical consequence, of the perpetual fall of humankind as nature's lords and cultivators.

N. P. Williams, *The Fall*, xv, 536–37, notes that the Pauline doctrine of the fall treats evil as a unified principle, encompassing the human, natural, and angelic realms. The idea of a fall of angels, or even the fall of a conscious "world-soul," allows one to attri-bute creation's original fallenness to some will other than God's. Perhaps this idea can hold even if creation's fallenness is anticipatory to the existence of created wills.

86. An eschatological redemption of ugliness, should we envisage it, would not mean that the ugly requires redemption simply because we may regard it with less love or care. Ugliness would require redemption because it is a privation in its own right. Such aes-thetic redemption, however, would not necessitate that all things become equally beauti-ful; rather, it allows for degrees of beauty and elements of plainness. Neither does the redemption of the ugly remove the odd or the interesting from nature: the hippopotamus may require no aesthetic redemption. But some creatures, which we sense *ought* to be beautiful, like human beings, would require redemption. This redemption would not eliminate every sort of transience from nature as improper to beauty or require that every beautiful form become statically permanent in the eschaton, since some beautiful forms, such as music and sunsets, unfold over time. These sorts of beauty have their appropriate progression and termination. In addition, aesthetic redemption would not necessarily re-quire every beautiful form to be present in the eschaton, although it would take seriously the particularity of individual beauties. Continuity of beauty between this world and the next would not necessarily require the continuity of precisely the same atoms of matter, but it would imply the continuity of material existence.

In an effort to come to terms with nature's perplexing mix of beauty and evil, Annie Dillard wrote her Pulitzer Prize winning *Pilgrim at Tinker Creek*. In the book, Dillard, who was later to become a Roman Catholic, takes a Walden-esque journey into the theology of nature.[87] Her work is remarkable for its poetic love of nature's beauties, yet brutal honesty toward nature's atrocities. Both emphases coincide with her affirmation of divine creativity. Dillard suggests a particular way of reading nature: she says that creation confronts us as a mystery in its beauty and violence; the hope is that there is yet something that we have failed to see or see rightly.[88] Dillard highlights the human factor in seeing, as illustrated by those who receive eyesight through surgery after being born blind. The new gift of seeing the world leads some to despair and others to exult in beauty. For the latter, a tree silhouetted against the sky is not just a tree but a "tree with lights in it"—a mysteriously beautiful object. It is this kind of vision for which Dillard believes one ought to live.[89]

The world certainly provides ample opportunity for both kinds of seeing. We can see creation's canvas as either a "Raphael" or a "Rembrandt,"— that is, permeated by grace or by fallenness.[90] But in this ambivalent context, creation's artistic grappling with fallenness suggests a hermeneutic for exegeting nature's vicissitudes. Much as art often does, nature concerns itself with what is, and not with what ought to be, whereas theology attempts to close this gap between *is* and *ought*.[91] Nature plagues us with a sense of what ought to be, yet it remains divine art, because, as Dillard says, "all things live by a generous power and dance to a mighty tune."[92] To read the world in this way one must possess wonder as a prerequisite; for God seems to delight in mystery, and to delight in our delight in mystery. From a perspective of wonder, nature's destructiveness (e.g., natural selection and natural disasters) does not muffle the voice of beauty speaking through creation's complex artistic text. Nonetheless, beauty's voice does not take away from the fact that death and destruction are built into biology: natural selection, left to itself, guarantees the eventual extinction of any particular biotic beauty,[93]

87. Coincidentally, Dillard wrote *Pilgrim at Tinker Creek* very near where both Holmes Rolston and I grew up in the Appalachians of Virginia.

88. See Dillard, *Pilgrim*, 15, 35.

89. Ibid., 37–38, 42.

90. O'Meara, "Aesthetic Dimension," 210, suggests this contrast between Raphael and Rembrandt.

91. Dillard, *Pilgrim*, 209, highlights nature's concern with "is" rather than "ought."

92. Ibid., 69.

93. Provine, "Evolution," 676, makes this observation about natural selection. Schloss suggests that "there is a purpose *for* evolution, but no discernible purpose *in*

for as environments change, species vanish and more fit species take their place. But this is simply the ambivalent and mysterious context from which biotic beauty shines forth. It is a context that does not always promote beauty, goodness, or love as ends, but promotes the opportunity and need for redemption toward such ends.[94] Within this context, one might experience creation's beauty much as one hears a musical fragment and anticipates its resolution.[95] In other words, the religious percipient could read beauty's repose not only as God's permanence, but through that permanence, as the "down payment," the hope of better things to come (cf. 1 Cor 1:22; 5:5; Eph 1:14)—the symbolic reassurance of God's perfection as holding ultimate sway over nature's eventual fulfillment.[96]

In this way, reposeful beauty, as a symbolic and revelatory leitmotiv, countervails artistically against the world's decay and destructiveness. Yet Augustine would seem to nullify this dramatic tension by including decay and destructiveness in the beautiful. He states, "To things falling away, and succeeding, a certain temporal beauty in its kind belongs, so that neither those things that die, or cease to be what they were, degrade or disturb the fashion and appearance and order of the universal creation; as a speech well composed is assuredly beautiful, although its syllables and all sounds rush past as it were in being born and in dying."[97]

This is an acceptable understanding of temporal beauty so far as it goes. Augustine describes how temporality and even *some* natural evil could be incorporated into the artwork of creation so as to render new beauties. But surely we cannot apply this statement universally. It is difficult to see how the rebirthing cycles of creation as it is now could compensate for the suffering, aging, and death of uniquely beautiful individuals, and thereby contribute to the overall greater beauty of creation. The comparison of these cases to a speech is a false analogy: surely suffering and death do "degrade or disturb the . . . appearance and order of the universal creation." As creatures who decay and die ourselves, we apperceive beauty to be not fully at home with our own dissolution or that of the beloved "other." And as percipients who contribute to what beauty and knowledge are as phenomena,

---

evolution" ("Evolutionary Theory," 201).

94. See Schloss, "Evolutionary Theory," 202, on nature's need of redemption toward such ends.

95. See Wynn, "Rolston's Footsteps," 59.

96. In Harrison's understanding of Augustine, "love or anticipation of the future in the present transforms present reality into a symbol or sacrament of future glory: loved and regarded in such a way the world is transformed into a world of forms which bear the traces of God's form" (*Beauty and Revelation*, 187).

97. Augustine, *Nature of Good* 8.

this apperception should not be rationalized as mere neurosis or thrown out of court. Though we can appreciate a Romantic artistry or "beauty" in evanescence, we are not quite convinced that it tells beauty's full story. Rather, beauty, through contrast with the world's harsh realities, speaks of fallenness. And through our unfulfilled longing, beauty points toward a redemption. Beauty offers a certain repose amid transience, and looks beyond transience toward the divine permanence. Here again Ruskin's typological approach to beauty suggests a better way forward. Beauty as a rubric allows us still to read the thread of God's perfection running through a dissonant and unstable tapestry. It becomes the unifying element in creation's drama, offering its more peaceable rationality.[98] This outlook contrasts with Augustine's, perhaps because, according to Carol Harrison, Augustine, unlike the earlier church Fathers, nowhere attributes fallenness explicitly to creation but only to human beings.[99]

But Augustine's attempt to incorporate decay and suffering fully into the goodness and beauty of creation is in the end only to diminish beauty. In this respect, Shaftesbury's solution is also unacceptable:

> The scaly serpents, the savage beasts, and poisonous insects, how terrible soever, or how contrary to human nature, are beauteous in themselves, and fit to raise our thoughts in admiration of that divine wisdom, so far superior to our short views. Unable to declare the use or service of all things in this universe, we are yet assured of the perfection of all, and of the justice of that economy to which all things are subservient, and in respect of which things seemingly deformed are amiable, disorder becomes regular, corruption wholesome, and poisons . . . prove healing and beneficial.[100]

Even if natural order contains disorder, true corruption is rarely wholesome, and we are not "assured of the [present] perfection of all," even though we are assured of God's justice. Shaftebury's response to natural evil and ugliness is in effect to deny their existence. Similarly, Rolston argues that science helps us appreciate the beauty in death and ugliness as part of natural processes. These processes may be the workings of divine art, and surely Rolston is correct insofar as aesthetics is much broader than my

98. Niebuhr, *Meaning of Revelation*, 109–10, sees revelation as unifying one's personal drama.

99. Harrison, *Beauty and Revelation*, 123–24. Nevertheless, Augustine's own statements about prickly or poisonous plants and animals complicate the matter by suggesting a fallen earth, at least in the way that it interacts with humankind. See *On Genesis* 1.19, and *Literal Meaning* 3.24, 3.27–28.

100. Shaftesbury, *Moralists*, 200.

own category of perceptual beauty. But even if science helps us appreciate the ecological complexities of a swamp as much as Rolston (who holds that "Thoreau in his swampy sanctuaries was nearer the truth than Linnaeus tramping his wetland hells"), we must acknowledge still that forbidding terrain is indifferent to human life.[101] In a similar way, nature's corruptibility does not always cater to our sense of beauty.

Nonetheless, beauty in nature does sometimes arise in the context of decay, as in the case of the brilliant colors of dying autumn leaves. But this is a transient effect and a pledge toward the renewed life and color of spring. One might also argue that autumn foliage is not decay properly speaking but a culmination of the nature of leaves, upon which true decay then follows. Of course the nature of plants allows uniquely for decay in a way that animal life does not, so that a bouquet of roses can progress appropriately into a dried floral swag. Still, we might find ourselves valuing a rose precisely *because* its petals are about to drop. Often this is not to value a lack of repose but, paradoxically, to wish for repose: we wish that roses could always be as beautiful as they are just before they fall. Or we wish that a tumbling petal could be slowed or suspended in time, and that our enjoyment of the moment could be prolonged without satiety. In this case, the wish for repose is a wish to stabilize the existing good. So in this sense, repose can apply to change and motion, and in no way undervalues the present or the temporary, but wishes to experience them more deeply. Repose does not require roses assume only one static form that is supposedly most beautiful. Repose only requires that we value the unique form for its own sake and not because it is about to be lost. On the other hand, if we value only the rose's transience and not the rose itself, this is not to value beauty. It is instead perhaps a Romantic melancholy that loses the form of the rose amid feeling for its loss.

In contrast with plant life, the wrinkled and age-weathered human form can exude a certain charm, though never quite the beauty of youth. The repose of Mother Theresa's visage is akin to reposeful beauty, but resides more appropriately in the convergence of wisdom, virtue, and peaceableness, as suggested by the deep but peaceful lines of her face. And distinct from aging bodies, mountains form by erosion, such that their "decay is sculpture";[102] yet this is not decay on the same order as it affects organisms, which possess the breath of life. The erosion of mountains, rather than being decay in a strict sense, is wrought by the energy of natural forces that work for both good and ill.

---

101. Rolston, "Swamps," 597.
102. Tyrwhitt, *Natural Beauty*, 142.

These cases do not require decay to be a central theme of beauty or ideal creation, even if the way that creation deals with decay is a theme of divine art. And similarly, though God chooses mercifully and artfully to raise compassion out of suffering and courage out of violence, these virtues do not quite seem to compensate for the original fact of evil. For there is still much tragedy and potentially gratuitous suffering in creation, and we do not know that what God achieves through evil is better than what he could achieve through other means. Whatever he does achieve through evil is made possible by his prescient accommodation to it—his artful interweaving of its dissonant themes.[103] Otherwise evil becomes integral to God's actions; he becomes dependent upon it to achieve the greatest good. Although God did achieve redemption through the evil of the cross, this was a response to evil already at work in the world and not necessarily an indication of God's unconditionally preferred means. Thus, there is no reason to see natural beauty as somehow conformed inherently and honorably to the cross as Rolston does.[104] Rather, it was Christ who by suffering conformed himself to the cruciform nature of the world. Cruciform elements arise in natural beauty as God addresses evil, but why should natural beauty not be liberated from these cruciform elements even as Christ's glorified body transformed the cross's deformities?[105] Despite fallenness, the earth is "no where unembellished by some trace / Of that first paradise"—"that cheer and charm of earth's past prime," which beauty anticipates renewed.[106] But it is the corrupt element of creation that God enters into and vanquishes through Christ's incarnation and suffering. Christ fully experienced ugliness and took the full brunt of evil and disorder,[107] but he did not thereby render evil, disorder, and ugliness equivalent to the good and the beautiful; rather, he achieved the victory over them through which beauty and goodness could reissue in resurrection and new creation.

Given evil and ugliness, there is truth in the assessment that our experience of the world is to some degree an experience of godlessness, even

---

103. See the interweaving of dissonant music in Tolkien's creation myth, *The Silmarillion*, 4–5.

104. Rolston, "Pasqueflower," 6–16. It is worth noting with Cramp, "Nature Redeemed," 124, that far from the crucifixion fitting in seamlessly with natural order, it was marked by a subversion of natural order—night replacing day.

105. Christ's resurrected body may be scarred, but this does not take away from the contrast between a glorified body and a crucified one.

106. Wordsworth, Fourteen-Book *Prelude*, 3.111–12; Hopkins, "Sea and Skylark," 68.

107. Begbie, *Voicing Creation's Praise*, 173–75, suggests Christ's entering into, fully experiencing, and vanquishing corruption.

if God in Christ has partaken of that godlessness.[108] Just as much as there is a *splendor formae*, there is also a ubiquitous stigma upon the world, the stigma of privation or non-being.[109] In fusing this stigma with repose, even Wordsworth sounds too much like Shaftesbury and Augustine:

> Tumult and peace, the darkness and the light—
> Were all like workings of one mind, the features
> Of the same face, blossoms upon one tree;
> Characters of the great Apocalypse,
> The types and symbols of Eternity[110]

But what if tumult and darkness are not "types and symbols of Eternity" but primarily of evil, sin, chaos—the absence of God? Even so far as tumult and darkness can symbolize God, they connote his mystery and absence rather than his presence, and his presence in veiled wrath rather than in revealed benevolence. And this typology could extend into the biotic world: in his later writings Ruskin observes that the lamb and the crocodile may indeed share a common ancestry; nevertheless, lambs and crocodiles could be contrasting symbols "of destruction or redemption, and, in the most literal sense, "Words" of God." Our admiration of the crocodile and tyrannosaurus resembles our admiration of violent and dangerous men, and the spider in its web-spinning is a cunning villain. After all, no dramatic plot succeeds without a villain that demands our respect and captures our imagination. These villainous creatures, says Ruskin, are intended to refer to the human moral intelligence and perception.[111] Through such reference they become "myths of the betrayal and the redemption, as the Spirit which moved on the face of the wide first waters, taught them to the heathen world."[112] If nature can teach religious perception in this way, then our negative feelings toward the wasteful destruction of nature are not entirely misguided or in need of suppression. Otherwise we find ourselves in the odd situation in which our emotions toward creation belie what we claim to know about creation. But our protest against destruction is as much a part of creation as the destruction itself and demands no less explanation. What is more, our protest arises out of a human perception that originates in God—the Being who judges all evil and ugliness to be essentially states of non-being.[113] Thus we can read

108. Bauerschmidt, "Aesthetics," 211, describes the world as godlessness and Christ's entering into godlessness.

109. Tillich, *Systematic Theology*, 1:129, speaks of the stigma of non-being.

110. Wordsworth, Fourteen-Book *Prelude*, 6.636–40.

111. Ruskin, *Queen of the Air*, 358–59, 378.

112. Ruskin, *Deucalion*, 98–99.

113. Haught, "God and Evolution," 710, links evil with non-being, and describes

evil and ugliness as endemic to the culture of nature yet as coexisting in tension with the culture of a benevolent God and the peaceableness of his kingdom. This appeal to the kingdom through symbolism in nature is no theodicy, for it does not justify God's ways; nonetheless, it provides a theological context for evil and ugliness within natural revelation. It harmonizes the world's "storied identity" with the character of God.[114]

Within this storied (i.e., narratively mediated) context, beauty is better left, in one sense, indifferent to human woe. Novelist Gloria Naylor is thus justified in her observation: "The sunsets don't give a damn. They were as heartbreaking in their beauty illuminating the bleached skulls of the killing fields of Cambodia as they were reddening the sails of Newport yachts. The stars came out just as brilliantly on the ruins of a bombed church in Birmingham, Alabama, as they did for night skiers on the pristine mountaintops of Denver, Colorado."[115] But Naylor is only right at one level, because there are two facets to beauty's repose, one deeper than the other. Beauty maintains its repose through indifference, yet in its indifference is no less revelatory. It is this deeper, revelatory element that Ruskin highlights and that plays out eschatologically. Without beauty's deeper message—that is, if God did not exist or had not invested beauty with transcendent value—we would be right to rebel against beauty's indifference; for then beauty would be utterly meaningless or even a mockery in the face of suffering. But we are also right, for that matter, to rebel against Augustine and Shaftesbury, or Henry More's God as the great Dramatist who produces a "Tragick Comedy," or Philipp Otto Runge who sees the harshness and love in the world as both having their source in God, or anyone else who dissolves evil and ugliness into the beautiful, thus making the whole world unsavory.[116] The savor of divine perfection is best preserved by a separate and indifferent beauty. Beauty retains its integrity as beauty whether or not it is attended by suffering, and in its aloofness it highlights creation's need for redemption. But natural beauty ceases to be indifferent, inasmuch as we experience it condemning evil through its aloofness, or mourning fallenness through its wasteful self-dissolutions. Natural beauty amid evil manifests an artistic style that, in Tillich's words, "shows ultimate reality by judging existing

---

our protest against evil as an aspect of creation needing explanation.

114. "Storied identity" is Wynn's phrase, in *Faith and Place*, 249.

115. Naylor, *More Reflections*, 10. One might object that Naylor merely personifies beauty without cause. But she might be suggesting that if God really existed, he would withdraw incongruous beauty out of dismay at human suffering, as he darkened the sky at Christ's crucifixion.

116. More, *Divine dialogues*, 2:147. See Runge, "Letter," 263.

reality."[117] One might argue that this sense of beauty's judging or condemning is a defect in our experience,[118] but this conclusion implies that humanity is not fallen. On the contrary, it is reasonable to sense our own lack in comparison to beautiful objects that are less corrupted and less corruptible than ourselves: thankfully, sage and heather in bloom are less corruptible and do not suffer as we do. Yet our measure of suffering is also the measure of our potential glory, for we sense too well what we are not, but could be. Beauty can seem indifferent, then, because it stands over us in judgment; but, like God, it also stands over us in hope. There is a sense in which God, like beauty, is indifferent to our suffering, in that he is eternal and incorruptible happiness. But he has also chosen to create and to relate to creatures, for whom he manifests a savor of himself in the beautiful.

Thus, it is actually a comfort that the springtime leaf and blossom do not stoop to weep for us, that beauty does not wallow with us in our misery; for therein is hope that we shall attain to such repose. We do well to accept that nature in her purposes is indifferent to our emotion, because this recognition grounds us in a larger reality more so than the weak sympathy of our fellows.[119] Nature's beauty can comfort us even in the midst of overwhelming personal difficulties, as Wordsworth experienced through the Somersetshire landscape after a five-year emotional crisis.[120] Even amid such connection with the landscape, beauty speaks to us through its aloofness, says Joan Chittister:

> In the midst of struggle, in the depths of darkness, in the throes of ugliness, beauty brings with it a realization that the best in life is, whatever the cost, really possible.... Whatever the dullness of a world stupefied by the mediocre, in the end beauty is able, by penetrating our own souls, to penetrate the ugliness of a world awash in the cheap, the tawdry, the imitative, the excessive and the cruel.... It shouts to us always, "More, There is more."[121]

Natural beauty in its contrast with the mundane proclaims the transcendent and offers hope—as, for instance, through the signal flare that the diurnal fire kindles once or twice daily—an incongruous display of light and color in the

---

117. Tillich, "Art and Ultimate Reality," 147, gives Daumier's *The Butcher* as an example of this artistic style. The painting focuses on a butcher's expression of disgust while going about his work.

118. Carritt, *Theory of Beauty*, 235–36, suggests this argument.

119. See Dowden, *Beauty of Nature*, 12, on beauty's ability to minister better than human sympathy.

120. Coletta, "Wordsworth," 75.

121. Chittister, "Monastic Wisdom," 173–81.

atmosphere that all may see. Burning through the confining dark or softening an oppressive glare, it proclaims however briefly that there is perfection and repose.[122] Perhaps every sunrise and sunset should be taken as a personal message from God, even if it does cast its light on commingled good and evil.

In the face of such commingling, we can affirm that creation as a work of art longs to be re-created: the lines yearn to be redrawn, the colors to intensify, because all beings, as combinations of actuality and possibility, have the potential to become more substantial, more real than they are.[123] In this respect, G. K. Chesterton's words apply fittingly to creation's ambivalent beauties:

> "As things tending to a greater end, they are even more real than we think them. If they seem to have a relative unreality (so to speak) it is because . . . they are unfulfilled, like packets of seeds or boxes of fireworks. . . . And there is an upper world of what the Schoolman called Fruition or Fulfilment, in which all this relative relativity becomes actuality in which the trees burst into flower or the rockets into flame."[124]

Through this fulfilled natural beauty and our place within it, the new creation, lacking corruption, could reflect God fully. And in such a context, our beatific vision could be more radically linked to our repose within a beautiful world—a world in which the glorified Christ is embodied. Beauty, as a leitmotiv, anticipates such a fulfillment of creation: a repose and a beatitude not yet actual.

Divine Love and Redeemed Life

The message of reposeful beauty can also be applied more specifically to the biotic world. Biotic beauty is beauty in the delicate, because life is delicate, and its beauty fades readily. Biotic beauty in all its motion, striving, and competition still seeks a delicate repose as a breath of life poised on the brink of an inanimate universe. Biotic beauties also find a living, dynamic repose as they adapt to their environment and find sustenance in it. For example, a horse is built to run, and it exhibits as much repose mid-stride as a sheep does safely grazing. Life is always seeking repose in being warm, safe, well-fed, and fecund, and when obtained, this living repose contributes

---

122. Tyrwhitt, *Natural Beauty*, 136, describes sunrise and sunset as universal proclamations.

123. Blond, "Perception," 237, stresses objects' potential to become more real.

124. Chesterton, *Aquinas*, 144.

especially to beautiful forms. Thus natural beauty has a complex relationship with biotic life, in that beauty is often but not always indifferent toward life: beauty can contribute to life and life to beauty. Not all living things are beautiful, but life and health contribute to beauty, while death and disease bring ugliness.[125] For example, in the human form, beauty belongs particularly to the face, where the presence of sensibility, intellect, and life are most evident. Similarly, the increased sense of life in vertebrates relates to a more complex curvature than in lower animals, allowing more freedom and grace in motion and contributing to survival (cf. 2:107). Another aspect of survival is reproduction, and beautiful forms are often linked directly with the renewal of life. In flowers, reproduction is marked notably with the integration of beauty and functionality, art supervening upon science.

For the non-religious person, such biotic beauty might only jar slightly against the hypothesis of life as a cosmic accident. But for religious perception, flowers reviving after the death of winter symbolize life after death, as expressed in flowers placed on graves since prehistoric times.[126] These prehistoric humans also etched into stone and painted on cave walls the earliest known art, depicting the powerful and graceful beauty of wild animals. Animal life in its beauty can certainly appear less "fallen" and more reposeful within creation than human life. And for this reason, shamanic religion, by ritually imitating animals, seeks to appropriate and communicate with their higher spiritual life of power and beauty.[127] For the religious person, animal life could speak of a universal striving toward a redeemed world—a world more conducive to the repose that living things seek—a world more infused with the life of God.

---

125. Vitality and proper function often contribute to beautiful forms, while lack of vitality (e.g., wounds, scars, and deformities) often detracts (2:153–54, 164). Thus, death in animal life brings the ultimate ugliness as exemplified by a decaying corpse. The corpse becomes the ugliest form, primarily because it has the most potential for beautiful form—and this is notwithstanding the emotions surrounding death and the value we place on life. Still death may sometimes grace the countenance with repose in comparison to the expressions wrought by the pain of prolonged illness. This repose may be related to having completed one's allotment of years; however, it is more proper to restful life than to the absence of life. Thus death can be euphemized as sleep. The beauty of a dead child is only what remains of the beauty of a living child, and this temporary agreeableness is more than offset by the chemical changes that soon affect the body's form.

126. Rolston, "Pasqueflower," 9, 15, describes flowers as art supervening upon science, noting their presence on graves and the connection with resurrection. Eliade observes, "It is for religious man that the rhythms of vegetation simultaneously reveal the mystery of life and creation and the mystery of renewal, youth, and immortality" (*Sacred and Profane*, 150).

127. See Eliade, *Myths, Dreams and Mysteries*, 61, on shamanism.

Also linked to life is brilliant color. In clown fish and iridescent dragonflies, colorful patterns strike us as an aesthetic extravagance, which we experience as related to the extravagance of life in all its flourishing. And since the color of flowers and fruits also connects directly with procreation, religious perception can experience color's procreative extravagance as God's extravagant love, which is always creating new life. Ruskin sees color as typifying God's love, mercy, and sparing of life as signified in the Noahic rainbow (5:417–19). Color as a type accords with perceptual beauty as an image of the divine nature, since color is an aspect of beauty as love is an aspect of God. God's love seems to be ultimately a desire that created life participate in his more abundant life, and so brilliant color also suggests the passion and emotion of erotic love, which is communicated through the colorful human eye, and leads to new life that can also participate in God. In humans and possibly other animals, reproduction is linked to the attractiveness of beauty (e.g., the color of mating plumage and display in birds). We seek beautiful mates and research correlates beauty with health and reproductive potential. Nature also encourages the survival of our offspring through the beauty we see in the faces of young children. But along with this functionality, Roger Scruton observes that the beauty of human beings "affects us as sacred things affect us, as something that can be more easily profaned than possessed."[128] When we are drawn to beautiful people, we are being drawn to beautiful images of God. Yet our preference for beautiful people is also haunted by fallenness, in that it marginalizes the life of the less healthy and attractive, and runs counter to Jesus' compassion for the disabled. Still we cannot deny the power of beauty in this regard; for in a mythological sense, the beauty of life's renewal images the redemption of creation, as we come to see "a Heaven in a wild flower."[129] As we would expect, this redemption is expressed only fleetingly in nature, as Robert Frost laments:

> Nature's first green is gold,
> Her hardest hue to hold.
> Her early leaf's a flower;
> But only so an hour.
> Then leaf subsides to leaf.
> So Eden sank to grief,
> So dawn goes down to day.
> Nothing gold can stay.[130]

128. *Beauty*, 53.
129. Blake, "Auguries of Innocence," 481.
130. Frost, "Nothing Gold can Stay," 84.

Indeed, living beauty is a spark that dies quickly, and we experience a measure of grief at its loss. Yet as life constantly renews itself, its beauty images God's unbounded life:

> there
> Breathed immortality, revolving life,
> And greatness still revolving; infinite:
> There littleness was not; the least of things
> Seemed infinite.[131]

Such experience displays our unsatisfied longing for beautiful life and points not only toward the living God and the redemption of creation, but also, for the Christian, to the redemptive, vivifying character of beauty itself as seen in light of Christ's incarnation and glorification. Christ's assuming and redeeming of flesh inaugurates nature's redemption, and beauty as an augury of that redemption anticipates that all creation, including ourselves, will be perfected ultimately in Christ. The beautiful, then, reflects our own participation in Christ and can even begin to transform us as it orients us toward him. Beauty orients us toward God by expressing his nature to us; and by participating in this symbolism, we can enter into beauty as a divine operation in creation: that is, we can perceive beauty as redemptive, as a purifying and illuminating force that culminates in praise. Thereby we can adopt a more consciously worshipful way of living in a beautiful world.[132] Beauty not only leads us to worship by reminding us of the redemption that God will accomplish, but also places a redemptive calling upon us that we might actualize more beauty. This actualizing is the only appropriate *aesthetic* response we can make to the more invidious side of natural beauty, which would ignore and exclude the unlovely. The appropriate response is not to ignore the beautiful in return as irrelevant to the good or the spiritual, but to make more of it, to expand its boundaries and dominion. This aesthetic operation must be included in the process of sanctification, working parallel to the moral, bringing not just our will into conformity with God, but our senses, our desires, our creativity, and every other aspect of our being.[133] Surely eternal *life* must entail nothing less.

131. Wordsworth, *Excursion*, 1.248–52.

132. Ward, "Beauty of God," 58–60, suggests the ideas of beauty as a divine operation, beauty as christologically redemptive, and beauty as influencing our way of living in the world.

133. Rahner, "Theology and the Arts," 28, says "the truly holy person is identical with the person who has developed fully all the dimensions of his human existence."

NATURAL BEAUTY AND HUMAN DESTINY

As we begin thus to indwell natural beauty as an operation in creation—as a heuristic and symbolic practice—beauty's symbolism brings with it its own connections, not only to God, but to humankind in relationship to God and creation. As we indwell the epistemic community of the beauty-skilled, entering into its desires and idioms, the poets begin to whisper rumors of a human destiny revealed in the beautiful. Drawing upon this shareable experience, we might push humanity's relationship with natural beauty further toward teleological and eschatological conclusions.

In this connection, Gerardus van der Leeuw remarks that "true art is eschatological art . . . the building which is lost in the stretches of the infinite landscape."[134] And similarly, Shelley, though no friend of religion, in "Ode to the West Wind" expresses the desire that not just a building but he himself might become lost in the landscape, or become one with the beauty of nature.[135] Through such artistic sentiments, humankind expresses the desire to be enveloped in some way by natural beauty, and although there may be pantheistic connotations, these can be translated easily into theistic terms. Of course the non-religious person might see such experience only as a recognition of our reducibility to the world from which we arose. But religious humanity desires to become one with nature's beauty, because natural beauty's order, in its difference from human order, is a desirable difference that speaks of God's otherness, as God highlighted it to Job (Job 38–39). As in the shamanic imitation of animals, humans desire to "put on" natural beauty, like princely robes and finery, partly because we sense in natural forms—like the curve of an antler or the silkiness of beaver fur—a simple dignity and grandeur that is proper to our glorified human nature. Surely this is also why pagans worshipped amid reposeful beauty on mountaintops, in shady groves, and beneath great trees. This desire to "put on" or indwell natural beauty points toward beauty's imaging of God's nature, and reflects our deeper desire for integration with God's order and repose. It reflects our being made for God and speaks of our proper place within the future blessing that he bestows in ways proper to our created nature, such as through beauty. This eschatological integration with God could take on many forms, but one form, as van der Leeuw suggests, concerns our desire to be enveloped in natural beauty (an image of God) within an eschatological landscape.

---

134. van der Leeuw, *Sacred and Profane Beauty*, 333.
135. Shelley, "West Wind," 325–26.

Ruskin maintains that the sky is an essential part of this landscape: we can experience the sky as an unbounded distance, an infinity typifying God's incomprehensible nature. The light evening or morning sky over a dark horizon is "of all visible things the least material, the least finite, the farthest withdrawn from the earth prison-house, the most typical of the nature of God, the most suggestive of the glory of His dwelling place" (2:81). In line with Ruskin's observation, the "height" of the sky symbolizes transcendence cross-culturally, and some cultures pray looking upward, with eyes and hands open toward the heavens.[136] In light of modern astronomy, the night sky also reminds us of the potentially infinite expansion of space, and Ruskin suggests that the experience of the sky allows for "countless" other associations related to "heavenly hopes" (2:87).

Such hopes seem bound up in our experience of the sky's beauty and distance. In dawn, night, or midday glories, we sometimes have the Icarus-urge to take flight over the landscape, to occupy the beauty and distance presented to us there as an aspect of our destiny. Thus the sky's beauty images not only God's unbounded nature but, as we seek to integrate with that image, our unbounded destination in God. Similarly, in landscapes there is the emotion caused by wide open spaces, especially a sunlit distance behind a darker horizon, suggesting hope in distance and "joyfulness in the apparent, though unreachable, nearness and promise" (2:79, 87). Thus Wordsworth: "How temptingly the landscape shines!—The air / Breathes invitation," and Emerson: "The health of the eye seems to demand a horizon. We are never tired, so long as we can see far enough."[137] In paintings, this beckoning from the horizon is achieved by objects such as sun rays, mountains, cloud formations—anything partially revealed that can represent the cosmic "Beyond."[138] Beauty in the landscape, as it suggests this destination beyond, is thus a "language of futurity."[139] But this onward gesturing of beauty is obscured if we accept Augustine's reconciling of beauty with temporal decay. The futurity of beauty accords better with the notion that art (human or divine), in contrast with the temporal, should proclaim the eternal horizon of our endless human questing and desire. Indeed, humankind is ever open toward an elusive future goal.[140]

136. Eliade, *Sacred and Profane*, 117–18, discusses the sky and transcendence.

137. Wordsworth, *Excursion*, 9.426–27. Emerson, *Nature*, 22.

138. D. Brown, *Enchantment*, 116, notes how landscape painters use such objects to evoke the cosmic "Beyond."

139. "Language of futurity" is Blond's phrase in, "Theology before Philosophy," 56.

140. See Rahner, "Theology and the Arts," 29, on art's eternal horizon. Migliore, *Faith Seeking Understanding*, 147, notes the theological implications of insatiable human desire and striving.

Thus we find in natural beauty an outwardly expansive eschatological impulse—the beauty of humanity lost in an infinite landscape—a beauty that speaks to the lure of frontier. The American frontier-paradise eschatology is exemplified powerfully in Mormonism, with its retreat to the Utah desert in order to establish the kingdom of God on earth. But such eschatology was also part of Columbus's and the Puritans' hopes, and the frontier ideal has remained a pervasive enough ideology that John F. Kennedy needed only to refer to a "new frontier" to capture the hearts of Americans for space exploration. Frontier and wilderness evoke the biblical imagery of wandering and a paradoxical route to paradise.[141] America as wilderness was once seen as "'fresh from the hands of the Creator,' a holy place, 'the unedited manuscript of God.'"[142] And this description also accords with contemporary experience of beautiful wilderness unmarred by human development. This same mythological pull today draws Americans to Alaska—"The Last Frontier."

Of course the frontier ideal has never succeeded entirely in practice; it has been marked by war and environmental disaster. Nineteenth-century America witnessed the extermination of both native peoples and wildlife in the name of a "manifest destiny" bolstered by postmillennialism. So of course theologies of nature can go badly wrong. And the non-religious person might reductively explain frontier's mythological pull in terms of a human evolutionary history of seeking food and shelter. But today, amid environmental crises and urban overcrowding, even Europeans are relocating to the far-flung isolation of the Outer Hebrides, and one suspects that these patterns allow us to say more about human experience of God through nature. The persistence of the frontier ideal, despite its shadowed history and impracticabilities, speaks all the more to its revelatory implications.

The frontier ideal combines the symbolic openness of wilderness with an idealized harmony between nature and humanity. This ideal harmony also seems to produce the ideal natural beauty, which many find not in wilderness but in European landscapes, such as Tyrolean villages, or villas hanging over azure waters of the Amalfi coast. This harmony of nature and humanity seems to contribute to our sense of perceptual beauty, even if wilderness holds as much symbolic appeal as "the unedited manuscript." Such beauty can also be experienced religiously through the beliefs that humankind is a created, intended part of the world and inseparable from its (subjective-objective) beauty. Through this religious connection, the ideal beauty can be experienced as our eschatological harmony with

141. Whitson, "Wilderness and Paradise," 7–15, makes the connections between Mormonism, Kennedy, and biblical wilderness imagery. Eliade, *Quest*, 91, describes similar themes in Columbus's and the Puritans' writings.

142. Porteous, *Environmental Aesthetics*, 78.

an endlessly expansive frontier—a fulfillment of both the hominess and wildness of Eden.

As we push back the frontier, we unveil further beauty in nature and our rightful place within it. Landscape painter Claude Lorraine evokes this idea well in his uniting of past glories with future expectation. He draws viewer into the painting as a wayfarer who beholds beautiful prospects with beckoning horizons.[143] This pursuit of beauty as a wayfarer also parallels the pursuit of knowledge: every page turned is a step taken; every concept grasped is a prospect viewed; every breakthrough in understanding is a new country explored. The most satisfying investigations are those that push the boundaries of our understanding, and yet any conclusions reached thereby are the hardest to justify. But our joy in understanding the world is tied to its ever greater mystery, and researchers in psychological aesthetics have found that the property of "mystery" in landscape—that is, the potential for new perspective to be gained through topographical exploration—is correlated with judgments of beautiful landscape.[144] Beauty resides not only *in* the landscape but arises as we move *through* the landscape in its unfolding mystery. Thus beauty as a function of exploration offers what Ricoeur calls "a meaning in motion." In "the phenomenology of the spirit," he says, "each figure finds its meaning, not in what precedes, but in what follows. Consciousness is thus drawn outside of itself, in front of itself," like the wayfarer.[145] And as we move through the landscape, our desire for beauty is renewed like our daily thirst. We experience beauty as an unending source of delight and fascination. Yet our beauty-judgments also correlate with the familiarity of landscapes, such that we partake continually of both the excitement of the undiscovered and the comfort of the familiar.[146] This trade-off can be experienced as an attunement to both Eden's bountiful provision and the creation mandate to subdue the earth and rule over it (Gen 1:28). Both the provision and the mandate require ultimately a harmony with, and repose in, an unbounded creation—that is, a convergence of the types of order, repose, and infinity. And so, as Wordsworth says, "Our destiny, our being's heart and home, / Is with infinitude, and only there."[147] Sought in these images of infinitude and unbounded

143. See, for example, his *Seaport with the Embarkation of the Queen of Sheba* in the National Gallery, London.

144. See Porteous, *Environmental Aesthetics,* 121, on research regarding beautiful landscape.

145. Ricoeur, *Conflict of Interpretations,* 21–22.

146. See Porteous on the new and the familiar in beauty-judgments. *Environmental Aesthetics,* 126.

147. Wordsworth, Fourteen-Book *Prelude,* 6.604–5.

creation, beauty constitutes an aspect of our destiny—a manifest destiny of the spirit, which also accounts for C. S. Lewis's Narnian eschatology of "farther up and farther in."[148]

Our harmony and repose in this unbounded creation gives rise to beauty and knowledge (as I have maintained epistemologically), and consequently, to know and to perceive the beautiful is to recover a lost link with divinity, an Edenic human integrity.[149] For this reason, primal religion understands sense experience to be the ideal means of access to God, while recourse to non-sensory, mystical experience implies fallenness with its unnatural separation of humanity's physical and spiritual activity. But as humanity returns to God, hierophanies appear in the commonest objects.[150] It is no coincidence, then, that we anticipate increased beauty and knowledge, in all their commonness, in our heavenly reward, and so Emerson's Romantic vision becomes fully true when realized eschatologically: "How does Nature deify us with a few and cheap elements! Give me health and a day, and I will make the pomp of emperors ridiculous."[151] This deification through knowledge and beauty is unending, because we can never fully represent or express what creation is; we cannot complete its story, for reality is an overflowing, unfathomable plenitude.[152] Indeed, the entire sensible world is, as Merleau-Ponty says, a horizon, "a being of porosity, pregnancy . . . and he before whom the horizon opens is caught up, included within it."[153] As we are caught up in this landscape, a divine mystery unfolds with it—a mystery that expresses himself aptly in the beautiful. As beauty commingles with the sublime, this mystery also holds a certain terror, yet it accompanies us on an unending and expectant journey of beauty and knowledge that contrasts happily with the cold certainties and foundationalisms from which I initially distinguished creational theology. As we continue this journey—as sensuous, embodied beings-in-the-world—we wonder how, apart from natural beauty, we could even contemplate such eschatological destinations.

148. Wolterstorff, *Art in Action*, 193, suggests a link between beauty and human destiny. See also Lewis, *Last Battle*, 176.

149. See Milbank, Pickstock, and Ward, "Suspending the Material," 10, on Edenic integrity and recovering a link with divinity.

150. Eliade, *Myths, Dreams, and Mysteries*, 73, 92–93, describes this theme in primal religion.

151. Emerson, *Nature*, 23.

152. Blond, "Perception," 241, discusses creation's unending plenitude and its eluding of full description. The unbounded nature of creation expressed in the frontier ideal also alleviates the problem of an overcrowded eschaton.

153. Merleau-Ponty, *Visible and Invisible*, 148–49.

6

Concluding Thoughts

TILLICH OBSERVES THAT "SYMBOLS cannot be produced intentionally. They are born and grow and die." Therefore, in his terms, beauty's symbolisms must be verified by their power to relate us and our world to ultimate reality.[1] I conclude by commending the power of this interrelationship of God, beauty, and ourselves, which I have described at various levels, from the perceptual to the mythological. But it is ultimately a power actualized by others who would indwell the symbolic practice of natural beauty. If Tillich is correct, my argument can only be confirmed by such use, as theology engages creation and its beauty as a theological source and continues to refine ideas such as I have put forward. This engagement with creation becomes especially necessary as science teaches us more about our world and as natural beauty continues to speak to us of our alienation from a more comprehensive reality—continues to reveal, even, a reality beyond the quotidian. If our experience of the world constantly "interrogates" us as to possibilities of what lies beyond the world, then certainly a symbolic relationship with beauty amplifies this interrogation.[2] Beauty could disclose humankind's frontier or "boundary situation"—not merely a situation within history but a situatedness within the larger scheme of the cosmos and on the boundaries of the transcendent. This situation of humankind is

1. Tillich, "Art and Ultimate Reality," 142; idem, "Environment and the Individual," 203. This is not to deny that symbols are produced creatively. Tillich is denying that one can set out to produce a trans-cultural symbol intentionally. The symbol has a way of arising on its own, yet still through our creativity.

2. See D. Brown, *Continental Philosophy*, 10, on experience's interrogation.

such that by a simple yet deeply felt consciousness of our interaction with nature and her rhythms, such as our watching the days and seasons and our moving through the landscape, we also sense something of the meaning and goal of our own existence. We sense something of the dignity and drama of our humanity as it is mirrored in that of nature, and as natural beauty speaks to our restlessness and desire. We come to participate in a way of being with nature that wards off our tendencies toward nihilism and superficiality without thereby transporting us inaptly out of history, creation, and our embodied experience of the world.[3]

In support of such a role for natural beauty, Ruskin says, "the laws, the life, and the joy of beauty in the material world of God, are as eternal and sacred parts of His creation as, in the world of spirits, virtue; and in the world of angels, praise."[4] Moreover, "the Spirit of God is around you in the air that you breathe,—His glory in the light that you see; and in the fruitfulness of the earth, and the joy of its creatures. He has written for you, day by day, His revelation."[5] In apperception of this revelation, we should sketch out the penumbra of the invisible in creation, making it seen and known; for in perceiving the beautiful, desire may yet lead us through the landscape into "worlds not realised" for which our eye is the gateway.[6] In so doing we respond to the phenomenality of God for his creatures that is beauty.[7] Natural beauty then functions as mythic reality and revelatory image in the "cosmic Christian liturgy." And through participation in this liturgy, our lives progress toward and take on their truer meaning, that of a glorious human condition realized in God.[8] Beauty begins the unveiling of this glorious condition, and in this way Ruskin's intuition is confirmed that a proper spiritual understanding of beauty is "the fulfilment of our existence."[9]

---

3. See Eliade, *Images and Symbols*, 34–36, on our "boundary situation" and experience of nature's rhythms.

4. Ruskin, epilogue to *Modern Painters*, 5:464.

5. Ruskin, *Deucalion*, 266.

6. Wordsworth, "Ode."

7. See Blond, "Theology before Philosophy," 57–58, on making the invisible seen and beauty as a phenomenality of God.

8. Eliade, preface to *Quest*, n.p. Cf. Eliade, *Images and Symbols*, 36.

9. Ruskin, *Modern Painters*, 2:362. "The call of beauty," for Jean-Louis Chrétien also, "is not one particular call as opposed to others, but the call par excellence that convokes us to our final destiny" *(Call and Response*, 13).

Bibliography

Adams, Richard. Introduction to *Pilgrim at Tinker Creek*, by Annie Dillard. London: Picador, 1980.

Anselm of Canterbury. *Monologion*. Translated by Simon Harrison. In *Anselm of Canterbury: The Major Works*, edited by Brian Davies and G. R. Evans, 5–81. New York: Oxford University Press, 1998.

———. "Prayer to St. Mary." Translated by Benedicta Ward. In *The Prayers and Meditations of Saint Anselm with the Proslogion*, 115–26. London: Penguin, 1973.

———. *Proslogion*. Translated by M. J. Charlesworth. In *Anselm of Canterbury: The Major Works*, edited by Brian Davies and G. R. Evans, 82–104. New York: Oxford University Press, 1998.

The Ante-Nicene Fathers [ANF]. Edited by Alexander Roberts and James Donaldson. 10 vols. Edinburgh: T. & T. Clark, 1885–1887.

Aquinas, Thomas. *De Veritate*. Translated by Robert W. Schmidt. 3 vols. Chicago: Regnery, 1954.

———. *Summa Contra Gentiles*. Translated by Vernon J. Bourke. Garden City, NY: Hanover House, 1956.

———. *Summa Theologica*. Translated by the Fathers of the English Dominican Province. 5 vols. Rev. ed., 1920. Notre Dame: Ave Maria, 1981.

Augustine of Hippo. *Confessions*. Translated by R. S. Pine-Coffin. Harmondsworth, UK: Penguin, 1982.

———. *On Free Will*. In *Augustine: Earlier Writings*, edited by John Baillie et al., translated by John H. S. Burleigh. The Library of Christian Classics 6. London: SCM, 1953.

———. *On Genesis: A Refutation of the Manichees*. In *On Genesis*, edited by John E. Rotelle, translated by Edmund Hill. 39–104. The Works of Saint Augustine: A Translation for the 21st Century 1/13. Hyde Park, NY: New City, 2002.

———. *The Literal Meaning of Genesis*. In *On Genesis*, edited by John E. Rotelle, translated by Edmund Hill, 155–506. The Works of Saint Augustine: A Translation for the 21st Century 1/13. Hyde Park, NY: New City, 2002.

———. *On Order [De Ordine]*. Translated by Silvano Borruso. South Bend: St. Augustine's, 2007.

———. *Unfinished Literal Commentary of Genesis*. In *On Genesis*, edited by John E. Rotelle, translated by Edmund Hill, 105–54. The Works of Saint Augustine: A Translation for the 21st Century 1/13. Hyde Park, NY: New City Press, 2002.

Balthasar, Hans Urs von. *Seeing the Form*. Translated by E. Leiva-Merikasis. Volume 1 of *The Glory of the Lord: A Theological Aesthetics*, edited by Joseph Fessio and John Riches. Edinburgh: T. & T. Clark, 1982.

Barth, Karl. *Church Dogmatics*. 1/1, *The Doctrine of the Word of God*. Translated by G. T. Thomson et al. G. W. Bromiley and T. F. Torrance. Edinburgh: T. & T. Clark, 1936.

————. *Church Dogmatics*. 2/1, *The Doctrine of God*. Translated by T. H. L. Parker et al. Edited by G. W. Bromiley and T. F. Torrance. Edinburgh: T. & T. Clark, 1957.

————. *Church Dogmatics*. 3/1, *The Doctrine of Creation*. Translated by J. W. Edwards, O. Bussey, and H. Knight. Edited by G. W. Bromiley and T. F. Torrance. Edinburgh: T. & T. Clark, 1958.

Baudelaire, Charles. "The Exposition Universelle 1855." In *Art in Paris 1845–1862: Salons and other Exhibitions Reviewed by Charles Baudelaire*, translated and edited by Jonathan Mayne, 121–43. London: Phaidon, 1965.

Bauerschmidt, Frederick Christian. "Aesthetics: The Theological Sublime." In *Radical Orthodoxy: A New Theology*, edited by John Milbank, Catherine Pickstock, and Graham Ward, 201–19. London: Routledge, 1999.

Beardsley, Monroe C. *Aesthetics from Classical Greece to the Present: A Short History*. New York: Macmillan, 1966. Reprint, Tuscaloosa, AL: University of Alabama Press, 1977.

Begbie, Jeremy S. *Voicing Creation's Praise: Towards a Theology of the Arts*. London: Continuum, 1991.

Beiser, Frederick. "Romanticism, German." In *Routledge Encyclopedia of Philosophy*, edited by E. Craig. London: Routledge, 1998. Online: http://www.rep.routledge. com/ article/DC094SECT2.

Bentley, Richard. *The folly and unreasonableness of atheism demonstrated from the advantage and pleasure of a religious life, the faculties of humane souls, the structure of animate bodies, & the origin and frame of the world : in eight sermons preached at the lecture founded by . . . Robert Boyle*. London, 1699.

Blake, William. "Auguries of Innocence." In *The Poetry and Prose of William Blake*, edited by David V. Erdman, 481. Garden City, NY: Doubleday, 1965.

————. "The Marriage of Heaven and Hell." In *The Poetry and Prose of William Blake*, edited by David V. Erdman, 34–37. Garden City, NY: Doubleday, 1965.

————. "The Tyger." In *The Poetry and Prose of William Blake*, edited by David V. Erdman, 24–25. Garden City, NY: Doubleday, 1965.

Blond, Phillip. "Emmanuel Levinas: God and Phenomenology." In *Post-Secular Philosophy: Between Philosophy and Theology*, edited by Phillip Blond, 195–228. London: Routledge, 1998.

————. "Perception: From Modern Painting to Vision in Christ." In *Radical Orthodoxy: A New Theology*, edited by John Milbank, Catherine Pickstock, and Graham Ward, 220–42. London: Routledge, 1999.

————. "Theology before Philosophy." Introduction to *Post-Secular Philosophy: Between Philosophy and Theology*, edited by Phillip Blond. London: Routledge, 1998.

Boethius. *The Consolation of Philosophy*. Translated by P. B. Walsh. Oxford, Clarendon, 1999.

Bonaventure. *Breviloquium*. Volume 2 of *The Works of Bonaventure*. Translated by Jose de Vinck. Paterson, NJ: St Anthony Guild, 1963.

————. *Collations on the Six Days*. Volume 5 of *The Works of Bonaventure*. Translated by Jose de Vinck. Paterson, NJ: St Anthony Guild, 1970.

————. *Commentaria in Quatuor Libros Sententiarum*. Translated by The Franciscan Archive. Franciscan Archive Publications, 2009. Online: http://www.franciscan-archive.org/bonaventura/opera /bono2292.html.

Bonhoeffer, Dietrich. *Letters and Papers from Prison*. Enlarged ed. Edited by Eberhard Bethge. London: SCM, 1971.

Brown, Colin. *Philosophy and the Christian Faith*. Downers Grove, IL: Intervarsity, 1968.

Brown, David. *Continental Philosophy and Modern Theology: An Engagement*. Oxford: Blackwell, 1987.

————. *God and Enchantment of Place: Reclaiming Human Experience*. Oxford: Oxford University Press, 2004.

————. "God and Symbolic Action." In *Divine Action: Studies Inspired by the Philosophical Theology of Austin Farrer*, edited by Brian Hebblethwaite and Edward Henderson, 103–22. Edinburgh: T. & T. Clark, 1990.

Brown, Francis, S. R. Driver, and Charles A. Briggs. *A Hebrew and English Lexicon of the Old Testament [BDB]*. Oxford: Clarendon, 1907.

Brown, Frank Burch. *Religious Aesthetics: A Theological Study of Making and Meaning*. London: Macmillan, 1990.

Brunner, Emil. *The Divine Imperative: A Study in Christian Ethics*. Translated by Olive Wyon. London: Lutterworth, 1937.

Burnet, Thomas. *Sacred Theory of the Earth*. 2 vols. Glasgow, 1753.

Byron, George Gordon. *Childe Harold's Pilgrimage*. In *Lord Byron: The Major Works*, edited by Jerome J. McGann, 19–206. New York: Oxford University Press, 1986; reprint, New York: Oxford University Press, 2008.

————. *Manfred*. In *Lord Byron: The Major Works*, edited by Jerome J. McGann, 274–314. New York: Oxford University Press, 1986; reprint, New York: Oxford University Press, 2008.

Calvin, John. *Institutes of the Christian Religion*. Edited by John T. McNeill. Translated by Ford Lewis Battles. Library of Christian Classics 20. Philadephia: Westminster, 1963.

Carlyle, Thomas. *Sartor Resartus: The Life and Opinions of Herr Teufelsdröckh. In Three Books*. London, Chapman & Hall, 1869.

Carritt, E. F. *The Theory of Beauty*. London: Methuen, 1962.

Charlton, W. *Aesthetics: An Introduction*. London: Hutchinson, 1970.

Chesterton, G. K. *St. Thomas Aquinas*. London: Hodder & Stoughton, 1962.

Chittister, Joan. "Monastic Wisdom for Seekers of Light." *Religious Life Review* 40 (2001) 173–81.

Chrétien, Jean-Louis. *The Call and the Response*. Translated by Anne A. Davenport. New York: Fordham University Press, 2004.

Clark, David K. *To Know and Love God*. Wheaton, IL: Crossway, 2003.

Clark, Tony. *Divine Revelation and Human Practice: Responsive and Imaginative Participation*. Eugene, OR: Cascade, 2008.

Cochrane, Arthur, editor. "The Belgic Confession A.D. 1561 Revised 1619." In *Reformed Confessions of the Sixteenth Century: Edited, with Historical Introduction*, 189–219. London: SCM, 1966.

Coletta, W. John. "William Wordsworth, 1770–1850." In *Fifty Key Thinkers on the Environment*. Edited by Joy A. Palmer et al., 74–83. London: Routledge, 2001.

Cooper, Anthony Ashley, third Earl of Shaftesbury. *The Moralists: A Philosophical Rhapsody*. London, 1709.

Couch, Beatriz Milano. "Religious Symbols and Philosophical Reflection." In *Studies in the Philosophy of Paul Ricoeur*, edited by Charles E. Reagan, 115–32. Athens, OH: Ohio University Press, 1979.

Cramp, Rosemary. "Nature Redeemed." *The Sense of the Sacramental: Movement and Measure in Art and Music, Place and Time*, edited by David Brown and Ann Loades, 122–36. London: SPCK, 1995.

Cross, F. L., and E. A. Livingstone. "Bentley, Richard." In *Oxford Dictionary of the Christian Church*, 191. 3rd rev. ed. Oxford: Oxford University Press, 2005.

Curtius, Ernst Robert. *European Literature and the Latin Middle Ages*. Translated by Willard R. Trask. London: Routledge, 1953.

Davies, Brian. *An Introduction to the Philosophy of Religion*. 3rd ed. Oxford: Oxford University Press, 2004.

Davies, G. Henton. *The Interpreter's Dictionary of the Bible [IDB]*, edited by G. A. Buttrick. 4 vols. New York: Abingdon, 1962.

Dawkins, Richard. "The God Delusion Debate" with John Lennox. University of Alabama, Birmingham, 3 October 2007. Online: http://fixed-point.org/index.php/video/35-full-length/164-the-dawkins-lennox-debate.

Descartes, René. *Discourse on Method*. In *French and English Philosophers: Descartes, Voltaire, Rousseau, Hobbes*, edited by Charles W. Eliot, 5–62. Harvard Classics 34. New York: Collier & Son, 1965.

Diderot, Denis. *Recherches philosphiques sur l'origine et la nature du beau*. Vol. 6 of *Variétés: Oeuvres Choisies de D. Diderot*. Jouhaust ed. Edited by Paul Albert. Paris: Librairie des Bibliophiles, n.d.

Dillard, Annie. *Pilgrim at Tinker Creek*. London: Picador, 1980.

Douglas, Mary. *Natural Symbols: Explorations in Cosmology*. Rev. ed. London: Routledge, 1996.

Dowden, John. "The Beauty of Nature a Revelation of God. A Sermon Preached in the Parish Church of Grasmere, St. Mary's Cathedral, Edinburgh, and Elsewhere, with a Preface and Notes." Pamphlet. Edinburgh: Douglas, 1884.

Dryden, John. *Select Essays on the* Belles Lettres. Glasgow: n.p., 1750.

Dulles, Avery. *Models of Revelation*. Garden City, NY: Doubleday, 1983.

Eco, Umberto. *The Aesthetics of Thomas Aquinas*. Translated by Hugh Bredin. Cambridge, MA: Harvard University Press, 1988.

Edwards, Jonathan. "The Beauty of the World." In *Scientific and Philosophical Writings*. Vol. 6 of *The Works of Jonathan Edwards*, edited by Wallace E. Anderson, 305–6. New Haven, Conn.: Yale University Press, 1980.

———. "The Excellency of Christ." In *"Miscellanies,"* edited by Thomas A. Schafer, 278–80. Works of Jonathan Edwards 13. New Haven: Yale University Press, 1994.

———. "Images or Shadows of Divine Things." In *Typological Writings*, edited by Wallace E. Anderson et al., 50–130. Works of Jonathan Edwards 11. New Haven: Yale University Press, 1993.

———. "The Mind." In *Scientific and Philosophical Writings*, edited by Wallace E. Anderson, 332–93. Works of Jonathan Edwards 6. New Haven: Yale University Press, 1980.

———. "The Nature of True Virtue." In *Ethical Writings*, edited by Paul Ramsey, 537–628. Works of Jonathan Edwards 8. New Haven: Yale University Press, 1989.

Edwards, L. Clifton. "Artful Creation and Aesthetic Rationality: Toward a Creational Theology of Revelatory Beauty." *Theology Today* 69 (2012) 56–72.

———. "The Beauty of Frontier: A Revelation of the Human Destination in God." *American Theological Inquiry* 3/2 (2010) 15–19.

———. "Re-envisaging Ruskin's Types: Beautiful Order as Divine Revelation." *Irish Theological Quarterly* 77 (2012) 165–81.

Eliade, Mircea. *Images and Symbols: Studies in Religious Symbolism.* Translated by Philip Mairet. Paris: Librairie Gallimard, 1952. Reprint, London: Harvill, 1961.

———. *Myth and Reality.* New York: Harper & Row, 1963.

———. *Myths, Dreams and Mysteries: The Encounter between Contemporary Faiths and Archaic Reality.* Translated by Philip Mairet. London: Collins, 1968.

———. *The Quest: History and Meaning in Religion.* Chicago: University of Chicago Press, 1969.

———. *The Sacred and the Profane: The Nature of Religion.* Translated by Willard R. Trask. New York: Harvest, 1959.

Emerson, Ralph Waldo. *Nature, Addresses, and Lectures.* Riverside ed. London: Routledge, 1883.

Erickson. Millard J. *Christian Theology.* 2nd ed. Grand Rapids: Baker, 1998.

Farley, Edward. *Faith and Beauty: A Theological Aesthetic.* Aldershot, UK: Ashgate, 2001.

Farrer, Austin. *The Glass of Vision.* Glasgow: Dacre, 1948.

———. *Love Almighty and Ills Unlimited.* London: Collins, 1962.

———. *A Rebirth of Images: The Making of St John's Apocalypse.* Glasgow: Dacre, 1949.

Finley, C. Stephen. *Nature's Covenant: Figures of Landscape in Ruskin.* University Park, PA: Pennsylvania State University Press, 1992.

Frost, Robert. "Nothing Gold Can Stay." In *New Hampshire: A Poem with Notes and Grace Notes,* 84. New York: Holt, 1923.

Green, Garrett. *Imagining God: Theology and the Religious Imagination.* Grand Rapids: Eerdmans, 1989.

Häring, Bernard. *Free and Faithful in Christ.* Vol. 2 of *The Truth Will Set You Free: Moral Theology for Priests and Laity.* Slough, UK: St Paul, 1979.

Harries, Richard. *Art and the Beauty of God: A Christian Understanding.* London: Continuum, 1993.

Harrison, Carol. *Beauty and Revelation in the Thought of Saint Augustine.* Oxford: Clarendon, 1992.

Hart, David Bentley. *The Beauty of the Infinite: The Aesthetics of Christian Truth.* Grand Rapids: Eerdmans, 2003.

Haught, John F. "God and Evolution." In *The Oxford Handbook of Religion and Science,* edited by Philip Clayton and Zachary Simpson, 697–712. Oxford: Oxford University Press, 2006.

Heaney, Seamus. *The Redress of Poetry: Oxford Lectures.* London: Faber & Faber, 1995.

Heidegger, Martin. *Being and Time.* Translated by John Macquarrie and Edward Robinson. London: SCM, 1962.

Hemming, Laurence Paul. "*Analogia non Entis sed Entitatis*: The Ontological Consequences of the Doctrine of Analogy." *International Journal of Systematic Theology* 6 (2004) 119–32.

Hilton, Tim. *John Ruskin: The Later Years.* New Haven: Yale University Press, 2000.

Hopkins, Gerard Manley. *The Sermons and Devotional Writings of Gerard Manley Hopkins.* Edited by Christopher Devlin. London: Oxford University Press, 1959.

———. *The Poems of Gerard Manley Hopkins.* 4th ed. Edited by W. H. Gardner and N. H. Mackenzie. London: Oxford University Press, 1967.

Howell, Russell W. "Does Mathematical Beauty Pose Problems for Naturalism?" *Christian Scholar's Review* 35 (2006) 493–504.

Hume, David. *An Enquiry Concerning Human Understanding.* In *English Philosophers of the Seventeenth and Eighteenth Centuries: Locke, Berkeley, Hume,* edited by Charles W. Eliot. Harvard Classics 37. New York: Collier & Son, 1965.

———. "Of the Standard of Taste." In *Essays Moral, Political, and Literary,* edited by Eugene F. Miller. Rev. ed. Indianapolis: Liberty Fund, 1987.

Hutcheson, Francis. *An Inquiry into the Original of our Ideas of Beauty and Virtue,* edited by Wolfgang Leidhold. Indianapolis: Liberty Fund, 2004.

Irenaeus of Lyons. *St. Irenaeus of Lyons Against the Heresies.* Translated by Dominic J. Unger. Ancient Christian Writers 55. New York: Paulist, 1992.

John of the Cross. *Ascent of Mount Carmel.* In *The Complete Works of St John of the Cross.* 3 vols. Edited and translated by E. Allison Peers. London: Burns, Oates & Washbourne, 1934.

Jones, David. "Art and Sacrament." In *Epoch and Artist: Selected Writings by David Jones,* edited by Harman Grisewood, 143–79. London: Faber & Faber, 1959.

Jung, C. G. "Archetypes of the Collective Unconscious." Translated by R. F. C. Hull. In *The Archetypes and the Collective Unconscious,* edited by Herbert Read et al., 3–41. Collected Works of C. G. Jung 9. London: Routledge, 1959.

Jüngel, Eberhard. "Even the Beautiful Must Die." Translated by A. Neufeldtfast and J. B. Webster. In *Theological Essays,* 2:59–81. Edinburgh: T. & T. Clark, 1995.

Kant, Immanuel. *Critique of Judgment.* Translated by J. H. Bernard. London: MacMillan, 1892.

———. *Critique of Pure Reason.* Translated by Norman Kemp Smith. New York: Palgrave Macmillan, 1929.

Keats, John. *Endymion: A Poetic Romance.* London: Printed for Taylor and Hessey, 1818.

Kerr, Fergus. *After Aquinas: Versions of Thomism.* Malden, MA: Blackwell, 2002.

Kierkegaard, Søren. *Søren Kierkegaard's Journals and Papers.* Vol. 1. Translated and Edited by Edna H. Hong and Howard V. Hong. Bloomington, IN: Indiana University Press, 1967.

Kuyper, Abraham. *The Antithesis between Symbolism and Revelation: Lecture Delivered before the Historical Presbyterian Society in Philadelphia, PA.* Edinburgh: T. & T. Clark, n.d.

Leeuw, Gerardus van der. *Sacred and Profane Beauty: The Holy in Art.* Translated by David E. Green. London: Weiderfeld & Nicolson, 1963.

Lewis, C. S. *The Great Divorce: A Dream.* San Francisco: HarperSanFrancisco, 2001.

———. *The Last Battle.* London: Bodley Head, 1984.

———. *The Problem of Pain.* San Francisco: HarperSanFrancisco, 2001.

———. *The Screwtape Letters.* San Francisco: HarperSanFrancisco, 2001.

———. "Transposition." In *The Weight of Glory and Other Addresses,* 91–115. San Francisco: HarperSanFrancisco, 2001.

Lewis, Hywell D. *The Self and Immortality.* New York: Macmillan, 1973.

Lonergan, Bernard J. F. *Topics in Education.* Vol. 10 of *The Collected Works of Bernard Lonergan,* edited by Robert M. Doran and Frederick E. Crowe. Toronto: University of Toronto Press, 1993.

MacDonald, George. *A Dish of Orts.* London: Sampson Low, Marston, 1893.

Marion, Jean-Luc. *In Excess: Studies of Saturated Phenomena.* Translated by Robyn Horner and Vincent Berraud. New York: Fordham University Press, 2002.

Maritain, Jacques. *Art and Scholasticism*. Translated by Joseph W. Evans. New York: Scribner's Sons, 1962.

———. "An Essay on Art." In *Art and Scholasticism*. London: Sheed & Ward, 1930.

Mazur, Barry. "Dialogue between Barry Mazur & Peter Pesic: On Mathematics, Imagination & the Beauty of Numbers." *Daedalus* 134 (2005) 124–30.

McGrath, Alister E. *Nature. A Scientific Theology* 1. Grand Rapids: Eerdmans, 2001.

———. *The Open Secret: A New Vision for Natural Theology*. Malden, MA: Blackwell, 2008.

———. *Reality*. Vol. 2 of *A Scientific Theology*. Grand Rapids: Eerdmans, 2002.

———. *Theory*. Vol. 3 of *A Scientific Theology*. Grand Rapids: Eerdmans, 2003.

McIntyre, John. *Faith, Theology and Imagination*. Edinburgh: Handsel, 1987.

Meek, Esther Lightcap. *Longing to Know: the Philosophy of Knowledge for Ordinary People*. Grand Rapids: Brazos, 2003.

Merleau-Ponty, Maurice. *The Visible and the Invisible*. Edited by Claude Lefort. Translated by Alphonso Lingis. Evanston, IL: Northwestern University Press, 1968.

Milbank, John. "Beauty and the Soul." In *Theological Perspectives on God and Beauty*, 1–34. Harrisburg, PA: Trinity, 2003.

———. "Knowledge: The Theological Critique of Philosophy." In *Radical Orthodoxy: A New Theology*, edited by John Milbank, Catherine Picstock, and Graham Ward, 19–37. London: Routledge, 1999.

Milbank, John, Catherine Picstock, and Graham Ward. "Suspending the Material: The Turn of Radical Orthodoxy." In *Radical Orthodoxy: A New Theology*, edited by John Milbank, Catherine Picstock, and Graham Ward, 1–20. London: Routledge, 1999.

Moltmann, Jürgen. *God in Creation: An Ecological Doctrine of Creation*. London: SCM, 1985.

Montag, John. "Revelation: The False Legacy of Suárez." In *Radical Orthodoxy: A New Theology*, edited by John Milbank et al., 38–63. London: Routledge, 1999.

Moore, G. E. *Principia Ethica*, edited by Thomas Baldwin. Rev. ed. Cambridge: Cambridge University Press, 1903.

More, Henry. *Divine dialogues, containing disquisitions concerning the attributes and providence of God . . .* 3 vols. Glasgow, 1743.

Mullins, Justin. "Truth plus Beauty: the Elegance of Mathematics is Rarely Celebrated as Part of our Culture. But Equations Can Be an Art Form in Themselves." *New Scientist* 189 (2006) 18.

Murdoch, Iris. *The Fire and the Sun: Why Plato Banished the Artists*. Oxford: Oxford University Press, 1977.

Muth, Michael P. "Beastly Metaphysics: The Beasts of Narnia and Lewis's Reclamation of Medieval Sacramental Metaphysics." In *C. S. Lewis as Philosopher: Truth, Goodness, and Beauty*, edited by David Baggett et al., 228–44. Downers Grove, IL: InterVarsity, 2008.

Navone, John. *Toward a Theology of Beauty*. Collegeville, MN: Liturgical, 1996.

Naylor, Gloria. In *More Reflections on the Meaning of Life*, edited by David Friend, 10. Boston: Little, Brown, 1992.

The Nicene and Post Nicene Fathers [*NPNF*]. Edited by Philip Schaff. 14 vols. Edinburgh: T. & T. Clark, 1886–1889.

Nichols, Aidan. *The Art of God Incarnate: Theology and Image in Christian Tradition*. London: Darton, Longman, & Todd, 1980.

Creation's Beauty as Revelation

Nicholson, Michael W. "General Revelation and Beauty." Portland: Theological Research Exchange, 1997.

Nicholson, Octavia. "Hirst, Damien." In *Grove Art Online*. No pages. Online: http://www.oxfordartonline.com/subscriber/article/grove/art/ T094002.

Nicolson, Marjorie H. *Mountain Gloom and Mountain Glory: The Development of the Aesthetics of the Infinite*. Cornell University Press, 1959. Reprint, Seattle: University of Washington Press, 1997.

Niebuhr, H. Richard. *The Meaning of Revelation*. New York: Macmillan, 1941.

O'Meara, Thomas Franklin. "The Aesthetic Dimension in Theology." In *Art, Creativity, and the Sacred: An Anthology in Religion and Art*, edited by Diane Apostolos-Cappadona, 205–18. New rev. ed. New York: Continuum, 2001.

Osborne, Harold. "The Golden Section." In *The Oxford Companion to Western Art*, edited by Hugh Brigstocke. *Oxford Art Online*. No pages. Online: http://www.oxfordartonline.com/ subscriber/article/opr/t118/e1081.

———. *Theory of Beauty: An Introduction to Aesthetics*. London: Routledge & Kegan Paul, 1952.

Outler, Albert. Introduction to *John Wesley*. Oxford: Oxford University Press, 1964.

Panofsky, Erwin. *Meaning in the Visual Arts: Papers in and on Art History*. Garden City, NY: Doubleday, 1955.

Pelikan, Jaroslav. *Human Culture and the Holy: Essays on the True, the Good and the Beautiful*. Philadelphia: Muhlenberg, 1955. Reprint, London: SCM, 1959.

Petrarca, Francesco. "To Dionigi da Borgo San Sepolcro of the Augustinian Order and Professor of Sacred Scripture, concerning some personal problems." In *Rerum familiarium libri I–VIII*, translated by Aldo S. Bernardo 172–80. Albany: State University of New York Press, 1975.

Plantinga, Alvin. "The Reformed Objection to Natural Theology." *Christian Scholar's Review* 11 (1982) 187–98.

———. *Warranted Christian Belief*. New York: Oxford University Press, 2000.

Plato. *Parmenides*. Translated by Mary Louise Gill and Paul Ryan. Indianapolis: Hackett, 1996.

———. *Philebus*. Vol. 3 of *The Dialogues of Plato*. 4th ed. Translated by B. Jowett. Oxford: Oxford University Press, 1953.

Plotinus. *The Enneads*. 4th ed. Translated by Stephen MacKenna. London: Faber & Faber, 1969.

Polanyi, Michael and Harry Prosch. *Meaning*. Chicago: University of Chicago Press, 1975.

———. *Personal Knowledge: Towards a Post-Critical Philosophy*. London: Routledge, 1962.

———. *The Tacit Dimension*. London: Routledge, 1966.

Porteous, J. Douglas. *Environmental Aesthetics: Ideas, Politics and Planning*. London: Routledge, 1996.

Price, H. H. *Essays in the Philosophy of Religion*. Oxford: Clarendon, 1972.

Prickett, Stephen. *Romanticism and Religion: The Tradition of Coleridge and Wordsworth in the Victorian Church*. Cambridge: Cambridge University Press, 1976.

Provine, William B. "Evolution, Religion, and Science." In *The Oxford Handbook of Religion and Science*, edited by Philip Clayton and Zachary Simpson, 667–80. Oxford: Oxford University Press, 2006.

Rahner, Karl. "Art Against the Horizon of Theology and Piety." Translated by Joseph Donceel and Hugh M. Riley. In *Theological Investigations*, 23:162–8. New York: Crossroad, 1992.

———. "Faith Between Rationality and Emotion." Translated by David Morland. In *Theological Investigations*, 16:60–80. New York: Crossroad, 1979.

———. "Theology and the Arts." *Thought* 57 (1982) 17–29.

———. "Thomas Aquinas on Truth." Translated by David Bourke. In *Theological Investigations*, 13:13–31. New York: Crossroad, 1975.

Raine, Kathleen. "Word Made Flesh." In *Collected Poems*, 45. Berkeley: Counterpoint, 2001.

Raven, Charles. *The Creator Spirit: A Survey of Christian Doctrine in the Light of Biology, Psychology, and Mysticism*. London: Hopkinson, 1932.

Richards, Jay Wesley. *The Untamed God: A Philosophical Exploration of Divine Perfection, Simplicity and Immutability*. Downers Grove, IL: InterVarsity, 2003.

Ricoeur, Paul. *The Conflict of Interpretations*. Evanston: Northwestern University Press, 1974.

———. *Freud and Philosophy: An Essay on Interpretation*. Translated by D. Savage. New Haven: Yale University Press, 1970.

———. "The Language of Faith." *Union Seminary Quarterly Review* 28 (1973) 213–24.

———. *The Symbolism of Evil*. Translated by Emerson Buchanan. Boston: Beacon, 1967.

Robinson, Richard. *Definition*. Oxford: Clarendon, 1950.

Rolston, Holmes, III. "Aesthetics in the Swamps." *Perspectives in Biology and Medicine* 43 (2000) 584–597.

———. "Celestial Aesthetics: Over our Heads and/or in our Heads." Paper presented at the "Celestial Aesthetics: Aesthetics of Sky, Space, and Heaven" conference, Finland, March 2009.

———. "Does Aesthetic Appreciation of Landscapes Need to be Science-Based?" *British Journal of Aesthetics* 35 (1995) 374–86.

———. "Environmental Ethics and Relgion/Science." In *The Oxford Handbook of Religion and Science*, edited by Philip Clayton and Zachary Simpson, 908–28. Oxford: Oxford University Press, 2006.

———. "The Pasqueflower." *Natural History* 88/4 (1979) 6–16.

Rookmaaker, Hans. *Art, Artists and Gauguin*. Vol. 1 of *The Complete Works of Hans Rookmaaker*, edited by Marleen Hengelaar-Rookmaaker. CD-ROM. Carlisle, UK: Piquant, 2005.

———. *Modern Art and the Death of a Culture*. Vol. 5 of *The Complete Works of Hans Rookmaaker*, edited by Marleen Hengelaar-Rookmaaker. CD-ROM. Carlisle, UK: Piquant, 2005.

———. *New Orleans Jazz, Mahalia Jackson and the Philosophy of Art*. Vol. 2 of *The Complete Works of Hans Rookmaaker*, edited by Marleen Hengelaar-Rookmaaker. CD-ROM. Carlisle, UK: Piquant, 2005.

———. *Our Calling and God's Hand in History*. Vol. 6 of *The Complete Works of Hans Rookmaaker*, edited by Marleen Hengelaar-Rookmaaker. CD-ROM. Carlisle, UK: Piquant, 2005.

———. *Western Art and the Meanderings of a Culture*. Vol. 4 of *The Complete Works of Hans Rookmaaker*, edited by Marleen Hengelaar-Rookmaaker. CD-ROM. Carlisle, UK: Piquant, 2005.

Rota, Gian-Carlo. "The Phenomenology of Mathematical Beauty." *Synthese* 111 (1997) 171-82.

Rubenstein, A. R., L. A. Kalakanis, and J. H. Langlois. "Infant Preferences for Attractive Faces: A Cognitive Explanation." *Developmental Psychology* 35 (1999) 848-55.

Runge, Philipp Otto. "Letter to Daniel Runge (1802)." Translated by Michael Snideman. In *Nineteenth-Century Theories of Art*, edited by Joshua C. Taylor, 260-9. Berkeley, CA: University of California Press, 1987.

Ruskin, John. *Fors Clavigera: Letters to the Workmen and Labourers of Great Britain*. Vols. 27-29 of *The Works of John Ruskin*, edited by E. T. Cook and Alexander Wedderburn. London: Allen, 1907.

———. Introduction to *Deucalion: Collected Studies of the Lapse of Waves, and Life of Stones*. In Vol. 26 of *The Works of John Ruskin*, edited by E. T. Cook and Alexander Wedderburn. London: Allen, 1906.

———. *Love's Meinie*. Vol. 25 of *The Works of John Ruskin*, edited by E. T. Cook and Alexander Wedderburn, 5-190. London: Allen, 1906.

———. *Modern Painters*. Vols. 3-7 of *The Works of John Ruskin*, edited by E. T. Cook and Alexander Wedderburn. London: Allen, 1903.

———. *On the Old Road*. In *The Works of John Ruskin*, edited by E. T. Cook and Alexander Wedderburn, 34:263-394. London: Allen, 1908.

———. *The Bible of Amiens*. Vol. 33 of *The Works of John Ruskin*, edited by E. T. Cook and Alexander Wedderburn. London: Allen, 1908.

———. *The Queen of the Air*. Vol. 19 of *The Works of John Ruskin*, edited by E. T. Cook and Alexander Wedderburn. London: Allen, 1905.

———. *The Sea Stories*. Vol. 2 of *The Stones of Venice*. London: Allen, 1903.

———. *The Seven Lamps of Architecture*. London: Allen, 1900.

Sayers, Dorothy L. *Further Papers on Dante*. London: Methuen, 1957.

Schiller, Friedrich. *On the Aesthetic Education of Man in a Series of Letters*. Edited and translated by Elizabeth M. Wilkinson and L. A. Willoughby. Oxford: Clarendon, 1967.

Schloss, Jeffrey P. "Evolutionary Theory and Religious Belief." In *The Oxford Handbook of Religion and Science*, edited by Philip Clayton and Zachary Simpson, 187-206. Oxford: Oxford University Press, 2006.

Scruton, Roger. *Beauty*. Oxford: Oxford University Press, 2009.

Shelley, Percy Bysshe. "Ode to the West Wind." In *The Golden Treasury of the Best Songs and Lyrical Poems in the English Language*, 325-6. Rev. ed. London: Macmillan, 1891-97.

Sherry, Patrick. *Spirit and Beauty: An Introduction to Theological Aesthetics*. 2nd ed. London: SCM, 2002.

Singh, D. "Adaptive Significance of Female Physical Attractiveness: Role of Waist-to-Hip Ratio." *Journal of Personality and Social Psychology* 65 (1993) 293-307.

Smith, Richard. "John Ruskin, 1819-1900." In *Fifty Key Thinkers on the Environment*, edited by Joy A. Palmer et al., 118-22. London: Routledge, 2001.

Suger, Abbot, of St.-Denis. *Abbot Suger on the Abbey Church of St.-Denis and its Art Treasures*. 2nd ed. Edited by Erwin Panofsky and Gerda Panofsky-Soergel. Translated by Erwin Panofsky. Princeton, NJ: Princeton University Press, 1979.

Tennyson, Alfred. *In Memoriam A. H. H.* In *The Major Works*, edited by Adam Roberts, 203-92. New York: Oxford University Press, 2000; reprint, New York Oxford University Press, 2009.

Thiessen, Gesa Elsbeth, editor. *Theological Aesthetics: A Reader*. London: SCM, 2004. Reprint, Grand Rapids: Eerdmans, 2005.

Thomsen, Dietrick. "The Beauty of Mathematics." *Science News* 103 (1973) 137–8.

Thomson, James. Preface to *Winter: A Poem*. 3rd ed. London: Blandford, 1726.

———. *The Seasons*, edited by James Sanbrook. Oxford: Clarendon, 1981.

Thorne, J. O. and T. C. Collocot, editors. "Burnet, Thomas." In *Chambers Biographical Dictionary*, 198–9. Rev. ed. Edinburgh: Chambers, 1974.

Tillich, Paul. "Art and Ultimate Reality." In *On Art and Architecture*, edited by John Dillenberger, 139–57. New York: Crossroad, 1987.

———. "Environment and the Individual." In *On Art and Architecture*, edited by John Dillenberger, 199–203. New York: Crossroad, 1987.

———. Excerpt from Tillich's own draft of *Systematic Theology* vol. 3 in the Tillich Archives, Andover-Harvard Library, the Divinity School, Harvard University, edited by Robert Scharlemann. Quoted in *On Art and Architecture*, edited by John Dillenberger, 159–60. New York: Crossroad, 1987.

———. *Systematic Theology*. 3 vols. London: Nisbet, 1968.

Tolkien, J. R. R. *The Silmarillion*. London: Allen & Unwin, 1977. Reprint, London: HarperCollins, 1998.

Tyrwhitt, R. St. John. *The Natural Theology of Natural Beauty*. Oxford: Clarendon, n.d.

Vaughan, Henry. "The Tempest." In *Silex Scintillans*. London: Blunden, 1650.

Viladesau, Richard. *Theological Aesthetics: God in Imagination, Beauty, and Art*. New York: Oxford University Press, 1999.

———. *Theology and the Arts: Encountering God through Music, Art and Rhetoric*. New York: Paulist, 2000.

Wainwright, William J. "Jonathan Edwards and the Language of God." *Journal of the American Academy of Religion* 48 (1980) 519–30.

Ward, Graham. "The Beauty of God." In *Theological Perspectives on God and Beauty*, 35–65. Harrisburg, PA: Trinity, 2003.

Weil, Simone. *Gravity and Grace*. Translated by Emma Craufurd. London: Routledge, 1952.

———. *Waiting on God*. Translated by Emma Craufurd. London: Routledge, 1951.

Weinfeld, M. *Theological Dictionary of the Old Testament* [*TDOT*]. Edited by G. J. Botterweck et al. Translated by David E. Green. 8 vols. Grand Rapids, 1974–1995.

Weir, Jack. "Holmes Rolson III." In *Fifty Key Thinkers on the Environment*, edited by Joy A. Palmer et al., 260–68. London: Routledge, 2001.

Westphal, Merold. "Hermeneutics as Epistemology." In *The Blackwell Guide to Epistemology*, edited by John Greco and Ernest Sosa, 415–35. Malden, MA: Blackwell, 2004.

Wheeler, Michael. *Ruskin's God*. Cambridge: Cambridge University Press, 1999.

Whitson, Robley Edward. "Wilderness and Paradise: Symbols of American Religious Experience." *Religion and Intellectual Life* 5 (1987) 7–15.

Williams, A. N. "Argument to Bliss: The Epistemology of the *Summa Theologiae*." *Modern Theology* 20 (2004) 505–26.

Williams, N. P. The Ideas of the Fall and of Original Sin: A Historical and Critical Study. London: Longmans, Green, 1929.

Wittgenstein, Ludwig. *Philosophical Investigations*. Translated by G. E. M. Anscombe. Oxford: Blackwell, 1968.

Wolterstorff, Nicholas. *Art in Action: Toward a Christian Aesthetic*. Grand Rapids: Eerdmans, 1980.

Wood, W. Jay. *Epistemology: Becoming Intellectually Virtuous*. Downers Grove, IL: InterVarsity, 1998.

Wordsworth, William. "Airey-Force Valley." In *The Major Works*, edited by Stephen Gill, 369–70. Oxford: Oxford University Press, 1984. Reprint, 2000.

———. *The Excursion*, edited by Sally Bushnell et al. Ithaca, NY: Cornell University Press, 2007.

———. *Guide to the Lakes*. Estate of Ernest de Sélincourt, 1906. Reprint, London: Frances Lincoln, 2004.

———. "Lines Composed a Few Miles above Tintern Abbey, on Revisiting the Banks of the Wye during a Tour, July 13, 1798." In *William Wordsworth: The Poems*, edited by John O. Hayden, 1:357–62. New Haven: Yale University Press, 1981.

———. "Ode." In *The Major Works*, edited by Stephen Gill, 297–302. Oxford: Oxford University Press, 1984. Reprint, 2000.

———. Preface to *Lyrical Ballads*. In *Lyrical Ballads, and Other Poems, 1797–1800*, edited by James Butler and Karen Green, 741–60. Ithaca, NY: Cornell University Press, 1992.

———. *The Fourteen-Book* Prelude. Edited by W. J. B. Owen. Ithaca, NY: Cornell University Press, 1985.

———. *The Thirteen-Book* Prelude. Edited by Stephen Parrish. Ithaca, NY: Cornell University Press, 1977.

Wynn, Mark. *Faith and Place: An Essay in Embodied Religious Epistemology*. Oxford: Oxford University Press, 2009.

———. "From World to God: Resemblance and Complementarity." *Religious Studies* 32 (1996) 379–94.

———. "In Rolston's Footsteps: Human Emotions and Values in Nature." In *Nature, Value, Duty: Life on Earth with Holmes Rolston, III*, edited by Christopher J. Preston and Wayne Ouderkirk, 45–62. International Library of Environmental, Agricultural, and Food Ethics 8. Dordrecht, The Netherlands: Springer, 2007.

———. "Knowledge of God, Knowledge of Place and the Practice and Method of Philosophy of Religion." In *Contemporary Practice and Method in the Philosophy of Religion*, edited by David Cheetham and Rolfe King, 148–59. London: Continuum, 2008.

———. "Natural Theology in an Ecological Mode." *Faith and Philosophy* 16 (1999) 27–42.

———. "Primal Religions and the Sacred Significance of Nature." *Sophia* 36/2 (1997) 88–110.

———. "Religion, Phenomenology of," in *Stanford Encyclopedia of Philosophy*. Online: http://plato.stanford.edu/.

———. "Representing the Gods: The Role of Art and Feeling." *Religious Studies* 36 (2003) 315–31.

———. "Towards a Broadening of the Concept of Religious Experience: Some Phenomenological Considerations." *Religious Studies* 45 (2009) 147–66.

———. "Valuing the World: The Emotions as Data for the Philosophy of Religion." *International Journal for the Philosophy of Religion* 52 (2002) 97–113.